Saints and Scoundrels

SAINTS
AND
SCOUNDRELS

from King Herod to Solzhenitsyn

ROBIN PHILLIPS

canonpress
Moscow, Idaho

Robin Phillips, *Saints and Scoundrels: From King Herod to Solzhenitsyn*
Copyright © 2011 by Robin Phillips.

Published by Canon Press
P.O. Box 8729, Moscow, ID 83843
800.488.2034 | www.canonpress.com

Quotations and excerpts from the author's previous writings are used by permission of (and with thanks to): *Christian Voice, Christianity & Society, Salvo,* and the Colson Center.

Cover design by Rachel Rosales.
Interior design by Laura Storm.
Printed in the United States of America.

Library of Congress Cataloging-in-Publication Data

Phillips, Robin.
Saints and scoundrels from king Herod to Solzhenitsyn / Robin Phillips.
   p. cm.
ISBN 978-1-59128-104-7
1. Christian biography. 2. History--Religious aspects--Christianity. I. Title.
BR1700.3.P5 2011
920.02--dc23
[B]
                                    2011035560

12 13 14 15 16 17 18 19 20   9 8 7 6 5 4 3 2 1

To Joseph, Miriam, Matthew,
Timothy, and Susanna.

Walk in the footsteps of the saints
and shun the path of the scoundrels.

For if history records good things of good men, the thoughtful hearer is encouraged to imitate what is good: or if it records evil of wicked men, the devout, religious listener or reader is encouraged to avoid all that is sinful and perverse and to follow what he knows to be good and pleasing to God. Your Majesty is well aware of this; and since you feel so deeply responsible for the general good of those over whom divine Providence has set you, you wish that this history may be made better known both to yourself and to your people.

—The Venerable Bede, from his letter to King Ceolwulf[*]

[*]The Venerable Saint Bede, *A History of the English Church and People* (New York: Penguin, 1968), 33.

CONTENTS

ACKNOWLEDGMENTS

A project like this could never have come to completion without the help and support of numerous individuals. I want to thank those friends who took time to read and comment on various chapters or who contributed ideas about which figures to include, including Esther Phillips, Stuart Bryan, Nick Harrison, Father Phil Lewis, Tracy van den Broek, Patty-Chris Marr, Mark Woodruff, Steve Hayhow, Joel Hayhow, Tim Enloe, Arthur Eedle, Laurence Kubiak, Bruce Gore, and those on the Wingfold e-group. Special thanks goes to John Davis, who devoted many hours to patiently proofreading each chapter for me.

Appreciation is also due to Bruce Evans, my original editor at Canon Press, who first caught the vision for this project and encouraged me to expand it, and to Brian Kohl, who saw the project to completion.

I remain deeply grateful to my parents, who helped alleviate some of my family's financial burdens while I was working on this project so I could devote the time required to research.

Special thanks must also be given to those scholars who took time out of their busy schedules to look over select chapters, in particular Eric Metaxas, Benjamin Merkle, George Grant, Rolland Hein, Mike

Aquilina, and Greg Wilbur, as well as my own father, whose discussions with me about George MacDonald were a valuable asset to my chapter on the Scotsman.

I also remain in debt to Stephen Green, who helped to ignite my interest in heroes of the faith when he asked me to contribute a monthly column about heroes to *Christian Voice* newsletter. I am also grateful to *Christian Voice* for giving me permission to republish in this book some of the material that originally appeared in their newsletter; reprint is with permission of www.christianvoice.org.uk.

I am grateful to Stephen Perks and the Kuyper Foundation for letting me republish in this book material on Thomas Chalmers that previously appeared in their journal *Christianity & Society*. I am grateful to *Salvo Magazine* for letting me use material from my article on Marcuse. And I am grateful to the Colson Center for letting me republish material on Bonhoeffer, the Frankfurt school, Solzhenitsyn, and George MacDonald which originally appeared on their website; reprint is with permission of the Colson Center (copyright 2011, www.colsoncenter.org).

Above all, I want to thank my wife, Esther, who remained patient when this project ended up taking a year longer than I initially anticipated.

PREFACE

When I was eleven years old, I traveled to West Germany with my family. I will never forget the afternoon my dad drove us to the wall separating West and East Germany. The electric fence dividing the free world from the "evil empire" looked ominous.

As we emerged from the car, we were met by a chill, drizzling rain. On the other side of the fence a lone guard stared gloomily at us. The rest of my family had their picture taken in front of the fence but I was too afraid to venture near. A few minutes later I plucked up the courage and asked my dad to photograph me next to the terrible barrier, or as close to it as I dared approach.

Three years later, in 1989, the wall was torn down. Communism had collapsed and Eastern Europe was free. A year after these momentous changes (when I was fifteen), I went back to Germany with my family. This time there was nothing to prevent us driving into the Eastern section. We traveled to Berlin where the remnants of the wall still zigzagged through the city like a serpent. In some areas there were portions of the wall still intact. Here and there I saw people dismantling what remained of the hated emblem of **totalitarianism**.

Though I was only fifteen at the time, the experience had a marked effect on me. There was something strangely moving in seeing the broken concrete all over the ground and thinking, "So this is all that is left of a regime that tried to crush truth and freedom." I stooped down and collected some big chunks of the rubble, determined to show them to my own children one day.

A few years ago my parents came to visit and they brought the box containing the fragments of the wall. Since then I occasionally take out the pieces and show them to my children. I tell them how amazed I was when I learned about the collapse of Soviet communism. Yet I am also careful to emphasize that within the perspective of all of history the collapse of the Soviet empire should not come as such a surprise. After all, hasn't every other evil empire been reduced to rubble? The Assyrian Empire, for all its boasting, was dismantled by the work of God. The Babylonian kingdom rose to glory but collapsed in ruin. The proud, grandiose claims of the Persians, the Romans, and the Nazis were all likewise brought down to the dust by the hand of the Almighty.

It was this confidence in God's continued victories over the forces of darkness that led the Russian exile Aleksandr Solzhenitsyn to predict in 1983 that Christianity would one day triumph over communism. Speaking of the militant atheists that rekindled "the frenzied Leninist obsession with destroying religion," he said:

> But there was something they did not expect: that in a land where churches have been leveled, where a triumphant atheism has rampaged uncontrolled for two-thirds of a century, where the clergy is utterly humiliated and deprived of all independence, where what remains of the Church as an institution is tolerated only for the sake of propaganda directed at the West, where even today people are sent to labor camps for their faith and where, within the camps themselves, those who gather to pray at Easter are clapped in punishment cells—they could not suppose that beneath this Communist steamroller the Christian tradition would survive in Russia . . . . It is here that we see the dawn of hope: For no matter how formidably Communism bristles with tanks and rockets, no matter what

successes it attains in seizing the planet, it is doomed never to vanquish Christianity.[1]

What Solzhenitsyn said of Communism is true of all systems, empires, and worldviews that have attempted to crush the gospel: God's kingdom eventually brings them to ruin.

In toppling His enemies, God does not work alone but uses the faithfulness of His people throughout the ages to accomplish His purposes. From my perspective as a young boy, it seemed as though the collapse of communism had come out of the blue. Since then, I have had the opportunity to study the men and women of faith who played a part in the accomplishment of God's plans. The destruction of Soviet communism was made possible by people like Solzhenitsyn, Brother Andrew, Pope John Paul II, Lech Wałęsa, and countless other individuals who rendered their service to God in the positions in which He placed them.

My boyhood experience helped to ignite my interest in the men and women of faith who fought against evil in various times, cultures, and situations. Some of these heroes, like Saint Columbanus, Boniface, and Jim Elliot, took the gospel to new and unexplored lands, laboring to dismantle pagan cultures and replace them with worshiping Jesus. Others, like Alfred the Great in the ninth century or Edmund Burke in the nineteenth, strove to defend Christian civilization against barbarian attacks or oppressive ideas. Still others, such as William Wilberforce, Thomas Chalmers, and Dietrich Bonhoeffer, set themselves against the threat of a corrupting evil springing up from within a nominally Christian society.

The more I have studied the heroes and heroines of faith, the more I have become convinced that the fight against evils like communism is only half of the job. When Boniface converted the native German tribes to Christianity, or when Jim Elliot laid the foundation for the conversion of the Waodani, that was the beginning and not the end. What is just as important as defeating or converting God's enemies is the positive work of building up the culture of Christendom. For

1. Aleksandr Solzhenitsyn, *The Solzhenitsyn Reader: New and Essential Writings, 1947–2005*, 2nd ed. (Wilmington: Intercollegiate Studies Institute, 2009), 580–581.

every Berlin wall that crashes to the ground, there are dozens of churches to be raised up, schools to be created, homes to be established. For each Roman coliseum that decays into ruins, there remain hundreds of libraries to be built, hymns to be composed, families to be nurtured in the faith. Here again, God does not work *ex nihilo* but calls men and women to be agents in His kingdom-building work. Saints like George Herbert, C.S. Lewis, and Dorothy Sayers lived in times of relative peace and were able to pour their energies into strengthening and beautifying Christian culture. When Nazi bombs rained down on London, Sayers was not able to conspire against Hitler like Dietrich Bonhoeffer, yet her reading and interpretation of Dante enabled her to leave behind just as valuable of a legacy.

Throughout the Christian era, there have been numerous heroes and heroines who have embodied both aspects of this call to service. Some were slayers of dragons, others builders of kingdoms. Some, like Charlemagne and Ronald Reagan, cried out to the enemies of God, "Thus far and no farther!" Others, like George MacDonald, G.K. Chesterton, and T.S. Eliot defended Christendom by showing that the faith is lovely. They knew that the greatest defense against evil is to enjoy the good, that the strongest bulwark against unbelief is our capacity to love what is beautiful, that the surest support against the lies of the devil is to be attracted to what is true. Some heroes have exemplified both sides of this noble calling: men like Constantine and Alfred the Great were great builders of Christendom, not merely because they led souls to Christ or defended civilization from pagan attack, but because they worked to advance a distinctly Christian vision of culture—a vision that found expression in art, literature, painting, technology, and hundreds of other areas.

I have not had time to write about all the heroes I would have liked to cover, or even all the ones referred to above. But I have attempted to include a fair selection of dragon-slayers and kingdom-builders. My hope is that these stories will be an inspiration in your own God-given vocations. Like those saints listed in Hebrews 11, the brave men and women in the following pages comprise a vast cloud of witnesses who reach down through the ages to show us what it means to put the gospel into action. Let them encourage you to expand your vision beyond what you thought possible, to never cease striving against the dragons and arch-villains that confront us in our own day.

In order that the virtues of these noble men and women may stand out in sharper relief, I have also included some chapters about the dragons. The witness of a woman like Perpetua is all the more remarkable when she is contrasted with the murderous aspirations of a despot like Herod. The stately wisdom of Edmund Burke shines all the clearer when we compare it to the egotistical foolishness of Rousseau or Joseph Smith.

But there is another reason for the presence of scoundrels in this volume: they teach us the same lesson I learned on that rain-soaked day in Berlin when I gazed on the shattered remains of the hated wall. The lesson is this: though villains may rise and fall, the people of God will always be there, pocketing their remains to show the next generation.

Robin Phillips
Post Falls
Feast of the Nativity of John the Baptist, 2011

INTRODUCTION

by George Grant

"Biography may well be," Paul Johnson argues, "the most powerful inducement for us to understand the history of the world and the flow of its great movements."[1] Likewise, Thomas Carlyle famously asserted, "Universal history, the history of what man has accomplished in this world, is at bottom the history of the great men who have worked here. They were the leaders of men, the great ones; the modelers, patterns, and in a wide sense creators, of whatsoever the general mass of men contrived to do or attain; all things that we see standing accomplished in the world are properly the outer material result, the practical realization and embodiment, of thoughts that dwelt in the great men sent into the world: the soul of the whole world's history, it may be justly considered, were the history of these."[2]

It should not be surprising to us then that biography has been one of the keenest tools used by historians through the ages—from the profiles of Plutarch and the hagiographies of the medieval saints to

1. Paul Johnson, *The Quotable Paul Johnson,* ed. John Willis (Chicago: Braeswood Publishing, 2007), 14.
2. Thomas Carlyle, *Heroes and Hero Worship* (New York: Fenelon Collier, 1897), 235.

the encyclopedic excavations of Boswell on Johnson and Hanna on Chalmers.

Alas, we moderns typically hold to a strangely disjunctive view of the relationship between individual lives and corporate history, between personal character and public accomplishment. As a result, we often nonchalantly separate prominent people from the flow of culture and private character from the attainment of public accomplishments. But this novel divorce of root from fruit, however genteel, is a ribald denial of one of the most basic truths in life: what we are begets what we do. Just as the good, the true, and the beautiful inevitably emerge from the lives of those committed to virtue, wrong-headed philosophies necessarily stem from wrong-headed philosophers; just as moral stalwartness is forged by the morally upright, wickedness doesn't just happen; it is sinners that sin.

Thus, according to the English historian and journalist Hilaire Belloc, "Biography always affords the greatest insights into sociology. To comprehend the history of a thing is to unlock the mysteries of its present, and more, to discover the profundities of its future."[3] Similarly, the inimitable Samuel Johnson quipped, "Almost all the miseries of life, almost all the wickedness that infects society, and almost all the distresses that afflict mankind, are the consequences of some defect in private duties."[4]

Or, as E. Michael Jones has asserted, "Biography is destiny."[5]

In a sense then, biography—even when it takes the forms of hagiography and nefariography—is a vital tool wise men and women will use to forge an understanding of the great sweep of events in the past and the trajectory of present circumstances into the future.

If for no other reason than this, these biographical sketches by Robin Phillips are valuable. But thankfully, there is another reason. In fact, there are many reasons: the vibrant story-telling, the clear moral philosophy portrayed therein, the broad selection, the diverse range—all these make *Saints and Scoundrels* not only an important

3. Hilaire Belloc, *The Biographer's Art: Excerpts from Belloc's Florrid Pen* (London: Catholic Union, 1956), 33.

4. Howard F. Pallin, ed., *Literary English and Scottish Sermons* (London: Windus Etheridge, 1937), 101.

5. E. Michael Jones, *Degenerate Moderns: Modernity as Rationalized Sexual Misbehavior* (San Francisco: Ignatius Press, 1993), 9.

book but a delightful one. I highly commend it to your attention, not only because of what you will learn but because of what you will enjoy.

I have always loved the sentiment of C.S. Lewis when he quipped, "You can't get a cup of tea large enough or a book long enough to suit me."[6] Thus, my only regret is that this small collection of short biographies is not a big collection of long biographies.

6. C.S. Lewis, *The Inklings: Collected Wit and Wisdom,* ed. James Caroll Thomas (New York: Hallowell and Sons, 1979), 47.

CHAPTER 1

A GENERAL CLIMATE OF HORROR

The Madness of Herod the Great (73–4 B.C.)

After Mary gave birth to Christ, certain wise men living in the Babylo-nian region saw a sign of Him in the night's sky. That was in the days before astrology had been separated from astronomy, and learned men still understood how to interpret the signs of the heavens.

Arriving in Jerusalem with their entourage, the foreigners couldn't help but arouse the attention of King Herod, who employed an elabo-rate system of espionage throughout Judaea. When Herod learned that the Magi were seeking one born "king of the Jews," he was in-dignant. There was only one king of the Jews as far as Herod was concerned: himself.

Herod had long known about the Jewish hope of a Messiah, yet he paid as little attention to God's prophecies as he did to God's com-mandments. That is, until the Magi arrived on the scene. Their words about the star made Herod begin to worry.

Throughout his career, the mere hint that someone might try to usurp his throne had been enough to trigger Herod into a series of murderous rages. In order to preserve or consolidate his own power, Herod had killed three of his sons, his son-in-law, his mother-in-law, his uncle, his brother, his wife, and numerous friends and associates. Now it seemed that the latest threat to his dynasty was a mere baby.

Determined to seek out and eliminate this usurper, Herod feigned a desire to worship the new king and asked the wise men to alert him to the child's whereabouts as soon as he was located. The wise men did eventually find the Christ-child. However, before they had a chance to tell Herod, the Lord warned them in a dream to return home by a different way.

When Herod learned that he had been tricked, he went into a frenzy. Having ascertained from the Old Testament that the Jewish Messiah would be born in Bethlehem, only a few miles away from his palace-fortress of Herodium, he ordered the massacre of all male children in the region two years old and under.

The slaughter of so many innocent children remains Herod's most memorable crime, yet it was only one in a career littered with similar brutalities. Who was this man and where did he come from? Why has history remembered him as Herod "the Great"? To answer these questions, we must backtrack several centuries and explore the background of the most fascinating region on earth.

A LAND OF BLOOD

There are few places that have witnessed as much conflict and bloodshed as the land of Israel. Almost every power in the ancient world coveted this strip of land west of the Mediterranean. It is not hard to see why: though now bordered by desert, in ancient times this area was composed of lush woodland and abundant wildlife. Moreover, it was an important trade route linking Egypt with Asia Minor.

The earliest recorded history shows tribal societies fighting for control of the land. Even after the descendants of Abraham were established in the region following their exodus from Egypt in the late fifteenth century B.C., times of peace were scarce. The people of God had to contend with the constant threat of violence from those tribes that the returning exiles had failed to drive out.

Only during the reign of Solomon in the tenth century B.C. did the nation achieve some measure of stability. Free from the demands of war, Solomon was able to direct his energies to building an elaborate temple, according to the design the Lord had given Moses.

The peace was not to last, however. In the reign of Solomon's son, Rehoboam, the kingdom was split in two: Israel in the north, Judah in the south.

The first foreign empire to lay claim to the Holy Land was Assyria, which conquered Samaria, the northern kingdom of Israel, in 722 B.C. The brutal Assyrian leader, Shalmaneser, put the kingdom under siege, while his successor (and probable usurper), Sargon II, forced the ten tribes into captivity. Sargon's army then proceeded to the southern kingdom of Judah and laid waste the entire land except for the city of Jerusalem, which remained under King Hezekiah's control.

The Assyrians' downfall began when the Chaldean king Nabopolassar (c. 658–605 B.C.) joined forces with the Medes, a tribe from the Persian hills, to wage an attack on the Assyrian stronghold of Nineveh in 612 B.C. Nabopolassar established a new Babylonian monarchy, while his son, Nebuchadnezzar, finally defeated the Assyrians and established Babylon as his own capital.

Though Nebuchadnezzar's empire was not as large as that of Assyria, he did eventually capture the southern kingdom of Judah in 586 B.C., carrying the Jews into captivity and destroying Solomon's temple. However, the neo-Babylonian or Chaldean empire was doomed from the start, as God had foretold through the prophet Jeremiah (Jer. 50–51). Its destruction occurred when the warrior Cyrus united all the Persian tribes—including the Medes—into one nation. In 539 B.C. he overthrew Babylon in an event predicted in Isaiah 13 and described again in Daniel 5.

Cyrus lived up to the prophecies about him, which had proclaimed that he would be a blessing to God's people (Is. 13, 45). In 536 B.C. he issued a decree allowing the people of Judah to begin returning to their land (2 Chron. 36:22–23; Ezra 1). Encouraged by the prophets Haggai and Zechariah, the Jews finished rebuilding the temple twenty years later.

Although the captives had returned, Judaea remained under Persian rule. Control passed to the Macedonians in 331 B.C., when Alexander the Great conquered Persia and asserted control over all the region. When Alexander died in 323 B.C., his empire was divided among his generals. However, it was never determined whether Judaea would be part of General Ptolemy's Egyptian-based empire or General Seleucid's empire of Syria. The struggle between Egypt and Syria would continue until the Syrian king, Antiochus III, secured the land following the battle of Panion in 199 B.C.

The Jews generally supported Antiochus III. However, his brother and successor, Antiochus Epiphanes (r. 175–164 B.C.), was a different matter. He immediately set himself up as the enemy of the Jews. He forced them to adopt the Greek religion, commanded the priests to offer sacrifices to Zeus, and forbade them from worshiping the Lord, circumcising their children, or keeping the Sabbath. He even made it a treasonous offense to avoid eating pork, a meat unclean according to Old Testament regulations. Moreover, Antiochus desecrated the Temple by sacrificing a pig on the brazen altar.

Thousands of Jews who refused to renounce their religion died by the sword. The second book of Maccabees (5:11–14) says that he ordered his soldiers to cut down without mercy those they met and to slay those who took refuge in their houses. The result was a massacre of young and old, women and children. In the space of three days, eighty thousand were lost: forty thousand meeting a violent death, and a similar number being sold into slavery.

THE HASMONEAN DYNASTY

Resistance to Antiochus was organized by the Maccabee family. The revolt started when the elderly priest Mattathias slew the leader of the king's messengers, in addition to killing a Jew who was prepared to offer the idolatrous sacrifices demanded by the king. In order to escape the authorities, Mattathias fled to the mountains with his sons, where they organized a resistance movement. After Mattathias' death, the revolt was continued by his son Judas Maccabeus ("the hammer").

Using guerrilla warfare, the rebellion succeeded in routing the forces of Antiochus. The Maccabees purified the temple and established an independent Jewish state. Two decades later Judas' brother Simon established a dynastic kingdom known as the Hasmonean dynasty. In this new kingdom, the monarch also occupied the role of High Priest (always before, the two positions had been kept carefully separate).

During the 103 years of Hasmonean rule, the Judaean state greatly expanded, capturing Samaria and Galilee in the North, the Idumaeans in the South and the Peraeans in the East. They also made treaties with Rome, the growing power in the West.

Meanwhile, the Hasmoneans began acting less like Jews and more like the nobility in the surrounding Hellenized culture. This prompted a religious reaction among the Pharisees, a group that arose in the second century B.C., who believed that Maccabean rule was an abomination to God. The Pharisees pointed out that the chief priests were supposed to be descended from the line of Zadok from the house of Aaron. The descendants of Mattathias and his sons could claim neither, being descended merely from common priests.

The Pharisees taught the people the Law of Moses, along with their growing body of authoritative interpretations of those laws. The Sadducees, a rival group, rejected many of the Pharisees' interpretations of the Torah and disbelieved in the resurrection of the dead. They tended to cluster around Jerusalem and attracted aristocratic or wealthy Jews more sympathetic with the Hasmoneans.

Conflict between the Pharisees and the Hasmoneans reached a climax during the reign of Alexander Jannaeus (r. 103 to 76 B.C.). The more liberal Sadducees supported Jannaeus, while the Pharisees rebelled against him after he intentionally broke their rules while officiating in his capacity as High Priest. Jannaeus showed little mercy to the Pharisees. Josephus records that he crucified eight hundred of his enemies in front of the palace in Jerusalem, while he and the women of his harem dined. To intensify his enemies' sufferings, Jannaeus had the throats of the rebels' wives and children cut at the foot of each cross.

FROM HASMONEANS TO HERODIANS

When Alexander Jannaeus died in 76 B.C., his wife, Salome Alexandra, ruled in his stead. Although she left the kingdom to her son Hyrcanus, his throne was coveted by his brother Aristobulus. Hyrcanus had no ambition to be king and conceded the throne to his brother, who was cruel and ruthless like their father had been.

Hyrcanus had a scheming friend and adviser named Antipater, the son of a military governor. Antipater urged Hyrcanus to assert his right to the throne, knowing that if Hyrcanus was in power he could manipulate things to his own advantage. He pressed the reluctant Hyrcanus first to wage a civil war against his brother and then to enlist the support of Rome.

Realizing that Hyrcanus would be easier to control than Aristobulus, the Roman general Pompey willingly assisted Hyrcanus in defending his throne. But help from Rome came at a high price. Pompey brutally defeated Aristobulus' forces, besieging Jerusalem and then slaying twelve thousand of its inhabitants, including the priests who were performing their sacrificial duties right up until the moment of their death. Worse still for the Jews, the Romans never left and Judaea became a client state of Rome. Hyrcanus was made High Priest and Ethnarch of Judaea, though most of the authority rested with his friend and chief minister, Antipater. But ultimate power now rested with Rome.

Antipater's loyalty to Pompey was short-lived. Antipater was a political genius and perceived that it would be beneficial to support the up-and-coming Julius Caesar in his civil wars. After Caesar defeated Pompey and made himself the supreme dictator, he repaid Antipater's loyalty by conferring Roman citizenship on him and making his family exempt from taxation. Caesar also named Antipater Procurator of all Judaea. With this title came power over all civil and religious matters. Antipater was even able to decide what happened with taxes, provided that he maintained the frontier forts and towns in good order.

The stage was being set for a new dynasty, which would take its name from Antipater's son: Herod.

GALILEE UNDER HEROD

Antipater's twenty-five-year-old son, Herod, was given command of the politically turbulent region of Galilee. This was no easy task. Antipater's family was not Jewish but rather descended from the Idumaeans that the Hasmoneans had conquered during the second century B.C. The Galileans were accustomed to being ruled over by a member of the Maccabees and resented this son of Esau.

Herod first ran into trouble with the religious leaders when he ruthlessly killed the brigands who lived in the Galilean hill country. The brigands included Jewish nationalists and rebels, but many were simply peasants who had been dispossessed of their houses and lands over the previous two generations and forced to become cave-dwellers. According to a Jewish law, which even Rome honored, the only agency that could legally condemn a Jew to death was the Grand Sanhedrin, the ruling council of Jews that met in Jerusalem and which consisted of seventy-one leading Pharisees and Sadducees. But

Herod was anxious to prove his sovereignty and disregarded the Sanhedrin's jurisdiction. He butchered those who opposed his rule and tortured Hezekiah, the leader of the Galilean brigands.

When the Sanhedrin learned about his violent treatment of the Galileans, they ordered Herod to come before them to stand trial. Because Herod ruled only in Galilee at this point, he had to at least pretend to cooperate with those in the other spheres of government. Though Herod consented to stand before the council of Jews, Josephus tells how he fled in the middle of the proceedings to escape an unfavorable verdict.

DONNING THE MACCABEAN MANTLE

The chance to become sole ruler of the nation presented itself to Herod when the Hasmonean prince, Antigonus II, joined with the Parthians and invaded Judaea in 40 B.C. After they captured Jerusalem, Herod fled to Rome to appeal for support. Eager for Judaea to be controlled by a competent ruler on good terms with their own nation, the Romans conferred on Herod the title "king of the Jews." Moreover, Rome offered him a detachment of soldiers with which to crush the rebellion.

Herod knew that the Jews would never accept him unless he could show a hereditary claim to the throne. Before laying siege to Jerusalem to crush the rebellion, Herod divorced his wife, Doris, and married Hyrcanus's granddaughter, Mariamne (Miriam in English), who was twenty years his junior. The marriage couldn't have been a better tactical move. By marrying a Hasmonean princess, Herod hoped to give legitimacy to his kingship. Since the House of Maccabees had permitted the marriage, they seemed imply their support for Herod, or at least that they considered him to be their peer.

Even this would not prove enough for Herod, who nursed a grievance that his pedigree prevented him from also serving as High Priest. Not one to be constrained by the facts, Herod drew up a fraudulent genealogy to demonstrate that he was descended from one of the priestly families who had been exiled to Babylon. But fearing that others would discover the document to be a forgery, Herod soon withdrew it. He would have to settle with being merely a king and leave the position of High Priest to his puppets.

JUDAEA UNDER HEROD

Herod remained subservient to the Romans, who claimed Judaea as part of their empire. It was in Rome's interests to allow client kings such as Herod to exercise a large degree of autonomy. These client kingdoms at the frontiers of the empire served as buffers between Rome and her powerful enemies. The key was for the client king to remain on good terms with Rome. Herod took after his father and was particularly adept in this. He accomplished the seemingly-impossible task of keeping on the good side of Rome all through the reigns of Julius Caesar, Cassius, Antony, and Augustus Caesar.

Herod had been nursing a grudge against the Sanhedrin for putting him on trial ten years earlier. Once installed as king he took his revenge, executing forty-five of the council's seventy members and restricting the Sanhedrin's authority in religious matters.

Far from solidifying his rule, however, this act of cruelty merely increased the hatred devout Jews felt for him. Throughout the remainder of his reign, Herod's worst enemies continued to be those in his own backyard. Samuel Sandmel summed it up well in his book, *Herod: Profile of a Tyrant:* "The Jewish opposition to Herod, where it existed, was relentless, and Herod was relentless in destroying it."[1]

Herod developed a highly organized network of informants who alerted him to anything suspicious. Those whom he suspected of disloyalty were quickly whisked away to one of the king's dreaded torture chambers.

FAMILY FEUDING

Herod may have been adroit at managing the various Roman emperors, but he failed miserably at managing his own household. He may have been able to bring order to Judaea, but he could never bring order to his home, which was continually plagued by intense rivalry and bitter feuding.

At the root of the family feud was the virulent hatred that Herod's sister, Salome, bore towards Herod's second wife, Mariamne, whose outspokenness and royal birth made Salome feel inferior. However,

---

1. Samuel Sandmel, *Herod: Profile of a Tyrant* (Philadelphia: Lippincott, 1967), 93.

nothing Salome said could diminish Herod's love for his Hasmonean princess. In fact, Herod's love for Mariamne verged on insanity. The thought that he might one day die, leaving Mariamne free to marry another man, nearly drove him mad with envy.

When Herod had to travel to Laodicea to meet Mark Antony, he left his uncle, Joseph, in charge. Unbeknownst to his wife, he also left secret orders that if he were to die, Mariamne should be killed along with her mother, Alexandra. On one occasion, when Joseph was telling Mariamne about his nephew's great love for her, he revealed these dreadful instructions, apparently thinking it would show the depths of Herod's passion for her. (It is possible that Joseph loved Mariamne and gave her the information in an attempt to turn her against Herod, but we will never know.)

Joseph was married to Herod's sister, Salome, who had begun to despise her husband almost as much as she despised Mariamne. The opportunity to rid herself of both Joseph and Mariamne in one stroke came when Herod returned from visiting Antony. Salome accused Mariamne of having committed frequent adultery with Joseph while the king was away. As Mariamne pleaded her innocence, she and Herod both broke into tears and fell into a lovers' embrace. As Herod clasped Mariamne to his bosom and whispered reassuring words of love, Mariamne said softly, "It was hardly a lover's gesture to command that if anything happened to you, I should be killed also."

At these words, Josephus tells us that "Herod went into a frenzy, crying and tearing his hair. This was damning proof of Joseph's intercourse with her, he said, for Joseph would not have revealed it if they had not been intimate."[2] Herod ordered his uncle's execution, but could not bring himself to kill his wife. Mariamne came to realize just how much control she wielded over her husband and began to use her position to manipulate the king against his sister, Salome, and his mother, Cyprus.

During Herod's next absence, he left one of his men in charge of Mariamne and her mother, Alexandra. Josephus tells us that, as before, Herod lodged secret orders for the women to be killed should

---

2. Josephus, *Josephus, the Essential Works: A Condensation of Jewish Antiquities and The Jewish War*, trans. Paul L. Maier (Grand Rapids: Kregel Academic, 1995), 242.

he fail to return, and once again, Herod's man disclosed the plot. On Herod's return, Mariamne dropped all pretense of love, ridiculing Herod and treating him with scorn.

Salome and Cyprus soon got their opportunity to do away with Mariamne. They hatched a plot designed to convict Mariamne of attempting to poison the king. Herod eventually succumbed to the pressure and had Mariamne executed.

Herod was never the same after his wife's death. Remorse over her death pushed him closer to madness, and for a while he refused to even acknowledge that she was no longer available to him. He would wander around the palace calling for her and ordering his servants to fetch her. Eventually Herod's remorse solidified into dark moods, violent rages, drunkenness, paranoia, and health problems, together with an increasing tendency to order the death of his closest friends.

Herod continued to put down plots and react to rumors of false plots. On each occasion he became more brutal and callous; the more brutal he became, the more conspiracies arose to rid the land of his cruelty; the more plots there were against him, the more plots Herod suspected; the more plots Herod suspected, the easier it was for members of his bickering household to plant poisonous suggestions in his mind against other family members that they hated.

As this suggests, the family bickering had not ended with the death of Mariamne. Four years after killing her, Herod married another Mariamne, the daughter of an insignificant priest. Herod then appointed her father, Simon, to the position of High Priest. Meanwhile, Herod sent the two boys the first Mariamne had borne to him—Alexander and Aristobulus—to be educated in Rome. Salome knew that Herod intended to make them his heirs, and as they grew older she began to look on them as a threat. When they took over the kingdom, they might try to avenge their mother's death, for which she was responsible. Salome thus focused all her attention on turning Herod against his sons, even as she had turned his mind against their mother.

The unhappiness of his household did not stop Herod from increasing its size. Whenever he tired of a wife, he set her aside and married another. As the household enlarged, so did the factions and intrigue. Each new wife took sides in the endless disputes, compounding the ever-shifting network of alliances and factions. By the end of Herod's life, there were nine rival wives, all living under the same roof, each vying for the welfare of her own children and trying to discredit the others in Herod's eyes. Herod himself hoped to reduce the strife and secure family interdependence through a network of interlocking marriages. However, the proliferation of so many children and intermarriages amongst them and their extended relatives merely added multiple layers of complexity to the continuous feuds within the dysfunctional family.

As Herod aged he became even more ruthless and unpredictable. Suspicious of everyone, he feared that those closest to him were plotting his overthrow. Josephus describes the resulting atmosphere:

> The whole court soon became a scene of suspicion, gloom, and distrust: suspects were tortured and killed, while spies were everywhere. People accused their enemies of plots so that the king would kill them, and there was a general climate of horror.[3]

When Herod was first presented with the false allegations about his intended heirs, Alexander and Aristobulus, he refused to believe them. But Salome, who was perpetuating the false charges, was relentless. Eventually the barrage of accusation overwhelmed Herod's ailing mind, so he recalled his first wife, Doris, and prepared to make her son, Antipater, his heir. Antipater immediately took sides with Salome against Alexander and Aristobulus, paying agents to circulate rumors against his half-brothers and their supporters. Yet to his father's face, Antipater defended his brothers. Eventually implicated in a plot himself, Antipater was killed, but not before he had succeeded in getting Alexander and Aristobulus butchered.

MADNESS AND DEATH

As Herod aged, his latent insanity began to dominate his mental disposition. He even tortured his own friends out of suspicion of their disloyalty. It is against this backdrop that the story of the Massacre of the Innocents must be understood. The biblical record of

3. Ibid., 252.

the Bethlehem murders has been doubted because the event is not mentioned by Josephus, who otherwise took care to record Herod's myriad crimes. However, the description of the event in Matthew's gospel fits with what we know of Herod's temperament. As Louis Matthews Sweet has put it in the *International Standard Bible Encyclopaedia*:

> Practically all of Herod's murders, including those of his beloved wife and his sons, were perpetrated under the sway of one emotion and in obedience to a single motive. They were in practically every instance for the purpose of consolidating or perpetuating his power. . . . The murder of the Innocents was another crime of the same sort. The old king was obsessed by the fear of a claimant to his petty throne; the Messianic hope of the Jews was a perpetual secret torment, and the murder of the children, in the attempt to reach the child whose advent threatened him, was at once so original in method and so characteristic in purpose as to give an inimitable verisimilitude to the whole narrative.[4]

In 4 B.C., Herod lay dying. Diseased in both body and mind, Herod's death agony was excruciating. His disease was probably syphilis, and included fever and pains in the colon, with severe itching, swollen feet, inflammation of the abdomen, convulsions, lung disease, and gangrene in his genitals.

Herod had many enemies who were eagerly awaiting the moment of his death. The king knew this and was determined that there should be grief rather than joy at his passing. To facilitate this, Herod ordered the Jewish notables of his kingdom to be shut up inside the hippodrome, with orders that, as soon as he was dead, these men should be murdered.

Though he had gained some favor among the Jews for his grand rebuilding of the temple, the temple itself was a mixed blessing since Herod had insisted on mounting the image of a golden eagle above the great door. This depiction of Rome's supremacy violated the strict

---

4. James Orr, ed., *The International Standard Bible Encyclopaedia* (Chicago: The Howard-Severance Company, 1915), 1472.

interpretations of Torah which forbade graven images. The eagle along with everything it stood for was bitterly resented by the more zealous Pharisees. Among these were two learned Pharisees named Sariphaeus and Matthias. When a rumor circulated that Herod was dead, Sariphaeus and Matthias urged a group of youths to remove the hated object. Forty were caught in the act and arrested. Though Herod was dying and could not even sit up, he insisted on hearing the case himself. All who had participated were to be killed with either the axe or the bowstring, while he ordered Matthias to be burned alive.

A few days later Herod expired. But contrary to his wishes, Salome released the Jewish leaders from the Hippodrome.

THE LEGACY OF HEROD THE GREAT

After Herod's death, the Romans divided his empire. They gave Iturea and the region of Trachonitis to his son Philip; Galilee and Perea went to his son Antipas; Judaea went to his son Archelaus.

In addition to receiving their father's land, the sons of Herod (with the exception of Philip) inherited his legacy of greed, malice, lust, treachery, and violence. It is not surprising that when Joseph heard that Archelaus was reigning over Judaea instead of his father Herod, he feared to enter the region, and took the holy family instead to Nazareth, which was part of the Roman province of Syria.

The immorality of Herod's house continued to be legendary. John the Baptist was beheaded because he opposed the unlawful remarriage of Herod Antipas (Mt. 14:1–12; Mk. 6:14–29). And Jesus Himself had to endure mockery at the hands of Antipas on the morning of His execution (Lk. 23:5–12).

Herod's grandson, Agrippa I, was no better, stretching out his hand to harass the church (Acts 12:1), killing James (Acts 12:2), and claiming for himself divine honors, for which he was struck down by God (Acts 12:19–23).

Evil as Herod's legacy was, it was not entirely negative. He was a remarkably able leader who seemed to genuinely care about his subjects. He may not have been able to sacrifice his lusts for the sake of his family, but he did make enormous sacrifices for the sake of his citizens. When a plague struck the land, he arranged for the infirm and elderly to get food from bread-kitchens. He even minted coins from the gold and silver ornaments in his own palaces in order to buy food from Egypt to feed his people.

It is not for nothing that he is remembered as "Herod the Great." He brought administrative order to the turbulent region, secured the borders, made the roads safe, and kept the various factions of the Jews intact. He created new harbors, opened trade routes, patronized the arts, and brought stability to the finances of the region. Moreover, he possessed enough political sagacity to accomplish the seemingly impossible task of making friends with both the Romans and the Jews. This same shrewdness was passed on to Herod's grandson Agrippa, whom Jesus perceptively called "that old fox" (Lk. 13:32).

The most famous testament to Herod's legacy was his impressive rebuilding of Solomon's temple. This was the most ambitious building project ever to be undertaken in that part of the world and exceeded the original temple in its magnificence. Herod also financed numerous other building projects throughout the East, even outside his own realm.

LESSONS FROM THE LIFE OF HEROD THE GREAT

Herod's ability to win the confidence of others, particularly those in positions of power, was truly remarkable. In his book *Herod: King of the Jews and Friend of the Romans*, Peter Richardson remarked that "his ability to win everyone's confidence was one of the hallmarks of his career: in succession he sided with Caesar, Caesar's assassins, Cassius and Brutus, their revengers Antony and Octavian, then with Antony and Cleopatra, and then with Octavian."[5] Herod also earned the adoration of huge segments of the Jewish population through his economic policies, building projects, and skillful leadership. What Herod could never win, however, was the respect of those that lived with him.

In Herod we see the abiding human tendency to successfully manage one's public life while failing pitiably to order one's private affairs. In his public policy, Herod was clever enough to know that

5. Peter Richardson, *Herod: King of the Jews and Friend of the Romans* (Minneapolis: Continuum International Publishing Group, 1999), 7.

sometimes rebellion could be overcome more effectively with kindness; in his own household, however, kindness was always in short supply. His aptitude in communicating with Roman emperors and foreign dignitaries contrasted sharply with his failure to properly communicate with the members of his own family. His adroitness as a military leader was juxtaposed by his abject failure as a father and husband.

In all this, we see how Herod represents the supreme folly of all those who would rule the world while neglecting responsibilities nearest to home. Though history has dubbed him "Herod the Great" for his public accomplishments, it would perhaps be more fitting to call him "Herod the Horrible."

A second lesson we learn from Herod's eventful and unhappy life concerns the nature of Christ's ministry. Herod attempted to kill the Christ-child on the assumption that the Messiah's reign would displace his own. And this assumption was not entirely erroneous.

Grounded in the Messianic prophecies woven throughout the Old Testament, first-century Jews looked forward to a climactic event that would establish the God of Israel as the sovereign God of the entire world. While many have supposed Christ's coming to be something which changes people's hearts but makes no difference to the public order, this was not the hope of the Jews. Had they expected that kind of a kingdom, Herod may not have lifted an eyebrow when the news reached him that the Messiah had been born in Bethlehem. As it was, however, Herod knew what Zacharias knew and had prayed about— that when the Messiah came, the game would be up for tyrants like himself, and a new order of justice and peace would be introduced (Lk. 1:67–79).

And yet in other ways, Herod misunderstood the nature of the Christ's kingdom, even as his successor, Antipas, would fail to comprehend the true nature of Jesus' kingship when he sent Him back to Pilot clothed in a royal robe (Lk. 23:11). When Jesus began preaching the gospel of the kingdom, He subverted many of the common notions of what the Messiah's kingship would look like. He taught that instead of ruling the world from an earthly throne like Herod, He would rule the world from heaven until His second coming (1 Cor. 15:24–26). Instead of toppling tyrants like Herod in a sudden catastrophic revolution, the redemption of the nations would be a gradual process accomplished through discipleship, baptism, and the work of missions (Mt. 28:18–20).

But though Jesus disrupted many false expectations of the Messiah's mission, He never disputed the idea that His kingdom would be a physical, earthy entity. Herod, along with all first-century Jews, was correct in anticipating that the Messiah's kingdom would be *of* and *for* this world.[6]

So Herod was right to fear Jesus, for the birth of Jesus was a portent of the imminent catastrophe against tyrants such as himself. God was beginning to judge the world, and this was reinforced in A.D. 70 when the Romans leveled the magnificent temple Herod had built. Centuries later, even the resilient Roman Empire would meet its doom, to be replaced with European Christendom. The kingdom of Herod and the empire of the Caesars were both outdone by the Christ-child of Bethlehem.

QUESTIONS FOR DISCUSSION

1. Is it appropriate for Christians to follow in the footsteps of the magi and discern meanings and portents from the stars?

2. If God is all-good, He would surely not have wanted the Massacre of the Innocents to take place; if God is all-powerful, He would have been able to stop the Massacre from happening; however, since the Massacre did occur, does it mean that God is either not all-powerful or not completely good?

6. Jesus never said that His kingdom is not of this world, despite wrong translations of John 18:36. The Revised Standard Version translates John 18:36 closest to the original Greek: "My kingdom is not from this world." Christ's kingdom is certainly of and for this world, but it does not arise from the authority of worldly powers in the way that Herod's kingdom did. Rather, it descends from heaven to earth, like Jesus. Thus, Christ taught us to pray, "Thy kingdom come on earth . . . as it is in heaven" (Mt. 6:10). As used in the gospels, the expression "kingdom of heaven" refers to God's lordship being brought to bear in the present reality. This draws on the theology of passages like Daniel 7: 26–27 and is the same crowning vision we find in Revelation 11:15: "The kingdoms of this world are become the kingdoms of our Lord, and of his Christ." For more information on this topic, see "Is Jesus' Kingdom of this world?" at http://tinyurl.com/2eydyn2.

3. Much of what the Bible says about the Herodians can be confirmed through extra-biblical textual evidence. Is it appropriate for such evidence to strengthen our conviction that the Bible is true? If so, does it logically follow that the converse should also be the case: that lack of extra-biblical textual evidence should weaken our conviction of the Bible's veracity?

4. During the reign of Antiochus Epiphanes, many Jews let themselves be tortured rather than disobey God's commandments. Would it be wrong to disobey God if someone forced you to?

5. Was Mattathias right to slay the leader of the king's messengers and the Jew who was prepared to offer the idolatrous sacrifices demanded by the king?

6. Until the Hasmonean kings came along, the positions of king and High Priest had been kept strictly separate. When King Uzziah tried to offer sacrifices in the temple, he was struck down with leprosy. Is there a lesson we can learn from this about "sphere sovereignty" or the necessary separation of church and state?

7. Herod married into the Maccabean family in an attempt to give hereditary legitimacy to his kingship. How important is it that a monarch have an impressive heredity?

8. First Timothy 3:4-5 specifies that before someone can be a leader in the church, they must first have learned to rule their own household. Why is this important? Would this be a useful rule for our political leaders to follow, too?

9. What evidences are there of Christ's kingdom making a difference in our present world?

10. Was it right for Joseph, and later Soemus, to reveal to Mariamne that Herod had ordered her death should he fail to return? If you work for someone and you know that your employer is plotting wrong against another person, is it always appropriate to tell that person?

11. It has been said that if ever there was an argument against polygamy, Herod was it. However, apart from the practical difficulties involved in having so many wives living under one roof, is

polygamy actually unbiblical? If a Christian moved to a polyga-
mous culture where women are economically dependent on men
and in which there is a surplus female population, would it be
unbiblical for a Christian to take more than one wife?

12. If someone's insanity leads him to commit evil, is he less guilty
than one who commits evil out of the calm deliberations of a rational mind?

13. Many people today think of Christ's kingdom as an invisible and
non-earthly reality. Is this the biblical view?

14. Many of the Pharisees considered the eagle that Herod mounted
on the temple to be a graven image of the type forbidden by the
second commandment of Exodus 20. Were they correct?

15. Some strict Protestants have argued on the basis of the Second
Commandment that there should not be any representative art-
work in churches. Is this application legitimate?

16. Is it unbiblical to execute criminals in an intentionally brutal way
as a deterrent to potential law-breakers?

17. Was Herod right to fear the Christ-child?

18. If Jesus' kingdom makes an actual difference in the real world,
why have tyrants like Herod continued to exist throughout the
Christian era? Has anything really changed in this regard since
the birth of Christ?

PERSONAL CHALLENGE

We have seen that Jesus' kingdom makes a real difference in the present space-time universe. How has Jesus made a difference in the part
of the world where *you* live? What are *you* doing to further extend
His kingdom?

CHAPTER 2

CONTENDING FOR THE FAITH

The Witness of Perpetua (181–203)
and Irenaeus (c. 130–202)

PERSECUTION UNDER SEVERUS

The date is A.D. 202 and the Roman emperor, Septimius Severus, has just enacted a law prohibiting the spread of Christianity and Judaism throughout the Roman Empire.

Alarmed by the steady growth of Christianity (which may have been increasing by as much as 40 percent each decade throughout the second century), Emperor Septimius hopes his decree will contain the Christian threat and strengthen his kingdom.

While persecution was nothing new to Christians in the early third century, this was the first time there was a universal decree forbidding conversion. If someone was discovered to have become a Christian, the choice offered by the emperor was simple: either curse Jesus and make an offering to the Roman gods or be executed.

"Many martyrs are daily burned, confined, or beheaded, before our eyes," observed Clement of Alexandria, describing conditions during the "terrible reign" of Severus.[1]

---

1. Philip Schaff, *History of the Christian Church Volume 2: Ante-Nicene Christianity* (New York: Charles Scribner's Sons, 1910), 75.

THE MARTYRDOM OF PERPETUA

One particularly moving story from this period concerns the martyrdom of a young mother named Perpetua.

Perpetua was a noblewoman living in Carthage at the beginning of the third century. Although it was unusual for women of that time to be educated, Perpetua was able to read and write. The account she left us of the events leading up to her martyrdom is the earliest known document written by a Christian woman.

In A.D. 203, when Perpetua was around twenty-one years old, she was preparing for baptism along with four other **catechumens** from Carthage, including a young woman named Felicity, who was eight months pregnant.

When the Roman authorities in Carthage learned of the conversions, Perpetua and her companions were taken to a dwelling and put under house arrest.

Though she was still nursing her newborn son and came under intense pressure from her pagan father to renounce the Christian faith, Perpetua was determined to remain faithful to Christ.

When it became clear that the company were soon to be moved to jail, the local church authorities allowed them to be baptized ahead of their formal training. Receiving the sacrament of baptism and the Eucharist, the five converts prayed for strength to endure to the very end. One can only imagine Perpetua's agony when the day finally arrived and she was sent to prison, while her baby, utterly dependent on his mother for sustenance, was taken from her.

A Roman prison was a foul place, and this one was no exception. The five converts were put in a windowless cellar, where there was no relief from the hot stifling air.

Upon entering the dark cell, Perpetua's worst torment was the thought of her child left helpless without her. However, two church deacons bribed the jailer to move the Christians to a better part of the prison. It was here that Perpetua received a visit from her Christian mother, who brought her son, now faint with hunger, to be suckled. For the remainder of her time in jail, Perpetua was allowed to keep the child. Because she was a woman of high birth, she was also allowed to keep a diary.

When the day of the trial finally arrived, the prisoners were brought before a tribunal, where Perpetua's father was also waiting.

Appealing to her love for him and for her child, the elderly man tried in vain to make his daughter renounce her beliefs. Hilarian the procurator urged Perpetua similarly, saying, "Spare your father's gray hairs. Spare the infancy of the boy. Make sacrifice for the Emperor's prosperity."

Perpetua answered simply, "I am a Christian." This left Hilarian with no choice but to pass sentence. Perpetua, along with the others, was condemned to be killed in the stadium for the amusement of the crowds. However, even at this point it was not too late for them to go free if they would simply agree to renounce Christ.

Thus it was that on March 7, 203, Perpetua and the other converts were marched to the Carthaginian amphitheater amid jeering crowds. Before entering the arena, both Perpetua and Felicity were stripped naked and forced to climb inside a net. A mad heifer had been prepared to kick, knock, and trample the netted girls to death. However, when they were brought into the arena, even the callous Romans shuddered to see the tender girls, milk still dripping from Perpetua's breasts. Consequently, Perpetua and Felicity were recalled and given robes to put on.

Even after being attacked by the cow, Perpetua did not die but stood up. Though covered in blood, she helped Felicity to her feet. Then turning to her Christians friends in the audience, she encouraged them, urging them to stand firm in the faith and to love one another.

A swordsman was appointed with the task of completing what the cow had been unable to complete. The man was a novice, so instead of piercing Perpetua right through, the blade accidently hit her collar bone. She shrieked but did not die. Unafraid of death, the bleeding Perpetua picked up the blade and set it upon her own neck, in order that the swordsman might finish the job.

WHY WERE THE CHRISTIANS PERSECUTED?

Why were gentle Christians like Perpetua considered such a hazard to Rome? Why did the emperor Severus believe that Christianity threatened the health of his empire?

This question is especially puzzling when we realize that Rome tolerated all manner of different religious movements. In the city of Rome, and throughout her empire, there was an array of various mystery cults. These were imported from all over the civilized world, but especially from the East. They offered their votaries privileged access to certain divinities but—and this point is crucial—*they did not dictate how life should be conducted in the public world.*

It is this last point which helps to explain why Christianity was so different. Like the New Age movement of today, the mystery cults occupied themselves entirely with one's interior spirituality. Christianity, by contrast, did not, and neither did the imperial religion of the Roman state.

But what was the religion of the Roman state? The main feature of the imperial religion was not emperor-worship, as is often imagined. It is true that many of the Julio-Claudian emperors claimed to be sons of a god, with some of them even claiming divine honors for themselves. However, the basis for such emperor-worship was the imperial religion, which revolved around loyalty to the empire. This loyalty involved more than merely paying taxes and defending one's country. It involved bringing all of one's external life and allegiance into subjection to the priorities of the state. As N.T. Wright wrote,

> The evidence now available, including that from epigraphy and archaeology, shows that the cult of Caesar was not simply one new religion among many in the Roman world. Already by Paul's time it had become the dominant cult in a large part of the Empire, certainly in the parts where Paul was active, and was the means whereby the Romans managed to control and govern such huge areas as came under their sway. Who needs armies when they have worship?[2]

It is not hard to see why the religion of Rome, or the "cult of Caesar," was attractive to so many. After all, the Roman state offered a vision of the good life. The state offered peace for its citizens, brought together previously warring pluralities, instilled a sense of eschatological progress, and provided a framework of meaning to answer the question, "How should we live?" In short, the commitment that

2. N.T. Wright, "Paul's Gospel and Caesar's Empire," N.T. Wright Page—An Unofficial Website Dedicated to Professor N.T. Wright, http://www.ntwrightpage.com/Wright_Paul_Caesar_Empire.pdf (accessed January 6, 2012).

Rome demanded of its citizens was so complete that it can only be adequately described in religious terms, even though many votaries of the state would not have considered themselves Rome-worshipers.

Unlike the mystery religions, which were private and personal, the religion demanded by Rome was *public* and *political*. As Stephen Perks has observed,

> The Eastern cults that were popular in ancient Rome, such as the cults of Mithras and Isis, did not structure the lives of their adherents—at least not if they were good Roman citizens. What structured the lives of the Romans was the religion of Rome, which was a political religion.[3]

Against this backdrop, it begins to make sense that Christianity threatened the imperial credo while the mystery cults did not. The Christians, like the Caesars, applied the language of *euangelion* ("gospel" or "glad tidings") to their movement. The Christians, like Rome, taught that they held the answer for bringing justice, order ,and peace to the world (Lk. 2:13–14; Jn. 14:27). The Christians, like the Romans, claimed that a single man had rightful dominion over the whole earth (Mt. 28:18). The Christians, like the imperial religion, offered a sense of community to previously warring pluralities (Gal. 3:28). The Christians, like the religion of Rome, were intent on evangelizing the world (Mt. 28:19).

But whereas the Caesars sought to Romanize the world through brutality, force, and bloodshed, the Christians sought to evangelize the world through love, self-giving, and sacrifice. The glad tidings of Jesus was therefore bad news for Caesar, since it proclaimed there was another way to transform the world that was superior to Caesar's way. It announced that God had called out a people whose vocation was to work for peace and justice on Jesus' terms, not Caesar's.

Had Christianity been merely one more mystery cult, offering its followers a new kind of spiritual experience, the Romans would have taken little or no notice of individuals like Perpetua. It was precisely

---

3. Stephen C. Perks, *Common-law Wives and Concubines: Essays on Covenantal Christianity and Contemporary Western Culture* (Taunton: Kuyper Foundation, 2003), 10.

for this reason—because the totalizing claims of Christ's lordship competed with the goals of the imperial idolatry—that Christianity could not be ignored. As Peter Leithart has observed in his book *Against Christianity,* the early church did not preach an essentially private gospel that existed within the public sphere, as if the public implications of the gospel were a second story built on the ground floor of private life. Rather, the gospel is the announcement that a new creation has burst in upon the old order, transforming not just individuals, but nations.[4] Such nations included the Roman Empire.

Even when the early Christians submitted to the ruling authorities, there was an implicit challenge. In writing to the Romans, Paul made clear that the reason Christians were to submit to the civil magistrates is because the rulers have been placed there by the higher authority of God (Rom. 13:1). Though the Caesars liked to think of themselves as subject to no one, Christians proclaimed that earthly rulers are God's ministers, responsible for carrying out His business here on earth (Rom. 13:2–7). The idea that Caesar's authority was *derivative* rather than *ultimate* was nothing less than fighting talk in the politically tumultuous days of the first and second centuries.

In light of this backdrop, one can easily understand why emperors like Severus felt threatened by the astronomical growth of the Christian movement. One can also imagine how strong the temptation must have been to rewrite the Christian faith as merely one more politically-correct mystery cult. And that is precisely what one group of heretics, known as the Gnostics, tried to do.

GNOSTICISM: AVOIDING CONFRONTATION

Gnosticism refers to a broad network of religious movements that developed independently of Christianity in the second century (and possibly earlier), but that quickly transformed themselves to take on a Christian hue.[5]

Although Gnosticism was never a monolithic movement and contained an almost infinite array of variants, there are certain key

---

4. Peter J. Leithart, *Against Christianity* (Moscow: Canon Press, 2003), 16.

5. For more information on the history of Gnosticism and its relevance today, see "Resources for Understanding Gnosticism," http://atgsociety.com/?p=1814 (accessed February 20, 2012).

commonalities which are shared by the various Gnostic sects. One of these characteristics was the belief that this world is corrupted beyond redemption—not because the world is *sinful,* but because it is *physical.* The basic human problem, according to the Gnostics, is not sin, but materiality.

Building on this, many Gnostics taught that our best hope is to receive secret knowledge that will enable us to escape into a paradise where we will no longer be burdened by matter. Such salvation is achieved through the attainment of hidden, esoteric knowledge (*gnosis,* in Greek).

What is needed to activate our escape is a revealer from the realms beyond (the upper spiritual realm undiluted by matter) to reveal to the chosen few that they have a divine spark within themselves. By responding to this divine spark instead of to the pressing influences of the shabby material world around us, the chosen ones can attain enlightenment in this life and disembodiment in the next.

For many of the so-called "Christian Gnostics," Jesus occupied the role of revealer. Significantly, Jesus was not seen as the creator of the world (the God who created matter must be bad, they reasoned, since matter is evil), but the one who shows us how to *escape* from the world. Unlike mainstream Christianity, which taught that God would renew the world and resurrect the bodies of the righteous, the Gnostics believed that disembodiment was the ultimate goal of salvation.

Most of the Gnostics agreed with the assumption behind the various mystery cults: namely, that spirituality is an intensely private affair. In attempting to reduce Christianity to this level, it left its devotees free to do what they liked in regards to imperial idolatry. After all, many of them reasoned, what happens in this world is of little importance and serves only to distract us from genuine enlightenment. Thus, while the early Christians were getting into trouble for rivaling the political priorities of Rome, many of the Gnostics (to quote a contemporary scholar of Gnosticism, M.A. Williams) "seemed intent precisely on pursuing a lessening of sociocultural tension between their religious movement and the larger social world."[6]

---

6. M.A. Williams, *Rethinking "Gnosticism": An Argument for Dismantling a Dubious Category* (Princeton: Princeton University Press, 1996), 264.

While saints like Perpetua were perishing under the sword for refusing to offer public allegiance to the religion of Rome, many of the Gnostics were teaching that what really counts is what goes on in your mind and heart. True faith, the Gnostics believed, is a matter of personal salvation, not public testimony. Like followers of the mystery cults, most of the Gnostics had no interest in the public, communal, and world-transforming categories of orthodox Christianity.

It is no surprise that Rome loved Gnosticism. It could truly be said of the Gnostics that they were too heavenly minded to be of any earthly good. The dualism they advocated between matter and spirit, together with their emphasis on private spirituality over and against public faith, conveniently avoided any confrontation with the ruling powers.

IRENAEUS AND THE CONFLICT WITH GNOSTICISM

One of Gnosticism's chief opponents was the Christian bishop Irenaeus, who was born probably sometime between 130 and 140 in the town of Smyrna, Asia Minor (modern Turkey). It was here that the young Irenaeus met Polycarp, the aged Bishop of Smyrna who had known the Apostle John personally.

Prior to Polycarp's martyrdom in 156, Irenaeus and his friend Florinus had often been inspired by the bishop's moving accounts of his conversations with John. Reflecting on this, Irenaeus would later write,

> I can tell the very place in which the blessed Polycarp used to sit when he preached his sermons, how he came in and went out, the manner of his life, what he looked like, the sermons he delivered to the people, and how he used to report his association with John and the others who had seen the Lord, how he would relate their words, and the things concerning the Lord he had heard from them, about His miracles and teachings. Polycarp had received all this from eyewitnesses of the Word of life, and related all these things in accordance with the Scriptures. I listened eagerly to these things at the time, by God's mercy which was bestowed on me, and I made notes of them, not on

paper, but in my heart, and constantly by the grace of God I meditate on them faithfully.[7]

When he grew up, Irenaeus eventually came to settle in Lyons, where he became a priest. Situated in France between Paris and Marseille, Lyons was the center of Roman Gaul and a thriving intellectual community.

During the rough days of the second century, the church was suffering from without at the hands of hostile emperors and within at the hands of mischievous heretics. Irenaeus was plunged into this turbulent milieu when he was made Bishop of Lyons, following the martyrdom of the town's previous bishop.

Irenaeus soon found himself having to confront Gnosticism head-on. Not only were the Gnostics gaining popularity in his bishopric, but Irenaeus's own boyhood friend, Florinus, embraced this politically-correct, sanitized alternative to Christianity.

Of particular concern to Irenaeus were the teachings of Valentinus. Described by Eric Osborn as a "pompous Platonist who turned his gifts to the confusion of the church and the fabrication of intricate fables,"[8] Valentinus developed a complex account of how a being called the "demiurge" created humans by mistake.

One of Irenaeus's chief criticisms against the Valentinian Gnostics was that they denied Jesus' physical body. "But according to none of the views of the heretics," he wrote, "was the Word of God made flesh. If one should read over all their creedal statements, he would find that they always bring in the Word of God and the Christ who is from above as without flesh and free from suffering."[9]

Because of their matter/spirit dualism, the Gnostics separated God the creator from Jesus the redeemer. Irenaeus opposed this by arguing forcefully for the unity of God. In his book *Against Heresies,* he proved from Scripture that the creator God was revealed in Jesus

7. Nicholas R. Needham, *2,000 Years of Christ's Power: Part One: The Age of the Early Church Fathers* (London: Grace Publications Trust, 1997), 98.

8. Eric Osborn, *Irenaeus of Lyons* (Cambridge: Cambridge University Press, 2001), 7.

9. Irenaeus of Lyons, "Selections from the Work Against Heresies," Christian Classics Ethereal Library: Early Christian Fathers, http://www.ccel.org/ccel/richardson/fathers.xi.i.iii.html (accessed February 18, 2012).

Christ, and that this God is *good*. The God who began the world is also the God who has been carefully overseeing it, bringing His plan to fruition through everything that happens. This plan, Irenaeus argued, culminated in the redemptive work of Christ and will be consummated when God renews the creation.

From this platform, Irenaeus vigorously opposed the idea that our physical experiences in this world are unspiritual. Rather, he suggested that a truly spiritual person should be able to glory in the world about him and in the life God has graciously given us. His oft-quoted words, "Man fully alive is the glory of God," bespeak an optimistic vision of life in which the salvation of our humanity and the physical experiences we have in our body become unified. This unity is an important consequence of the gospel.

Irenaeus understood redemption as being broader than something that merely affects solitary individuals. Rather, salvation comes for the sake of the larger world, which God is in the process of renewing. As Professor Mark McIntosh has put it, "For Irenaeus, salvation is fundamentally the recovery, renewal, and discovery of what the true glory and potential of creation might be."[10]

But Irenaeus' optimism also had an edge. Since this life is good, and since this world is the product of a good God, it follows that what happens in this world matters. Indeed, the good God who made all things by His word is sovereign over the world and has the power to judge it. It follows, Irenaeus believed, that the power exercised by earthly rulers like Caesar is derivative rather than ultimate since it comes from the higher authority of God. Consequently, Christians should not just be passive observers while the forces of evil carve up the world for themselves. Instead, Irenaeus taught, believers are called to act as agents of new creation, endeavoring to apply God's renewal to the here-and-now regardless of the consequences.

LEGACY AND LESSONS

Perpetua and Irenaeus lived very different lives in very different places. Yet they are linked by a common commitment to the proclamation of Christ's kingdom. They both shunned the life of ease that might have

---

10. Mark A. McIntosh, *Divine Teaching: An Introduction to Christian Theology* (Malden: Blackwell Publishing, 2008), 81.

been theirs had they only embraced the Gnostic idea—so popular in our own age as well—that faith is merely a private personal affair that ought to remain disconnected with what we do in the public world.

The idea of public truth played a key role in Irenaeus' polemic against the Gnostics. The Gnostics, like other heretical groups, attempted to interpret Scripture outside the apostolic tradition that had produced the Scriptures in the first place. For example, many of the Gnostics claimed they had special secret knowledge passed on orally from Jesus and the apostles. This secret knowledge had apparently bypassed mainline, institutionalized Christianity.

To combat this theory and underscore the public nature of Christian truth, Irenaeus developed the idea of apostolic succession. The church is the custodian of the truth, he argued, but only those churches that have continuity with the teachings of the apostles. To establish whether a church is within the apostolic tradition one must do two things. First, one must look to see if the church's theology is in line with the rule of faith passed down through the apostles in the sacred writings. Thus, Irenaeus used biblical exposition to show that the teachings of the Gnostic churches were incompatible with the apostles' doctrine.

Secondly, in determining whether a church is legitimate it was equally important to see if it was under a bishop who was the recipient of a chain of ordination going back to the apostles. This was because he believed that the apostles and their successors would have appointed only those leaders who agreed with their teaching and also because he believed that apostolic authority was transmitted by the laying on of hands in a transfer of real divine power and authority. As Irenaeus put it in *Against Heresies*,

> [W]e appeal again to that tradition which has come down from the apostles and is guarded by the succession of elders in the churches. . . . Even if the apostles had not left their Writings to us, ought we not to follow the rule of the tradition which they handed down to those to whom they committed the churches?[11]

11. Irenaeus, *Against Heresies* in Cyril Richardson, *Early Christian Fathers* (New York: Simon & Schuster, 1996), 371–374.

Although Irenaeus did not have time "to enumerate the successions of all the churches," he took the church at Rome as one example and traced the succession of ordinations back to Peter and Paul. This, he maintains, provides "a full demonstration that it is one and the same life-giving faith which has been preserved in the Church from the apostles to the present, and is handed on in truth."

The doctrine of apostolic succession provided a hedge around the interpretation of Scripture. Any church which taught private innovations, doctrines that were different from the public tradition of the other apostolic sees, was a church teaching heresy.

The appeal to public truth by Irenaeus was not mere abstract doctrine, but a matter of life and death. It was precisely because Christian truth is public that it is worth dying for. If Irenaeus had lived to see Perpetua pierced by the sword, he would not only have applauded her willingness to make a public stand against the imperial religion, he would certainly have joined her. We know this because one of his arguments against the Gnostics is that though many of them claimed the name of Christ, they were unwilling to die for Him. "During the whole time which has elapsed since the Lord appeared on earth," Irenaeus once commented, "only one or two of them . . . have occasionally, along with our martyrs, borne the reproach of the name . . . and been led forth with them to death."[12]

Irenaeus and Perpetua did have one thing in common with the religion of Rome. They both agreed with Rome (against the Gnostics and mystery cults) that the truth which demands our allegiance is public and accessible to all. But they denied that Caesar was the nexus of that truth. Ultimate truth, they maintained, can be found in none other than Jesus Christ. It was this faith that spurred on Irenaeus in his conflict against the Gnostics, and this faith that comforted Perpetua even as she lifted the sword to her bleeding neck.

12. Irenaeus, *Against Heresies* in Reverend Alexander Roberts, *The Ante-Nicene Fathers: The Writings of the Fathers Down to A.D. 325 Volume I: The Apostolic Fathers with Justin Martyr and Irenaeus* (New York: Cosimo, 2007), 508.

QUESTIONS FOR DISCUSSION

1. In the early church, a catechumen went through a period of training before receiving the sacrament of baptism. By contrast, many churches today will baptize converts simply on a confession of faith. Is either of these practices more biblical than the other?

2. Can the obligation to honor Christ ever conflict with the obligation to honor our parents?

3. What were some possible reasons why the mystery cults were so popular in Rome?

4. One of the reasons that Irenaeus taught apostolic succession is because he believed that the apostles "certainly wished those whom they were leaving as their successors, handing over to them their own teaching position, to be perfect and irreproachable, since their sound conduct would be a great benefit [to the Church], and failure on their part the greatest calamity." If Irenaeus was correct, might it be possible that the purity of this chain of succession could expire after a time, as the link to the first apostles becomes more and more distant?

5. Is Irenaeus' doctrine of apostolic succession a biblical doctrine?

6. If Irenaeus is correct in his doctrine of apostolic succession, which churches today satisfy the criteria for having apostolic succession?

7. How can the idea that "the glory of God is man fully alive" help in our approach to everyday life?

8. Discuss the following statement: "The early church was political, but not in the way that the church tries to be political today."

9. It has been noted that when the early Christians said, "Jesus is Lord," they were simultaneously saying "therefore Caesar is not." Going on information presented in the Bible, does this seem likely?

10. How were the goals and methods of the Caesars similar or different to the goals and methods of Jesus?

11. What does it mean in practice to say that Jesus has redeemed nations as well as individuals?

12. What are some Gnostic tendencies that contemporary Christianity has imbibed?

13. H. Richard Niebuhr discussed the relationship of the church and culture in terms of the following five paradigms: Christ against Culture, Christ of Culture, Christ above Culture, Christ and Culture in Paradox, and Christ Transforming Culture. Which of these models best illustrates the Gnostic approach to the faith? How many, if any, of these models describe the biblical approach?

PERSONAL CHALLENGE

If you were offered a choice to either curse Jesus and make an offering to a false god or accept death by execution, what do you think you might do? Is there anything you could be doing now to help prepare you for such an event?

CHAPTER 3

TAMING THE STORM

The Manly Strength of Saint Columbanus (540–615)

THE ANCIENT CELTS

"Their aspect is terrifying . . . They are very tall in stature, with rippling muscles under clear, white skin."[1] Thus wrote the Greek historian Diodorus Siculus in the first century B.C., to describe the legendary Celtic peoples. Diodorus continued:

> The Celtic way of fighting was alarming. They wore . . . bronze helmets with figures picked out on them, even horns, which make them look even taller than they already are . . . while others cover themselves with breast-armor made of chains. But most content themselves with the weapons nature gave them: they go naked into battle.[2]

As these words suggest, the Celts were feared by the Greeks and Romans, and with good reason. Emerging from central Europe around 1000 B.C., these fierce warlike people were among the most

1. Ted Olsen, *Christianity and the Celts* (Oxford: Lion, 2003), 10.
2. Ibid.

successful conquerors the world had ever known. Archaeologists have discovered Celtic artifacts as far north as Denmark and as far east as India. By the time of the Roman Empire, however, Celtic dominance had waned, being limited primarily to Gaul (modern France) and the British Isles.

In 390 B.C., the Romans were able to witness firsthand the ferocity of the Celts, when a Celtic tribe from Gaul sacked Rome. The tables were turned two centuries later when Julius Caesar tried to annex Gaul, and later Britain, for Rome. It would take nearly a hundred more years before Rome finally succeeded in bringing the British Celts into her empire. Even then, Rome had to send about an eighth of her entire fighting force to the island just to keep the Celts from revolting. Moreover, a heavily fortified seventy-six-mile-long barrier known as Hadrian's Wall (named after the emperor who commissioned it) was required to keep the wild confederation of northern Celtic tribes at bay.

Fierce as they may have been, the Celts were also sensitive to poetry, music, and the arts. They were great craftsmen, fine storytellers, and legendary for their hospitality.

TRANSFORMED BY THE GOSPEL

No one knows for sure how the Celts living in the British Isles first heard about the gospel. According to one set of legends, Christianity was introduced to Britain shortly after the resurrection by Joseph of Arimathea, a tin merchant who is thought to have been Jesus' great uncle. Whether there is any truth to such stories or not, it is clear from the writings of people like Tertullian (c. 160–220) and Origen of Alexandria (c. 185–254) that Christianity was well established in Britain by the second century, possibly earlier.

When these warrior-poets embraced Christianity, they lost neither their fierceness nor their poetry but put these qualities to the service of God's kingdom. Like King David, the prayers and hymns of the Celts show a vision of the Lord that was raw, rugged and untamed. It was a hardy faith that would later give birth to stalwart reformers such as John Knox.

If Christianity helped to mitigate the barbarism of the Celts, however, it diminished none of their natural temerity. Celtic monks were known to be just as courageous, and sometimes just as foolhardy, as their pagan forefathers.

"A SPIRIT OF RESTLESS ENERGY"

The Celts had always been keen explorers, eager to seek adventure through travel. After their conversion to Christianity, this dynamic energy found expression in some incredible missionary voyages. Never half-hearted about anything, Celtic missionaries sailed to wild Nordic lands or to rural areas in Gaul where the Christianizing influences of the late Roman Empire had not yet penetrated. Old Irish writings with Christian symbols have even been found as far afield as West Virginia, presenting a mystery for archaeologists and scholars to the present day.

While we do not know the extent of their missionary labors, it is clear that the Celts were some of the boldest evangelists the world has ever known. "A spirit of restless energy possessed them," wrote Katharine Scherman in *The Flowering of Ireland*. She spoke of the Irish Christians possessing a "seeking curiosity, the desire to expand mental boundaries along with physical, to find new ideas in new settings."[3]

It is one of these Celtic missionaries whose story concerns us now.

IN SEARCH OF EXILE

Columbanus was born around A.D. 543 in what is now south Leinster, Ireland. Not much is known about his childhood, but we do know that he grew up in a Christian community where he was nurtured in the faith by his God-fearing mother.

As he grew older, Columbanus lacked none of the native beauty of the Celts. In fact, according to his seventh-century biographer Jonas of Bobbio, his physical attractiveness began a series of events that would result in him coming to embrace the monastic life. The lad was not only handsome, but his fine figure, the splendid color of

---

3. Katharine Scherman, *The Flowering of Ireland: Saints, Scholars, and Kings* (New York: Barnes & Noble, 1996), 132.

his hair, and his noble manliness made him beloved by all, especially by the young maidens.

The attractions of the opposite sex did not go unnoticed by Columbanus, who began to find it increasingly difficult to resist the advances of beautiful girls. Fearing that he was on the brink of giving into the lusts of the flesh, Columbanus sought the council of a female hermit known for her wisdom. Twelve years earlier this woman had fled from the world to take refuge in a cell. She reminded Columbanus that Samson, David, and Solomon had all been led astray by females. Recalling her own example of pious exile, her advice to the young man was blunt: "Away, O youth, away! Flee from corruption, into which, as you know, many have fallen. Forsake the path which leads to the gates of hell."[4]

A true Celt, Columbanus took the injunction to "flee" literally. To him it could only mean one thing: he must seek exile as a monk.

Returning home, he immediately began to pack his bags, while his mother urged him to reconsider. It is not hard to guess why she opposed the idea: for the Celts, going into exile as a monk was always meant to be permanent. Indeed, if one ever returned home, it was looked upon as backsliding.

When it became clear that her words would not deter her son from the path he had chosen, Columbanus's mother changed her strategy. She barred the entrance to the cottage with her own body. Undeterred, Columbanus is said to have leaped "over both threshold and mother."

Columbanus traveled to the northwest monastery of Cleenish. From there he went to Bangor (in present-day Wales) where he studied under the fiery Irish Pict, Comgall.

Columbanus and Comgall got on well together. Both were bold, rough, and adventurous. Comgall was so rugged, in fact, that in his younger days he had taken a number of his followers to a remote island, where he ordered them to fast for days on end. However, emulating the lifestyle of desert monastics in the harsh climate of Ireland proved too much for many of Comgall's weaker followers, some of whom died before the exercise was complete. But the dead monks were soon replaced by hundreds of others attracted to the austere

---

4. Jonas of Bobbio, *Life of St. Columban* (Charleston: BiblioLife, 2009), 4.

lifestyle. These monks congregated at Bangor, where a thriving monastery was established.

Columbanus remained at Bangor for twenty-five years, gaining a reputation both as a scholar and a model of piety.

COLUMBANUS TAKES TO THE SEA

"[For] the Irish people," observed the Benedictine theologian Walafrid Strabo in the ninth century, "the custom of traveling to foreign lands has now become almost second nature."[5] Columbanus was no exception. By his mid-forties the desire to travel to far-off lands became too strong to resist. Although Comgall was initially hesitant to let him go, the abbot eventually approved a missionary voyage to Gaul.

Taking twelve disciples with him, Columbanus journeyed first to Britain. As they braved the elements in their small craft, Columbanus kept up the courage of his men by composing and singing songs such as the following:

The Boat Song of Saint Columbanus

Cut in the forests, swept down the two-horned Rhine,
Our keel, tight-caulked, now floats upon the sea.
Heia, men! Let the echoes resound with our heia!

The wild gusts swell, the slashing torrents fall,
But manly strength has force to tame the storm.
Heia, men! Let the echoes resound with our heia!

To earnest effort, clouds and tempest yield;
Zeal and unceasing labor conquer all.
Heia, men! Let the echoes resound with our heia!

Endure and save yourselves for better things;
Oh you who have suffered worse, this too shall end.
Heia, men! Let the echoes resound with our heia!

---

5. Olsen, *Christianity and the Celts,* 130.

So when the loathsome foe assaults our hearts,
Tempting and shaking the depths of our hearts with passion,
Let your souls, men, remembering Christ, cry heia!

In resolution fixed, scorn Satan's wiles.
By virtues armed, defend yourselves with valor.
Let your souls, men, remembering Christ, cry heia!

Firm faith and holy ardor conquer all.
The ancient fiend, defeated, breaks his arrows.
Let your souls, men, remembering Christ, cry heia!

The Source of Good and Being, the Highest Power,
Offers the warrior and gives the victor prizes.
Let your souls, men, remembering Christ, cry heia![6]

MINISTRY IN GAUL

From Britain, Columbanus and his companions traveled to Gaul,
where they were welcomed by the king of Burgundy, who offered
the monks a half-ruined Roman fortress in the Vosges Mountains
for a base.

Far away from civilization and nourished only by what the forest
provided, it was an ideal life for Columbanus, who once remarked
that he was "seeking the salvation of many, and a solitary spot of my
own." For better or worse, his effectiveness at the former rendered
him unsuccessful at the latter. Almost immediately the monastery
began to attract crowds who had heard about the sanctity of Columbanus and his men. To escape, he would often withdraw to a distant
cave, taking only a single companion to act as messenger between
himself and the brothers back at base.

In rapid succession Columbanus established monasteries at Anne-
gray, Luxeuil, and Fontaine. Country-dwelling aristocrats flocked to
these communities as a welcome alternative to the exclusively urban
monasteries that had characterized pre-Columbanian Gaul. Once a

---

6. Charles Till Davis, *Sources of Medieval History* (New York: Appleton-Century-
Crofts, 1967), 91–92.

monastery became too crowded, Columbanus would simply move on and start a new one.

Not everyone was happy about the influence of Columbanus on the Continent. In Ireland it was customary for an abbot, not a bishop, to supervise a monastic network. In Gaul, on the other hand, early sixth-century councils had handed Frankish bishops absolute authority over abbots and their monasteries, even ordering abbots to appear periodically before their bishops. Columbanus simply ignored these rules and carried on with the Celtic pattern he was used to, to the chagrin of the French clergy. While this alienated him from the church leaders, it endeared him to the people. This was because many Frankish bishops were perceived as pieces of a power-hungry political system, being appointed by kings as a way to reward royal servants. Historian Richard A. Fletcher notes that this practice made many French families apprehensive—sometimes with good reason—of the covetous designs of the nearby bishop on their endowments. The politically **autonomous** monasteries of Columbanus were a welcome alternative and attracted many aristocrats to the monastic lifestyle.

TEACHING ON FORGIVENESS

Columbanus also encountered opposition because of his radical views on forgiveness. By the sixth century an exceptionally harsh model of **penance** had emerged, whereby the church told sinners that they could only demonstrate repentance through a ceremony of public shaming, administered by a bishop in front of the entire congregation. Even after the ceremony a penitent was debarred from ever holding public office (a Spanish king in the seventh century who underwent penance had to abdicate). Moreover, the penitent person was segregated into a special part of the church building, where they had to listen to the communal intercessions for them. This meant that assurance of God's forgiveness was kept at arm's length for many Christians. Moreover, penance could only be undergone once in a lifetime, so anyone who transgressed again was cut off from any hope of pardon.

Not only did Columbanus preach the message of forgiveness to the pagans, he also helped to educate the church in the wonderful

news of God's forgiveness. He taught that penance could be administered by any priest and as many times as was necessary. Though
he commanded penitent sinners to perform acts such as fasting, the
central principle behind penance was repentance and turning away
from sin.

"True penance," he wrote, "is to not commit things deserving of
penance and to lament such things as have been committed."[7] This
held out hope to many Frankish nobles who, unwilling to face the
rigors of penance, would otherwise have believed themselves cut off
from all hope of salvation. However, the Frankish bishops did not
look kindly on these developments, which lessened their own control
over the population.

NOT THE PERSON BUT THE ARGUMENT

It was one thing to challenge the customs and hierarchies of French
bishops, and quite another to take on the pope himself. Yet that is
exactly what Columbanus did on more than one occasion. In fact,
he wrote to the pope in tones ranging from bemusement to ridicule.
"What makes me bold, if I may say so," he wrote in one of his milder
letters to the Roman pontiff, "is partly the freedom of speech which
is the custom of my country. For among us it is not the person but
the argument that carries weight."[8]

It wasn't just the pope and the Frankish bishops who drew the ire
of the feisty Irish monk. Columbanus had a run-in with the polyga-
mous king, Theuderic II, and his grandmother, Brunhilda, when he
refused to bless Theuderic's illegitimate heirs.

As a result of his conflict with Theuderic, Columbanus was thrown
out of Gaul. He remained on the Continent, however, preaching and
establishing monasteries in what would later become France, Germany, and Switzerland.

It was while living in Italy, working to convert the Arian Lom-
bards and build the monastery of Bobbio, that Columbanus died in
November, 615.

7. J. N. Hillgarth, *Christianity and Paganism, 350–750: The Conversion of Western Europe* (Philadelphia: University of Pennsylvania Press, 1986), 131.
8. Olsen, *Christianity and the Celts,* 134.

THE LEGACY AND LESSONS OF SAINT COLUMBANUS

The missionary journeys of Columbanus have remained an inspiration to evangelists throughout history. While others were content for the gospel to be confined to the urban centers of the late Roman Empire, Columbanus forged new ground in taking the message of Christ into rough rural regions dominated by centuries of paganism.

As he confronted rural paganism head on, Columbanus had much to fear, yet he remained steadfast because he believed that the devil was a defeated foe. As he sang in his boat song, "The ancient fiend, defeated, breaks his arrows."

The main reason Columbanus made such an impact throughout Europe was because of the love and good works which emanated from the communities he founded. Twenty-eight years after his death, the monk Jonas wrote an account of his life, based on the eyewitness reports of those who had worked with him. His book, *The Life of St. Columban,* gives us a glimpse into what was so attractive about these communities:

> Modesty and moderation, meekness and mildness adorned them all in equal measure. The evils of sloth and dissension were banished. Pride and haughtiness were expiated by severe punishments. Scorn and envy were driven out by faithful diligence. So great was the might of their patience, love and mildness that no one could doubt that the God of mercy dwelt among them. If they found that one among them was in error, they strove in common, with equal right, to restrain the sinner by their reproaches. They had everything in common. If anyone claimed anything as his own, he was shut out from association with the others and punished by penances. No one dared to return evil for evil, or to let fall a harsh word; so that people must have believed that an angelic life was being lived by mortal men. The holy man was reverenced with so great gratitude that where he remained for a time in a house, all hearts were resolved to practice the faith more strictly.[9]

9. Jonas of Bobbio, *Life of St. Columban*, 6–7.

QUESTIONS FOR DISCUSSION

1. Does the church have the right to give or withhold God's forgiveness to anyone? How does Matthew 18:18 fit into this question?

2. Columbanus dealt with sexual temptations by fleeing the company of all women. Is this an appropriate way to deal with this temptation?

3. When he came to Gaul, Columbanus brought with him a certain structure of church government that clashed with that of the Frankish authorities. Was this a right attitude? Should Columbanus have respected the customs of the Franks when he was living in their land?

4. Is there one right way for church government to be organized, or should different churches have the right to make up their own rules?

5. Columbanus opposed practices of penance that diminished or denied the truth of God's forgiveness. Are there ways in which we also diminish or deny this truth in our personal lives?

6. The story of Comgall represents the tendency among the Celts towards **asceticism**. Is asceticism biblical? Is it sinful?

7. Scherman describes the Celtic Christian as having "a seeking curiosity, the desire to expand mental boundaries . . . to find new ideas in new settings." Is this a good thing? Should the church try to cultivate an atmosphere of intellectual adventurism?

8. Was Columbanus wrong to disobey his mother, who asked him not to go into exile? Should we obey our parents even when we are grown?

9. The monastics believed that one of the most effective ways to evangelize the world was to withdraw from it and worship God in seclusion. Were they correct?

10. Is biblical repentance a purely private act, or is it ever appropriate that there should be a public ceremony to demonstrate it? Is it

appropriate for a pastor to require someone to do certain things as a proof of repentance?

11. Jonas tells us that the monks "had everything in common" and that "if anyone claimed anything as his own, he was shut out from association with the others and punished by penances."[10] Is this a worthy model to follow? What does the Bible teach about private property?

PERSONAL CHALLENGE

The Celts were some of the boldest evangelists the world has ever known. What are some ways your family could be more bold in its evangelism? What about you?

10. Ibid.

CHAPTER 4

AN EXCELLENT PILOT

The Leadership of Alfred the Great (849–899)

The year A.D. 793 would forever change the destiny of Britain. A writer in the late 800s wrote in *The Anglo-Saxon Chronicle* that "in the year 793 terrible portents came over the land of Northumbria, and miserably afflicted the people, there were massive whirlwinds and lightenings, and fiery dragons were seen flying in the air. Immediately after these things there came a terrible famine."[1]

The anonymous writer went on to describe the event that made 793 such a dark year in the annals of Anglo-Saxon history: "Six days before the Ides of January, the harrowing of heathen men miserably devastated the church of God on Lindisfarne, by plunder and slaughter."[2]

The monastery at Lindisfarne had been founded by Saint Aidan in 635, under encouragement from King Oswine of Deira (an Anglo-Saxon kingdom). Located on a small tidal island off the northeast coast of England, the monks who made their home there were completely unprepared for the savage assault that greeted them on January 8,

---

1. Benjamin R. Merkle, *The White Horse King: The Life of Alfred the Great* (Nashville: Thomas Nelson, 2009), 8.
2. Ibid.

793. The priests were cut down, their monastery pillaged, and their sacred altar stripped of its sacred treasures.

Never before had a terror like this been seen in Britain. "For nearly 350 years," wrote the Saxon monk and scholar Alcuin after hearing about the raid, "we and our fathers have dwelt in this most beautiful land, and never before has such a terror appeared in Britain, such as the one that we are suffering from this pagan nation."[3] Alcuin, who was serving at the court of Charlemagne at the time, went on to describe just how unexpected the attack at Lindisfarne was:

> Nor was it thought that a ship would attempt such a thing. Behold the church of Saint Cuthbert, splattered with the blood of the priests of God, plundered of all its treasures, a place more venerable than anywhere in Britain is given over to pagan nations for pillaging . . . the heritage of the Lord has been given over to a people who are not his own. And where the praise of the Lord once was, now is only the games of the pagans. The holy feast has been turned into a lament.[4]

The invaders were Vikings from Scandinavia. When they took their booty home, the thought that there might be more unguarded treasure was too much for their kinsmen to resist. The people of Britain hardly had time to recover from the Lindisfarne massacre when the Vikings sacked another monastery further south at Jarrow. After that they hit the community at Iona in the Hebrides islands, off the western coast of what is now Scotland.

Monasteries, usually situated near waterways, provided a perfect target for these greedy raiders. They could make a quick escape before the surrounding villages had time to mobilize against them. Moreover, the monasteries contained much portable, unprotected wealth.

As tales of easy gains reached the Danish homeland, more of these pillaging "dragon" ships began to make their way to the British coast, carrying small bands of raiding parties. Occasionally, even a whole fleet of a dozen Viking ships would make their way over.

---

3. Cited in ibid., 12.
4. Cited in ibid.

The Anglo-Saxons of Britain were helpless to defend themselves. The Vikings relied on three things that always gave them the advantage: speed, surprise, and fear. Their speed meant that they could strike and return to their ships before a town or monastery had time to sound the alarm. The element of surprise meant that no one could predict when or where they were next going to attack. The result was that the people of Britain became paralyzed with fear, and for good reason: Danish sagas show that the Vikings were not only ruthless but were proud of that fact, taking great delight in their cruelties.

But the Anglo-Saxons possessed one thing that the Vikings did not: they had Christ on their side. Ultimately it would be through the power of Christ that the Vikings would be repulsed.

The fact that the Vikings were attacking religious communities immediately put the conflict into a spiritual context for the Saxons. Alcuin wrote to the king of Northumbria, urging him to call the people to repentance, lest these attacks were God's judgment against this people for their sins: "Consider carefully, brothers, and examine diligently, lest perchance this unaccustomed and unheard-of evil was merited by some unheard-of evil practice."[5]

In another letter, he wrote, "This is the beginning of greater tribulation, or else the sins of the inhabitants have called it upon them. Truly it has not happened by chance, but it is a sign that it was well merited by someone. But now, you who are left, stand manfully, fight bravely, defend the camp of God."[6]

Alcuin was right: this was just the beginning of greater tribulation. Viking ships continued to attack the land, using fast, mobile armies to raid England's coasts in a relentless search for plunder. Utterly destroying everything that stood in their way, the Vikings became the terror of the countryside. Far and wide they ranged, riding stolen horses, killing with such terrible ferocity that the people prayed nightly, "From the fury of the Northmen, Good Lord, deliver us."

5. Angus Somerville and R. Andrew McDonald, The Viking Age: A Reader (Toronto: University of Toronto Press, 2010), 233.
6. Ibid., 845.

HISTORICAL BACKGROUND

When the Romans quit Britain early in the fifth century, the native Britons had suddenly found their shores undefended. Germanic tribes, known collectively as "Anglo-Saxons," had taken advantage of the situation and began coming over to Britain in droves. As more Anglo-Saxons spread over the island, the native Britons were forced to retreat north into Scotland, south into Cornwall, and east into Wales.

Though the Britons had been Christian, they harbored such resentment against their Anglo-Saxon conquerors that they refused to convert them. The job of bringing the Anglo-Saxons into God's kingdom was left to Augustine of Canterbury, a missionary sent to Britain by Gregory the Great (540–604).

In the ninth century, this same cycle was repeating itself. By the middle of the century the Vikings settled on a new goal: permanent conquest of the island. Once again, however, the conquest of Britain would lead to a new people being brought into God's kingdom.

ALFRED'S EARLY YEARS

During those turbulent years, Alfred was born to Æthelwulf and his wife, Osburga. Æthelwulf was king of Wessex, an Anglo-Saxon principality located on the far south of the English coast. At the time of Alfred's birth, only four Saxon kingdoms still remained. Of these, Alfred's father's kingdom of Wessex was the strongest.

Alfred and his four older brothers were trained in the art of war almost as soon as they could walk. Swordsmanship, hunting, and athletics were regular features of a prince's education. Significantly, however, the boys were not taught to read. Reading and writing was not considered necessary for a king's son, whose primary job was to lead his people in battle. Book-learning was left almost exclusively in the hands of the clergy, and not even all of them were literate. (The lack of literacy is not surprising when we consider that books were both rare and expensive. The books that did exist had to be copied out slowly by hand onto thin sheets of expensive parchment.)

Alfred loved to hunt and fight alongside his father and brothers, yet from his mother he also inherited a keen love for books. There is a legend that Queen Osburga offered a book of Saxon poetry as a prize to whichever of her sons could memorize it first. Alfred immediately coveted the volume, in which the poems were written in ornate script, beautifully worked onto calfskin. Not knowing how to read, Alfred enlisted the help of monks, who read the poems to him until he had them memorized and could claim the prize. With the help of tutors—possibly these same monks—Alfred learned to read by his twelfth year.

As the youngest child (he was about twenty-five years younger than his oldest brother), it was unlikely that Alfred would ever be king. Yet his parents gave him special attention and care, perhaps sensing that God had destined him for great things. When Alfred was four years of age, his father sent him to Rome in the company of Wessex pilgrims. Two years later, Alfred again had the chance to travel to Rome, this time with his father. Alfred's boyhood visit to Rome, the bosom of the apostolic faith, seems to have made a lasting impression on the young lad. In his later life he would write about the city's magnificent buildings, and he was always careful to maintain a close relationship with the church at Rome.

Despite his interest in spiritual matters and books, Alfred shared with his brothers a love for the "manly arts." He also had the invaluable opportunity of accompanying his father on various journeys to the towns of his kingdom. These travels gave Alfred an instinctive familiarity with the terrain of Wessex—a familiarity that would later prove invaluable in his guerrilla warfare against the Vikings.

THE FIGHTING BROTHERS

Three years after his second pilgrimage to Rome, Alfred's father died, leaving the kingdom to Alfred's eldest brother, Æthelbald, who did not live long and was soon succeeded by Alfred's next eldest brother, Æthelberht. When Æthelberht died five years later, Alfred's remaining brother, Æthelred, assumed the throne.

By now the future of Wessex was in doubt, as a gigantic Viking force had made its way into Northumbria. With its fall, the Danes used the Northumbrian capital, York, as a base from which to launch expeditions into two other major Anglo-Saxon kingdoms, East Anglia and Mercia.

When they heard that Mercia had been attacked, King Æthelred and Alfred led a force to aid their neighboring kinsmen, in an attempt to liberate Nottingham, the Mercian capital. They failed to drive the Danes from the city, but Alfred was successful in one respect: he met and married the Mercian noblewoman, Ealswith. The union proved fruitful and would eventually result in two sons and three daughters.

With the fall of the kingdom of East Anglia in 869, there was nothing to stop the Vikings from helping themselves to Wessex. When the brothers heard that the Vikings had attacked their city of Berkshire, they assembled a force to meet them. After an unsuccessful assault on the Danish forces at Reading, the two armies clashed in a field called Ashdown. Thousands of Vikings perished that day, securing temporary peace for the people of Wessex. Even so, minor skirmishes between the two forces continued. In one such skirmish Æthelred was mortally wounded. Shortly after Easter he died, and Alfred succeeded him as king of Wessex.

"DEATH OUT OF THE NORTH"

The burden that now rested on the shoulders of the twenty-one year old Alfred was enormous. It is little wonder that he felt incapable of the task that lay before him. In the paraphrase he would later make of Boethius's *The Consolation of Philosophy*, he wrote, "Look . . . you know that desire for and possession of earthly power never pleased me overmuch, and that I did not unduly desire this earthly rule."[7]

Given his circumstances, it is hardly surprising that Alfred did not desire earthly rule. His friend and biographer Asser tells us that in the spring of 871, when Alfred was crowned, "he did not think that he alone could ever withstand such great harshness from the pagans, unless strengthened by divine help, since he had already sustained great losses of many men while his brothers were alive."

Almost immediately after being made king, Alfred received news that a large Viking fleet was sailing up the Thames. One of these ships carried the man who would become his **nemesis**: the wicked heathen king Guthrum.

7. Anonymous, *Alfred the Great: Asser's Life of King Alfred & Other Contemporary Sources* (New York: Penguin Classics, 1984), 132.

"Guthrum" soon became synonymous with fear and terror. G. K. Chesterton's epic poem "The Ballad of the White Horse" captures something of the prevailing mood when he appropriately described Guthrum as "death out of the north."

> King Guthrum was a dread king,
> Like death out of the north;
> Shrines without name or number
> He rent and rolled as lumber,
> From Chester to the Humber
> He drove his foemen forth.
>
> The Roman villas heard him
> In the valley of the Thames,
> Come over the hills roaring
> Above their roofs, and pouring
> On spire and stair and flooring
> Brimstone and pitch and flames.[8]

Alfred's forces were no match for Guthrum's well-organized bands. Eager to avert a battle, Alfred secured a temporary peace by paying Guthrum large sums of money, known as the *Danegeld*. Though only a temporary solution, it did allow the men of Wessex to return to their farms for a few years. And in 876, when Guthrum's men returned and captured strategic towns in Wessex, Alfred was again able to buy peace. This time, Alfred made him swear on the holy ring of Thor— sacred to the pagans—never to return.[9] As a sign of good faith, Alfred allowed Guthrum to take hostages. It soon became apparent that an

---

8. G. K. Chesterton, *The Ballad of the White Horse* (San Fransisco: Ignatius Press, 2001), 45.

9. The fact that Alfred would make his enemy swear on a pagan object seems to have later been a source of embarrassment, and Alfred's official biographer, Asser, changed the ring into a Christian relic. *The Anglo-Saxon Chronicle* relates that this was "a thing which they would not do before for any nation," and were reduced to it "that they would speedily leave his kingdom" (Dorothy Whitelock, *The Anglo-Saxon Chronicle* (London: Eyre and Spottiswoode, 1965), 48). Alfred was indeed in a position of desperation.

oath sworn to a pagan god was meaningless. Alfred's ninth-century biographer, Asser, describes what happened next:

> But one night, practicing their usual treachery, after their own manner, and paying no heed to the hostages, the oath and the promise of faith, they broke the treaty, killed all the hostages they had, and turning away they went unexpected to another place, called Exeter.[10]

From the fortified city of Exeter, Guthrum waited for a larger force sailing up the river Exe to join him. However, during the temporary peace purchased by the Danegeld, Alfred had not been idle. He had enlisted the help of the Vikings' old enemies on the Continent, the Frisians, having heard that their ships were a match for those of the Vikings. From the Frisians, Alfred learned how to build vessels, and he constructed a small fleet. Though better designed than the Vikings' ships, Alfred's ships were few in number, and incapable of repelling the approaching armada.[11] Alfred's small navy would almost certainly have been obliterated had it not been for a sudden squall. The storm dashed the Danish ships against the rocky coast of Dorset, nearly destroying their whole fleet.

When Guthrum learned that his reinforcements had been destroyed, he was eager to leave Wessex as quickly as possible. Once more, Alfred agreed to let the Danish leader depart in peace, and once more Guthrum performed solemn oaths never to return. Guthrum retreated to Mercia, where his men went on a rampage of destruction: raping, destroying farms, gutting churches, and kidnapping children.

Guthrum had already proved that he could not be trusted to keep his word, and Alfred feared what would happen if the Viking leader attempted another invasion. The problem was not simply that Wessex had lost many of its valuable fighters in their engagements with the Vikings; the death of so many men also meant that the country

10. Anonymous, *Alfred the Great*, 83.

11. *The Anglo-Saxon Chronicle* numbers the Viking fleet at 120 ships. If this figure is correct, and if each ship was manned by about thirty men, then this was a force numbering around 3,600.

was depleted of farmers. When a man failed to return from battle, this created an extra workload for the other villagers, who would then provide for the widow and children of the deceased man. Not surprisingly, therefore, Alfred had difficulty recruiting and maintaining his army. Moreover, when one shire was conquered by the enemy, Alfred's soldiers from that shire tended to abandon the army to go back to their wives and children now vulnerable behind enemy lines. Even when they were successful in a battle, Alfred's men were reluctant to press their advantage, but would quickly return to their neglected farms, lest their villages have no food in winter.

TIME OF NEBUCHADNEZZAR

Although Alfred anticipated another attack, it came when he least expected it. Guthrum intentionally chose to wage his attack on Twelfth Night, when Alfred and his countrymen were celebrating the last day of Christmas on the Eve of Epiphany. The Christians, deep in their celebrations, had no idea that Guthrum and his men had slipped into the country. The Vikings struck before Alfred had a chance to mount a successful counter-attack, scattering Alfred and his men.

Guthrum followed up his success with a series of quick victories. It was clear he was after more than mere loot: he wanted to be king of Wessex. Realizing that resistance was futile, many Wessex noblemen either relocated to Europe or acknowledged Guthrum's kingship to save their lives. Alfred's family, accompanied by a small band of faithful friends, took refuge in the marshes of Somerset.

Alfred's biographer captured the mood of this time when he said that the king "led a restless life in great distress amid the woody and marshy places."[12] In his later years, Alfred would refer to this period of his life as his "exile" or "time of Nebuchadnezzar." Laid low and humbled, Alfred came to more fully appreciate the claims of Christ on his life.

Their hideout was the small isle of Athelney, consisting of high ground rising out of the marches and bordered on its north side by the River Tone. Athelney could be reached only by punt and even then only by those who knew where to look.

---

12. Anonymous, *Alfred the Great*, 83.

Many legends exist about this period of Alfred's life, including the famous story about him arousing the indignation of a swineherd's wife by accidentally burning her honey cakes. Whether or not the legend has any truth, it does reflect the fact that Alfred and his family had to rely on simple peasants to stay alive. Although Alfred could have taken his family to parts of Wessex that had not yet fallen, such as Hampshire or Dorset, he chose to remain with his people behind enemy lines. As the humbled king and his wife lived alongside his own people and their children, they developed lasting relationships with those who would later help him to reclaim the crown.

From his island refuge, Alfred began to wage hit-and-run warfare. Careful never to attack too many Vikings at a time, when his force did strike, they were deadly. A small party of Danes might be on a hunting expedition or traveling the roads at night, and then suddenly, as if from nowhere, Alfred and his men would ambush them, hacking them to pieces on the ground before the Vikings even realized what was happening.

Alfred became the terror of the countryside, yet he remained an invisible foe. Try as they might, the Vikings could never locate his lair. This was the hunting ground of Alfred's youth, and he knew how to elude those who were searching for him. As the eleventh-century chronicler William of Malmesbury put it,

> It was necessary to contend with Alfred even after he was overcome, after he was prostrate; insomuch that when he might be supposed altogether vanquished, he would escape like a slippery serpent, from the hand which held him, glide from his lurking-place, and, with undiminished courage, spring on his insulting enemies.[13]

The point of the guerrilla warfare was not so much to decrease his enemies' numbers, but to demoralize their spirits. Yet it also helped Alfred to gain support. As Abels explained in his 1998 biography:

13. William John Allen Giles, *William of Malmesbury's Chronicle of the Kings of England* (Charleston: BiblioBazaar, 2008), 117.

[B]y harrying the lands of his foreign enemies and the traitors who supported them, Alfred also reminded his subjects that their king had not abdicated and still had power to punish the disloyal. Guthrum, on the other hand, lacked the manpower to protect the lands and people he now claimed to rule. In a sense, Alfred and Guthrum were waging a war for hearts and minds; the former knew that he could not regain his kingdom, and the latter that he could not maintain even the pretense of rule, without the active support of the local elites.[14]

THE GATHERING OF THE CHIEFS

As Alfred continued to spy on the Danes and gather information about their ways and movements, he began to gradually formulate a plan. One thing was clear: if he did not strike soon, there would be no Wessex left to defend. Every day that Alfred tarried, Guthrum's men ransacked more churches, violated more women, kidnapped more children, raided more farms, and continued to destroy all that was good, true, and beautiful in the people's Christian heritage.

In what G. K. Chesterton called "the gathering of the chiefs," Alfred began to secretly call together the peasants he had come to rely on during his exile, as well as those in the surrounding shires. It was no easy task to meld into a single force the military resources of three shires, and to do so in complete secrecy. The plans culminated in his sending out a message that every able-bodied fighting man should meet him at Egbert's stone on Whitsunday or Pentecost, seven weeks after Easter.

Accounts say that when the men finally gathered at Egbert's stone and looked upon their king, it was as though he had been resurrected from the dead.

THE BATTLE OF EDINGTON

When finally assembled, the forces numbered four or five thousand. Gathered together in one place, it was now impossible to conceal

---

14. Richard Philip Abels, *Alfred the Great: War, Kingship, and Culture in Anglo-Saxon England* (London: Longman, 1998), 156.

their existence. Guthrum scurried to gather his own men to meet the Saxons in battle.

As they waited to engage the enemy, Alfred walked among his men, looking them in the eye, recalling stories of their families. He reminded them what they were fighting for, urging them not to forsake their vows but to stand bravely to the very last in defense of their homeland. He said that by the end of the day, the fields would be stained red with their own blood, yet he enjoined them to die with courage and honor.

Throughout the morning it was uncertain which side would win, as both armies seemed to be evenly matched. As the day progressed, however, it became clear that the men of Wessex had a psychological advantage. They knew that everything depended on this one battle. They held nothing back because they knew they were fighting for their farms, their wives, and their children. They knew it would be better to die than accept defeat. By contrast, the Vikings knew that if worsy came to worst they could always migrate north to one of the territories they had previously conquered. Consequently, the Vikings' motivation to win was not as great. The advantage on Alfred's side did not become apparent until the evening, when the Vikings lost courage and their forces fell into disarray. Asser describes Alfred's success:

> Fighting fiercely with a compact shield-wall against the entire Viking army, he persevered resolutely for a long time; at length he gained the victory through God's will. He destroyed the Vikings with great slaughter, and pursued those who fled as far as the stronghold, hacking them down.[15]

Guthrum only just managed to escape to his Chippenham fortress with some survivors. The rest of the Vikings, exhausted almost to the point of collapse, struggled to make it to the fortress before Alfred's men found them. However, the retreating Vikings were too slow. From the secure walls Guthrum watched helplessly as his exhausted men were mercilessly butchered by Alfred's pursuing army.

Guthrum himself was temporarily safe, but the fortress did not hold enough food to withstand even a short siege. Fearing that it was

15. Anonymous, *Alfred the Great*, 84.

only a matter of time before Chippenham fell to the fury of Alfred's army, Guthrum sent a message to the king, pleading for safe passage.

Although Alfred knew how to be terrible in battle, he did not share the Viking lust for blood. He knew how to fight, but he also knew how to show mercy. He agreed to let Guthrum retreat from Wessex, but on one condition: Guthrum must become a Christian and submit to Holy Baptism.

FROM GUTHRUM TO ÆTHELSTAN

It might be easy to think that Guthrum agreed to Alfred's terms merely to save his skin. However, his conversion to Christianity seems to have been genuine. While Guthrum had grown to respect Alfred for his bravery in battle, what impressed the Dane even more was the way this king showed mercy and kindness to an enemy who had repeatedly broken his promises. This was something completely new to Guthrum. The Vikings never showed mercy to their conquered foes, and the Icelandic sagas indicate that they believed cruelty to their defeated enemies was virtuous.

Three weeks after Guthrum accepted Alfred's terms, he was led by thirty of his noblemen to a small church in Aller, near to the marshy hideout Alfred's family had called home for so long. In the liturgy that preceded the baptism, Guthrum and his nobles were called upon to renounce the works of the devil and to put faith in Christ. When the liturgy had finished, the priest took Guthrum's head and immersed it in the water three times, baptizing him in the name of the Father, the Son, and the Holy Ghost. On the third and final immersion, Guthrum's head was lifted from the baptismal font by Alfred, who was now his godfather.

Alfred's decision to sponsor Guthrum's baptism was significant, as it bound the two men in spiritual kinship. In his book *Christianizing Kinship: Ritual Sponsorship in Anglo-Saxon England,* Joseph Lynch tells how "every baptism in medieval Europe had the potential to create a family-like relationship that theologians and canonists called 'spiritual kinship.'"[16] In practice, this meant that if Guthrum attacked

---

16. Joseph H. Lynch, *Christianizing Kinship: Ritual Sponsorship in Anglo-Saxon England* (New York: Cornell University Press, 1998), 7.

again, he would be attacking his own spiritual father. To solidify his new identity, Guthrum was given the Christian name of Æthelstan.

The baptism over, Alfred made Æthelstan swear by the Triune God never to return to Wessex in battle. Alfred hoped the Danish king would honor this vow more than the previous oaths he had sworn to the Norse deities. To solidify the new relationship with his godson, Alfred invited Æthelstan and his companions to twelve days of feasting, merry-making, and generous gift-giving after the fashion of Saxon hospitality. Æthelstan and his nobles were then released to join their forces at the Chippenham fortress, where they began making preparations for their withdrawal to Mercia.

Would Æthelstan keep true to his word? As much as Alfred believed in the power of baptism, he knew that sanctification did not happen overnight. To be on the safe side, Alfred kept his army on constant alert.

In autumn of the same year, Æthelstan was joined by a fresh force of Vikings who camped west of London. The new troops sent Æthelstan a message, seeking to form an alliance capable of overrunning Wessex once and for all. Alfred's spies knew about this and waited to see what Æthelstan's response would be. They knew that if this new force was combined with all of Æthelstan's men, there would be little Wessex could do to prevent complete obliteration.

By God's grace, Æthelstan remained true to his newfound faith in Christ. Unwilling to meet the legendary Alfred without Æthelstan's assistance, the force returned to the Continent.

Alfred and Æthelstan remained on good terms throughout the rest of their lives and even entered into alliances. Equally important, however, was the fact that all of Æthelstan's people began to be transformed as well. It would be naive to think that they abandoned their pagan ways overnight. The process of Christianization would take many more years. Alfred Smyth, Professor of Medieval History at the University of Kent, rightly observed that "it was Alfred's achievement, through the imposition of baptism on Guthrum and his warriors, to have influenced the lives and fortunes not only of the population of Wessex, but of all Æthelstan's too—English and Dane alike—from St. Albans to the Humber."[17] Alfred would have dis-

17. Alfred P. Smyth, *King Alfred the Great* (Oxford: Oxford University Press, 1995), 83.

puted that this was his accomplishment: in everything he achieved for God's kingdom, he was careful to give all credit to God.

REBUILDING THE KINGDOM

Alfred no longer had to contend with Æthelstan, but the possibility of invasion by other Viking armies remained a constant threat. Given the clumsiness of the Anglo-Saxon military structure, Alfred knew that his army would have to be completely restructured if the kingdom were ever to be adequately defended.

The core of a Saxon king's army was always his hearth-troop, a collection of noblemen that would feast and lodge with the king as well as fight beside him. If the king needed a larger force, he had to call for the shire *fyrd*, a voluntary territorial army assembled by the leaders of the different shires. The shire fyrd existed for the purpose of defending local territory but could also travel to remote locations if need demanded. The system worked well if there was sufficient time to assemble the fyrd, but it was almost useless for responding to sudden threats. As a solution, Alfred reorganized the army on a rota basis: half the men would take it in turns to be battle-ready, while the rest could attend to their farms. After a while, they would switch. Alfred also strengthened his navy so that the Southern coast could be defended. He made key alliances with other Saxon rulers, paving the way for the united nation of England to eventually emerge.

Once Alfred was confident that Wessex could be properly protected, he applied himself to developing the Christian culture that the heathens had nearly eliminated. At the heart of this was a renaissance of the liberal arts, which he spearheaded. William of Malmesbury tells us that Alfred "absorbed the liberal arts into his very lifeblood." While this is true, what is even more impressive is the way Alfred brought the liberal arts into the lifeblood of the common people. He showed his subjects that being human was about more than merely surviving; rather, it required giving glory to God through lives modeled on what was good, true, and beautiful. The liberal arts played a key role in this process, since through them one could be inculcated in the wisdom of the Christian tradition.

Alfred read Bede's *Ecclesiastical History of the English People* and was deeply impressed to find how the British monasteries had previously been centers of learning. By contrast, in the ninth century most of the monasteries had been destroyed. Those that remained had very few books (it is probable that the illiterate Vikings used valuable manuscripts as tinder), let alone people who could read them. Reflecting on the situation, Alfred wrote, "And I would have it known that very often it has come to my mind what men of learning there were formerly throughout England, both in religious and secular orders; and how there were happy times then throughout England."[18] He went on to compare these former times with the contemporary situation in which "learning had declined so thoroughly in England that there were very few men on this side of the Humber who could understand their divine services in English, or even translate a single letter from Latin into English; and I suppose that there were not many beyond the Humber either."[19]

To remedy the situation, Alfred gathered what writings remained and had copies made. A lesser man might have been satisfied with simply ensuring the clergy were literate. But Alfred settled on the ambitious goal of having every man in his kingdom learn to read. Believing that without Christian wisdom there could be neither prosperity nor success in war, Alfred aimed (in his own words) "to set to learning (as long as they are not useful for some other employment) all the free-born young men now in England who have the means to apply themselves to it."[20]

To facilitate this, Alfred installed a school in the royal household, where his children and the children of nobles could be taught by some of the top scholars in Europe. He also established schools throughout Wessex.

It was especially important to Alfred that those involved in his government either be taught to read or be given frequent opportunity to hear someone else read aloud. However, a constant hindrance to achieving this goal was that nearly all the books were written in Latin and therefore inaccessible to those that had not even learned to read the vernacular Anglo-Saxon dialect (a forerunner of English). In his preface to his translation of Gregory the Great's *Pastoral Care*,

18. Anonymous, *Alfred the Great*, 124.
19. Ibid., 125.
20. Ibid., 126.

Alfred reflected on the way the Greeks translated the Hebrew scriptures into their own language, observing that

> [I]t seems better to me—if it seems so to you—that we too should turn into the language that we can all understand certain books which are the most necessary for all men to know, and accomplish this, as with God's help we may very easily do provided we have a peace enough.[21]

Beginning in the 880s, Alfred began collecting scholars to his court who could translate and copy the great books of Western civilization into the Saxon tongue. During the latter part of Alfred's reign, the Wessex book-making industry boomed, as beautiful, illuminated manuscripts were produced which became treasures for later generations. By 887 the king himself learned Latin, and joined his team of scholars translating these texts into the common tongue. Bede's *Ecclesiastical History,* Augustine's *Soliloquies,* and Boethius's *The Consolation of Philosophy* were among Alfred's own translations and became classics. Since his goal was to produce texts that would help his people grow wise, the king did not always translate the Latin word for word, but would paraphrase things in a way he knew his people could grasp. When he translated part of the book of Psalms, however, he rendered it literally.

Since we tend to take literacy for granted, it is hard to appreciate just how revolutionary it was for a ninth-century monarch to insist that the ordinary man learn to read. Many of Alfred's contemporaries wondered if these reforms were really necessary. Battle-hardened men who had fought beside the king did not see the need to sit down and learn their letters with the school children. Yet the king was unrelenting: anyone who wanted to serve in his government must grow wise through reading. The sons of noblemen, he insisted, should learn to read before they mastered the skills of hunting, riding, and fighting. After they began their training in the martial skills, the king insisted that they should continue their book-learning.

Alfred believed that reading was not merely another activity alongside fighting. Rather, education could actually help the men of

21. Ibid.

Wessex defeat the Vikings. This is because he believed that Viking invasions were themselves a divine judgment against the people for falling from their earlier love of learning. Thus, in Alfred's mind his educational renaissance was just as important a protection against the Vikings as the restructured military. "Remember what punishments befell us in this world," he wrote, "when we ourselves did not cherish learning nor transmit it to other men."[22]

In the Viking wars, Alfred had set the example of bravery by fighting in the front lines beside his men. When it came to love of learning, he also set the example for his people. He devoted half of every day to studying and prayer. He even invented a special type of clock made out of candles in order to regulate his time.

FINAL CHALLENGE

Even while rebuilding the culture, Alfred kept one eye on the military. This proved providential, for in 892, seven years before the king's death, a fresh force of Vikings crossed the channel heading straight for Wessex. This great heathen army was significantly larger than anything the men of Wessex had previously encountered. The pagan force was led by Hæsten, a Viking with a reputation for piracy and murder that rivaled the reputation of Guthrum prior to his conversion. Moreover, the Vikings traveled in concert with their families, a sure sign that their plan was permanent conquest rather than quick plunder. Alfred could no longer count on his godson for protection, as Æthelstan had died two years earlier.

Alfred's first response was to try to prevent conflict by evangelizing the newcomers. He invited Hæsten to feast with him and his family. During the feast Alfred shared the gospel with him, urging the Viking leader to convert to the Christian faith. Hæsten replied that he had already undergone baptism. (Many Viking leaders submitted to baptism for purely political reasons, and Hæsten had probably been baptized in order to better conduct business with the Franks.) However, he did offer two of his sons for baptism, to whom Alfred and his son-in-law acted as godparents.

22. Ibid., 125.

It turned out that these baptisms, too, were purely political. Shortly after Hæsten withdrew from the region with promises of peace, he began plundering the border territories and followed up with a quick advance into Wessex.

As soon as he heard the news, Alfred led an army against the Danes yet failed to locate them in the thick forests of the country. Meanwhile, a different set of troops, led by Alfred's son Edward, found the pagans and dealt vengeance upon them. Even as they celebrated their victory, however, more Vikings continued to pour into the land. By God's grace, these new Vikings were also located and cut down by the unflagging Wessex military.

Alfred eventually captured the treacherous Hæsten and his family. According to common practice, Alfred should have executed him and pressed his sons into slavery. But Alfred did not forget that he and his son-in-law were godparents to the Viking princes. Although Hæsten did not take the baptism of his sons any more seriously than his own, there was one man who took their baptisms very seriously: King Alfred. Hæsten's family was astonished when, instead of executing and enslaving them, Alfred reminded them of their Christian obligations. Baptism, he pointed out, had given them a new identity and brought them into a new family. As such, it created loyalties and obligations that must be honored. He then invited the family to more days of feasting and gift-giving before sending them on their way once again.

THE LEGACY OF ALFRED THE GREAT

To date, the English have not seen fit to bestow the epithet "Great" on any king other than Alfred. Considering his remarkable legacy, this is not surprising.

Alfred's goal was not just to make England safe for his generation, but to develop a culture that would be a lasting monument for every generation that followed. One of the ways he did this was by creating a written law code based on biblical principles. He opened his constitution with an exposition of the Ten Commandments and the laws of Exodus 21, before moving on to a discussion of Christ's Sermon on the Mount. In discussing Christ's teachings the king was careful to show that Jesus did not abolish the Old Testament laws but simply applied them in a new way.

After laying the theological foundations, Alfred's constitution proceeded to codify many of the Saxon traditions already in place. In doing so, he was careful to emphasize that he was collecting rather than inventing laws.[23] Even so, the laws he collected underwent important modifications, showing us what things were important to the king. For example, none of the other Saxon law codes showed such concern about sexual crimes committed against women. Alfred, who had personally suffered betrayal and treachery from the Vikings, laid great stress on oath-keeping. His modifications also involved abolishing unbiblical practices left over from the Saxon's pagan past, such as settling feuds through bloodshed or conducting trials by ordeal.

Alfred's laws formed the foundation of English common law to the present day. But this was only one of the many areas where his legacy has exercised a lasting influence. The king was speaking for himself when he wrote (in his translation of Boethius), "My will was to live worthily as long as I lived, and after my life to leave to them that should come after, my memory in good works." His desire was certainly fulfilled, because when he died in 899, at around the age of fifty, he left behind a tremendous legacy of good works that has had a lasting impact. In addition to those areas already mentioned, Alfred's good works include rebuilding the monasteries, perfecting the administrative organization of his government, developing a system for the relief of the poor, and establishing a system of judges through the land to enforce the laws. He also brought together the fragmented Saxons and gave them an identity as Englishmen (he introduced the notion of being "English" halfway through his reign).

Had it not been for Alfred, the culture and language of England might have followed the template set by the Danes. As it was, the

---

23. "I, King Alfred, have collected these laws, and have given orders for copies to be made of many of those which our predecessors observed and which I myself approved of. But many of those I did not approve of I have annulled, by the advice of my councilors, while [in other cases] I have ordered changes to be introduced. For I have not dared to presume to set down in writing many of my own, for I cannot tell what [innovations of mine] will meet with the approval of our successors" (F. L. Attenborough, *The Laws of the Earliest English Kings* [Clark: The Lawbook Exchange, 2006], 63).

nation of England grew in the wake of Alfred's Wessex dynasty. As historian Richard Abels put it, "In the course of the tenth century Wessex was transformed into England, and Alfred's reign was the critical precondition for this process."[24] The inscription on a statue of Alfred at Wantage provides a fitting summary to these and all of Alfred's other remarkable achievements:

> Alfred found learning dead and he restored it, education neglected and he revived it, the laws powerless and he gave them force, the church debased and he raised it, the land ravaged by a fearful enemy from which he delivered it. Alfred's name shall live as long as mankind shall respect the past.

LESSONS FROM THE LIFE OF KING ALFRED

King Alfred's amazing life provides an almost endless array of lessons for men and women today. Space permits us to only focus on six.

First, Alfred shows us what it means to love our enemies. Jesus said, "Love your enemies, bless those who curse you, do good to those who hate you, and pray for those who spitefully use you and persecute you" (Mt. 5:44). Alfred understood that Jesus was not advocating pacifism, but that even when we have to use warfare against the wicked, our prayer and goal must continually be their conversion. Alfred was satisfied when he was able to conquer his enemies with the sword, but he was filled with joy when he was able to conquer them with the gospel. Even as he fought the heathen foe, his prayer was that the Lord would turn his enemies into brothers, united by the powerful bond of baptism.

Secondly, Alfred reminds us that the Christian life is both practical and intellectual, and that we separate these two facets at our peril. The Christian life should be practical, since the effectiveness of our witness for Christ depends on the gospel flowing out of our fingertips, being constantly applied to the material of our daily lives. But in order for a Christian to serve Jesus in practical ways, he must also grow in wisdom and understanding. At a time when ignorance and illiteracy were accepted as normal, this was a challenging position

24. Abels, *Alfred the Great*, 25.

to take. It is no less challenging in a period like our own, when the practical and intellectual dimensions of our faith are often pitted against one another, rather than being understood as two sides of the same coin.

Thirdly, Alfred appreciated that his strength came not from his own natural ability, but from God. In himself, Alfred was not particularly strong or impressive. In fact, it is said that people would travel from far places to see this great king, only to be disappointed by his short and unimpressive stature. But even though he did not have great strength in the flesh, he was a great leader because he had learned to depend on Christ. That was the hard lesson he learned during his time of humility and weakness in the marshes. Reading over some of the prayers he translated and personalized, we can see a man acutely conscious of his own weakness and utterly dependent on the Lord for his strength:

> Lord God Almighty, shaper and ruler of all creatures, I pray Thee for Thy great mercy, and for the token of the holy rood, and for the maidenhood of St. Mary, and for the obedience of St. Michael, and for the love of Thy holy saints and their worthiness, that Thou guide me better than I have done towards Thee.

> Guide me to Thy will, to the need of my soul, better than I can myself. Steadfast my mind towards Thy will and to my soul's need. Strengthen me against the temptations of the devil, and put far from me every unrighteousness. Shield me against my foes, seen and unseen; and teach me to do Thy will, that I may inwardly love Thee before all things with a clean mind and clean body. For Thou art my maker and my redeemer, my help, my comfort, my trust, and my hope. Praise and glory be to Thee now, ever and ever, world without end. Amen.[25]

25. Robert Chambers and David Patrick, *Chambers's Cyclopaedia of English Literature: A History Critical and Biographical of Authors in the English Tongue From the Earliest Times Till the Present Day, With Specimens of Their Writing* (London: W. & R. Chambers, 1901), 22.

Fourthly, Alfred teaches us the importance of spiritual warfare. With the enemies of God threatening the very fabric of Christian civilization, Alfred knew that the Lord called his children to be warriors, to strive against both the visible and invisible forces of darkness. The same is true today. There are many contemporary equivalents of King Guthrum rampaging about, seeking to undermine what is good, true, and beautiful in the Christian heritage. In many respects, the Guthrums of today are more dangerous because they are more subtle.

Fifthly, Alfred teaches us what it means to be an effective leader. It was not easy for Alfred to rule. The defense of the kingdom required taxes that were as unpopular as his campaign of universal literacy. However, he compelled the obedience of his subjects through his own love and generosity rather than by force and threat. As Asser wrote,

> Yet once he had taken over the helm of his kingdom, he alone, sustained by divine assistance, struggled like an excellent pilot to guide his ship laden with much wealth to the desired and safe haven of his homeland, even though all his sailors were virtually exhausted; similarly, he did not allow it to waver or wander from course, even though the course lay through the many seething whirlpools of the present life. For by gently instructing, cajoling, urging, commanding, and (in the end, when his patience was exhausted) by sharply chastising those who were disobedient and by despising popular stupidity and stubbornness in every way, he carefully and cleverly exploited and converted his bishops and ealdormen and nobles, and his thegns most dear to him . . . to his own will and to the general advantage of the whole realm.[26]

The sixth and final lesson we learn from Alfred concerns Christ's command to "make disciples of all the nations" (Mt. 28:19). Few people understood this command better than Alfred. He knew that the life of the nation, no less than the life of the individual, needs to be regulated by Christ's lordship. The Bible is not simply a devotional manual for our private lives, but a template for bringing all of culture

---

26. Anonymous, *Alfred the Great*, 101–102.

into subjection to Christ. Thus, Alfred's vision for England was one in which all aspects of human culture were brought together. Central to this was the notion of Christendom. "Christendom" is not simply a collection of Christians living together in society, but it comprises the institutions, literature, manners, works of arts, educational values—in short, the entire fabric of culture—which emanate from Christian civilization. A moment of time is all it takes for a person to turn from unbelief to faith in Christ, but it takes hundreds of years to build Christendom out of a previously pagan society. Alfred realized this, and that is why his vision was multi-generational.

QUESTIONS FOR DISCUSSION

1. When God's people are attacked by pagans, is it always a sign of God's judgment?

2. If Guthrum had remained successful in ruling Wessex, might there have come a time when revolting against him would be an act of rebellion against a God-ordained authority? After a certain amount of time is one obligated to consider an existing government a legitimate authority, even if the origin of its rule involved usurpation? If so, how is such a time-scale to be determined?

3. If we programmed our computers to send e-mails with beautiful illuminations and marginal pictures like the books that King Alfred had copied out, is it likely that unconsciously we would begin to take more care in what we wrote and become more eloquent? How do methods of communication affect the content coming through them?

4. Psalm 58:10 says, "The righteous shall rejoice when he sees the vengeance; He shall wash his feet in the blood of the wicked." Is this is the attitude that Christians should have when our enemies are destroyed? If so, how does this fit with Ezekiel 18:23, where we are told that God does not take delight in the death of the wicked?

5. Was it sinful for many Wessex nobles to acknowledge Guthrum's kingship to save their lives?

6. What are some of the ways that the practical and intellectual dimensions of our faith can be falsely pitted against each other?

7. Was Alfred wrong to make Guthrum swear on a pagan object?

8. In continually pardoning his enemies and giving them second chances, Alfred followed Christ's command to forgive those who despitefully use us. But would it have also been biblically acceptable for Alfred to *not* forgive Guthrum and Hæsten?

9. What are some ways that reading leads to wisdom?

10. Alfred did not require that baptism be preceded by evidence of a changed life, since he believed that a changed life would result from baptism. Was his position biblical?

11. Was it right for Alfred to give Guthrum and his nobles the choice of either being baptized or killed? Was that a case of trying to threaten someone into God's kingdom?

12. Many of the imprecatory Psalms, such as Psalm 58, invoke death and destruction on the enemies of God. How is this compatible with Christ's command to love our enemies?

13. Alfred believed that the Viking invasions were God's judgment against the people for falling into ignorance. Could he have been right?

14. Was Alfred right to pay the Danegeld to keep the Vikings away?

15. Was it murder for Alfred and his men to wage guerrilla warfare against the Danes?

PERSONAL CHALLENGE

If you had someone to constantly remind you of your baptism, how might that alter your day-to-day behavior?

CHAPTER 5

FOULER THAN HELL ITSELF

The Hypocrisy of Bad King John (1166–1216)

"Foul as it is, hell itself is defiled by the fouler presence of John," wrote the thirteenth-century monk and chronicler Mathew Paris.

As this remark suggests, King John (r. 1199–1216) has the distinction of being remembered as the worst monarch England has ever known, with the possible exception of Bloody Mary four hundred years later. Possessing an apparently endless supply of greed, violence, malice, rage, lust, sadism, treachery, and hypocrisy, it seems that there was no vice in which John did not excel.

But neither John nor his evilness arose out of a vacuum. The wickedness of King John was the product of a family culture stretching back many generations.

FEUDAL FRANCE

John's family background was deeply rooted in the feudal structure of medieval society. Throughout the Middle Ages, the kings of France derived legitimacy from their vassals who governed the provinces. By giving land and titles to these nobles, the French king—only marginally more powerful than his vassals—could strengthen his rule. In return, the vassals were expected to provide armies to help protect the throne. This model was replicated in the vassal's own land, where he protected peasants in exchange for service rendered to him.

This arrangement, known as feudalism, was far from straightforward. Vassals of the French king would often fight to gain one another's territory, and on occasion they would even engage in battle with the king himself.

In 1066, William, duke of Normandy, himself a vassal of the king of France, conquered England. From then on, whoever carried the title "duke of Normandy" also held claim to the throne of England. This situation created a thorny relationship between the kings of France and the kings of England/dukes of Normandy. In his capacity as duke of Normandy, the English king remained a vassal to the French monarch, but in his capacity as king of England, he liked to think of himself as equal to the king of France. This created a number of problems that would come to a head during the reign of King John.

A HOUSE OF DEVILS

One important vassal to the French king had been the ninth-century Frankish nobleman, Ingelger. He was appointed Count of Anjou by Louis II (r. 877–879). Not much is known of Ingelger, but his importance is derived from the fact that he stood at the head of the Plantagenet dynasty, which would become one of the most powerful houses in all of Europe.

Legends from the time, recounted by the chronicler Gerald of Wales, maintained that Ingelger and his progeny, the counts of Anjou, were descended from the daughter of Satan. The history of the Anjou rulers seemed to lend credence to this dubious pedigree. Fulk III ("The Black," 987–1040) had his first wife burnt to death in her wedding dress as a punishment for unfaithfulness. He later died during a holy pilgrimage. Fulk's son, Geoffrey II, called *Martel* ("The Hammer," 1040–1060), was known for his treachery and cruelty to neighbors. He enjoyed relations with a succession of different wives before becoming a monk in the final year of his life.

As these and other stories suggest, the Anjou propensity to wickedness was matched only by their quest to maintain the appearance of piety. True Pharisees, the counts of Anjou bestowed lavish gifts on the church, built impressive monasteries and abbeys, and went through all the outward motions of religious devotion while living lives of utter corruption and immorality.

THE ANGEVIN CURSE

Ingelger's descendants would probably have remained in relative obscurity were it not for the fact that one of the counts of Anjou, Geoffrey the Fair (r. 1129–1151), captured Normandy in 1144, securing the throne of England for his descendants. As Geoffrey had a custom of wearing a sprig of broom (or *genet* in French) in his hat, he was given the nickname "Plantagenet." The name stuck and remained with the Anjou rulers ever since.

Geoffrey's descendants derived more than just their name from him. They also inherited his relentless ambition, combined with a knack for increasing power through complex political games, shrewd diplomacy and open warfare. By the time of Geoffrey's son, Henry II of England (r. 1154–1189), Angevin lands had come to encompass half of France, in addition to all of England.

For all their power and wealth, the Plantagenets were not a happy family. Instead of looking out for the best interests of one another, the ambitious Plantagenet children feuded constantly. This ultimately weakened their empire. The problem, which came to be known as the "Angevin Curse," often centered on Plantagenet rulers attempting to divide their dominions among numerous children, all of whom vied for the best lands and titles. Over the years this led to a culture of jealousy and mistrust that would reach its climax in King John.

CHILDHOOD AND EARLY LIFE

John was born Christmas Eve, 1167, the fourth child of King Henry II and Eleanor of Aquitaine. From an early age he learned the art of treachery by seeing his older brothers and mother unsuccessfully conspire against their father. The conspiracy ended with John's mother being imprisoned. That did not end the trouble. John's brother, Richard, continued to fight against their father right up until the time of Henry's death.

John's own relationship with his father was not much better. Eclipsed by his older brothers and neglected by his father, he was sent to be raised in the household of his elder brother in order that he might learn to be a knight. He also spent time in the household of Ranulf de Glanvil, head of Henry's government, to learn the business of state. It is doubtful that John mastered either of these skills, but it is certain that none of his family's propensity for self-seeking and hypocrisy was lost on him.

King Henry gave his youngest son the nickname "Lackland" because there was no land left to give him as an inheritance. As a compensation for this, John was put in charge of governing Ireland. It only took John six months to alienate the entire native population. He achieved this by ridiculing the beards of the Irish chieftains, even going up to the warriors and tugging on their facial hair. The situation escalated out of control, and John was forced to slink back home to his father.

Four years later John's brother, Richard I (r. 1189–1199), succeeded as king of England and lord of the Plantagenet Empire in France. But Richard's heart, lion-like though it may have been, was not in England. He remained on the island only long enough to raise money for a crusade (now known as the "Third Crusade"). When Richard was able to leave for the Holy Land in 1190, he appointed William of Longchamp to oversee the kingdom. Hoping to keep his younger brother out of trouble, Richard gave John control of vast estates.

FROM REBEL TO KING

If John had any virtues at all, gratitude was not among them. As soon as his brother Richard was safely on his way to the Holy Land, John began scheming to overthrow Longchamp and make himself the supreme ruler. Because Longchamp was unpopular, John found it easy to rally the people to his side.

When news of the rebellion reached Richard, he dispatched Archbishop Walter de Coutances to put an end to it. Not willing to admit defeat, John conspired with King Philip II (r. 1180–1223) of France to stir up rebellion against Richard. The opportunity arose when Richard was returning from the Holy Land and fell prisoner to the duke of Austria. With Richard safely locked up, Philip seized strategic castles of Richard's in France, while John usurped the throne. However, by 1194 England had raised enough money to pay Richard's ransom and he was able to return home.

Unfortunately, Richard refused to punish his younger brother, who had never been forced to face the consequences of his actions. Though John was twenty-seven at the time, Richard considered him the family baby and made the excuse that he had merely fallen victim to bad company.

John knew when it suited his purposes to behave, and for the next five years he restrained himself. His piety proved beneficial, for when Richard was mortally wounded in a fight to regain one of his castles, he appointed John heir to the Plantagenet dominions.

Although Richard's wishes were respected in England and Normandy, the barons in Anjou, Maine and Touraine chose John's twelve-year-old nephew, Arthur of Brittany, as their overlord. John eventually took care of that: by bribing King Philip, he was able to capture and murder his young nephew.

"NO ANIMAL IN NATURE"

With his rival out of the way, John began to reveal his true colors. Yet for all his wickedness, John's character remained a complex mixture of traits. "Richard had embodied the virtues which men admire in the lion," wrote Winston Churchill in his *History of the English-Speaking Peoples*, "but there is no animal in nature that combines the contradictory qualities of John. He united the ruthlessness of a hardened warrior with the craft and subtlety of a Machiavellian . . . In him the restless energy of the Plantagenet race was raised to a furious pitch of instability."[1]

As Churchill's words suggest, John's character was something of an enigma. He was both impulsive and calculating, impetuous and highly intelligent. Always on the lookout for carnal pleasures, he also devoted much time to book-learning. Though he eschewed moral purity, he was careful about personal hygiene at a time when it was unusual for an Englishman to regularly wash. In order to advertise

1. Winston S. Churchill, *The Birth of Britain: A History of the English-Speaking Peoples,* vol. 1 (London: Cassell, 1956), 190.

his own righteousness, he conferred modest grants on numerous abbeys and helped to found the monastery at Beaulieu, in Hampshire.
Yet he also enjoyed advertising his wickedness and drew particular
delight from publicizing the shame of those women he had successfully seduced. Though in many respects he remained a spoiled child
who refused to grow up, he worked hard in the administration of
his kingdom at a time when it was customary for monarchs to leave
business matters in the hands of others. Though he was very kind to
his animals and regularly gave alms to the poor, he punished women
and children by starving them to death, and crushed old men under
heavy piles of lead.

Behind John's brutality was a mind of exceptional cunning. A
keen judge of human nature, John knew how to manipulate people
and circumstances to his advantage. Accounts from the time have
chronicled his wickedness, but they also describe him as judicious,
patient, and occasionally generous. This was partly because he was
subject to impetuous mood swings, but more often it was because
he possessed the same knack as his Anjou ancestors of being able to
perceive when it advanced his aims to adopt the pretense of piety.

The one constant in his character was that John could not abide being accountable to anyone other than himself. This quickly brought
him into conflict with his overlord, Philip. Though John had been
united with Philip as an enemy of his brother Richard, he did not
find the relationship to his liking now that he was subject to the
French king.

KING "SOFT-SWORD"

The trouble with Philip began when John became infatuated with
twelve-year-old Isabella of Angoulêm. Believing that a union with
her would be a political asset, John deserted his first wife for this girl
twenty years his junior. The only problem was that young Isabella
was already betrothed to Hugh of Lusignan, who had been patiently
waiting for his fiancé to come of age. John not only snatched Hugh's
bride, but also confiscated his lands in order to present them as a gift
to his new father-in-law.

Hugh appealed to the judgment of Philip, who summoned John to
Paris. As king of England, John felt it would be beneath his dignity

to comply. But Philip argued that he had not lost authority over John simply because his vassal had acquired the status of king of England.

As a result of John's refusal to appear in court, Philip dispossessed him of all his continental holdings, giving John's boyhood nickname "Lackland" a new significance. But now John had to contend with another nickname: "Soft-Sword," because of the way he had allowed Philip to so easily snatch up his lands. "When we reflect," observed Churchill, "that the French provinces counted just as much with the Plantagenet kings as the whole realm of England it is obvious that a more virtuous man than John would be incensed at such treatment, and its consequences."[2]

John did realize his mistake, but only after it was too late. Not only had he lost all the Plantagenet holdings in France, but he was looked upon as a coward for not putting up a fight. For the rest of his life, all of John's energies were bent on recovering both his territories and his reputation.

TAXING DRY THE LAND

For John, the solution to his problem was simple: he would tax the people until he could afford an army large enough to invade France. He had watched his brother Richard tax and spend and now it was his turn to prove that he was just as capable of implementing this unpopular policy.

The problem was that Richard had already wrung England dry to finance his Crusade. On top of that, the shires had then been forced to contribute an exorbitant amount to pay Richard's ransom. And during the last five years of Richard's reign, he had again bled England dry to recapture the castles Philip had taken. As a result, by the time of John's reign, the economy of England was depleted, poverty was rampant, and prices were soaring. All that was needed to push England into total ruin was another tax. And that is exactly what John introduced.

John invented creative new ways of taxing his subjects. He forced knights to buy themselves out of military service every year, even when the land was at peace. In 1207, he levied a surcharge on all rents

2. Churchill, *The Birth of Britain*, 80.

and moveable property (previously people's taxes were calculated on the basis of their land). In addition, he tightened the forest laws and appointed sheriffs in charge of enforcing them.[3]

John also let it be known that he was open to bribery. Corrupt officials could pay him not to peer too closely into their questionable activities. He even found ways to exact huge amounts of wealth from the native Jewish population, already subject to punitive taxation. His method was simple: blind and hang members of the Jewish community until they coughed up exorbitant sums of cash.

Behind this oppressive system of taxation was a philosophy of government that had been imported to England at the time of the Norman Conquest. Prior to the invasion of 1066, the kings of England had never thought they owned all the land they governed. However, William and the Norman rulers who followed in his wake, considered the entire island of England to be their own private backyard.[4] The French nobles that William placed in leadership throughout England followed their king's example by enslaving the populations in their territories. However, by the time of John's reign, these nobles had begun to think of themselves as Englishmen and had imbibed many of the ideas of liberty native to the English tradition. Moreover, many of them had grown powerful, capable of mounting a front to resist the king's oppressive taxation. The king, they argued, did not own the land he governed, but must himself be subject to the rule of law.

3. This forms the backdrop to the legends of Robin Hood. We know very little about the historical Robin Hood, but we do know that he is unlikely to have been the proto-socialist he is commonly perceived to be, stealing from the rich to give to the poor. The historical context makes it more probable that if such a figure did exist, he merely attempted to give back to the people what the king's officers had already taken from them.

4. For example, in order to create an ideal hunting ground for himself, William destroyed thirty-six parishes of the New Forest and declared that one-third of southern England's forests were reserved for the king's chase. In order to have lands with which to repay his French supporters, William began to systematically dispossess English landowners of their property. The year following his invasion, some Thanes in the West and North had tried to revolt. In order to prevent the English from revolting again, William passed through the North, massacring entire villages, burning crops to the ground, sowing salt into the fields, and destroying tools so that the native populations couldn't support themselves. Many starved as a result.

Thinking it would be perceived as weakness to listen to these complaints, John stepped up his demands. He was determined to raise enough funds to get back at Philip. Yet he knew that the people would not support an expedition of English soldiers into the Continent. Instead he waged war on Philip indirectly by paying the anti-French emperor, Otto, one thousand marks a year to make trouble for France. He also paid the Count of Boulogne for a similar purpose. Additionally, large sums went to the Dukes of Limburg and Brabant, and the Counts of Flanders and Holland to encourage proxy wars against Philip. John also maintained an expensive army himself, which included hundreds of Flemish knights and a navy with the capability to demolish French fleets. As all of this required yet more money, John continued to raise taxes.

In addition to money, John built up a large collection of jewels and fine clothes, with which he loved to decorate his person. He also had expensive tastes when it came to food. For one Christmas celebration he ordered fifteen hundred chickens, five thousand eggs, twenty oxen, one hundred pigs, and one hundred sheep.

John's greed for money, jewels, and food was surpassed only by his lust for women. In his court the "royal prerogative" took on a new and more sinister meaning. It soon became evident that no woman could be safe around the king. The barons knew that John often cast an envious eye on the more attractive of their own wives, daughters, and sisters, always looking for opportunities to add to the growing population of his illegitimate children.

THE CHURCH GOES ON STRIKE

Unable to get all the money he needed from the barons, John turned his attention on the wealthy church. Opportunity to seize control of the English church had presented itself in 1206 when the Archbishop of Canterbury, head of the English church, died. John appointed his own man, John de Gray, to the vacancy. But the bishops of Canterbury had already elected one of their own company to the post. When the rival archbishops arrived in Rome, each one claiming authority, Pope Innocent III declared both appointments invalid and set forth his own candidate, the English cardinal and theological professor, Stephen Langton.

John refused to recognize the papal choice and forbade Langton to even set foot in his kingdom. Unperturbed, Pope Innocent responded by placing all of England under an interdict—formally suspending all activities of the national church. This essentially meant that the church had to go "on strike." For over five years no one in England could get legally married, receive a blessing at death, or even partake of the sacraments. Only private baptism and last rites (the sacraments deemed necessary for salvation) were allowed. Even on the holidays of Christmas, Good Friday, and Easter, the church bells remained silent.

John was incredibly skillful adapting to changing circumstances and manipulating them to his own advantage. Although the work of the English churches could have carried on as normal, even without formal sanction from the pope, John made sure the churches did not operate. Then because the churches were no longer functioning, John reasoned that they no longer needed funds. He therefore ordered his men to plunder the churches' buildings and confiscate her wealth. Churchmen who resisted were imprisoned until they agreed to pay, while others were hung or put to the sword. Some escaped to the Continent.

Surprisingly, John's persecution of the church actually found support from many of the barons, as the new stream of revenue temporarily diverted the king's attention from the little that remained of their own wealth. John eventually stole from the church £100,000 (hundreds of millions of dollars in today's currency) and used this money to wage successful wars in Ireland, Scotland, and Wales.

But Pope Innocent was not finished with John. The most powerful of all the medieval popes, he was not a man to brook opposition. As the first pope to style himself "Vicar of Christ," Innocent regarded all resistance to himself as opposition to Almighty God. Seeing that John would not admit Langton into England, Innocent unleashed the final weapon at his disposal. On November 1209, he excommunicated the king.

The sentence meant that John was no longer considered a Christian. Furthermore, it mean that John's subjects were absolved from the oaths of loyalty they had sworn to him. By thus placing John outside Christendom, the pope made it morally permissible for anyone to invade and conquer the island. Moreover, any Christian that invaded the land of an excommunicant was considered by the church to be a Holy Crusader.

It did not take long for John's nemesis, Philip of France, to grasp the import of the situation and stake his claim to the English throne.

FROM EXCOMMUNICANT TO CHURCH DARLING

John may not have possessed the Plantagenet aptitude for effective rulership, but he lacked none of his family's propensity for hypocrisy. Faced with the threat of losing his throne, and with it the amorous relationships he cultivated, John announced in May 1213 that he would repent.

Not one to do anything half-heartedly, John decided to prove the genuineness of his conversion by offering all of England as a gift to the pope. This meant that from then on England would be a papal fiefdom. Moreover, it meant that John and all subsequent monarchs of England would be obliged to do homage to the pope as their feudal overlord.

It was a stroke of tactical genius. Convinced that the king was being genuine, Innocent returned the country to John as a gift five days later. Now John was more powerful than he had ever been since he had the pope as his political ally, in addition to all the diplomatic powers at Rome's disposal. (Prior to this transaction with the pope, John had persuaded the church prelates to sign an acknowledgment that the revenue he had stolen from them had, instead, been freely donated.)

King Philip quickly abandoned his invasion plans, unwilling to make an enemy of the pope. In July, Langton was able to return to England and assume his position as archbishop. In the ceremony to install Langton, John prostrated himself on the ground, his eyes streaming with tears and his heart filled with sorrow for his sin. Embarrassed by this public display of emotion, the king's men urged him to desist, but John could not hold back tears of what appeared to be bitter remorse. Langton absolved him. In return, John swore to uphold the liberties England had enjoyed under his father's reign and to repeal any unjust law.

DISPUTE WITH THE BARONS

John was characteristically swift to break his promises, revealing his newfound piety to be nothing more than the dramatics of Plantagenet hypocrisy.

Although the pope may have been fooled by John, Archbishop Langton was not. But Langton was tactful and knew that outright opposition to the king could make matters worse. He talked with the barons and waited for the right time to act.

John's standing with the people plummeted still further in 1214, when he attempted an unsuccessful invasion of France. Nor did it help when, returning from the Continent, he imposed a tax on all the barons who had not joined him in the war.

While he would have liked to have ruled as an autocrat and simply ignored the barons' grievances, no medieval king could govern without some support from his aristocracy. This was especially true in John's case, as he had numerous foes abroad that would have taken advantage of a civil war. Thus John was forced to negotiate with the barons, both before and after his failed French expedition. But though the barons pleaded with him to preserve their historic rights, John continued to abolish their ancient freedoms in his ongoing quest for more wealth and power.

Although the dispute with the barons had been brewing for many years, John's relationship with the pope gave him a new determination not to yield. With the "Vicar of Christ" now on his side, John began to mistake his own egotism for piety.

Believing they had no other recourse, a group of barons in the North conspired against the king. John marshaled his forces in preparation for open war and marched to confront the rebels. Learning of this, Langton rode from London to Northampton to meet the king's army. The archbishop, as much a shrewd politician as an able Bible scholar, persuaded the king to negotiate with the barons. Realizing that this time he had no other option, John consented.

THE MAGNA CARTA

Instead of negotiating, John appealed to the pope. Before he had a chance to receive a reply it became clear that his life would be in danger if he did not submit. As the barons marched on London, John agreed to a series of meetings in the spring of 1215.

Langton and the barons had grown to distrust all the king's promises and pressed for a written charter outlining their liberties. The negotiations culminated in the two parties meeting near a marshy meadow by the Thames riverside, known as Runnymede. There they signed the Magna Carta (Great Charter). In drafting the agreement, Langton had urged the barons to look beyond their own class interests and root their demands in the customs of English common law, as well as an earlier charter issued by John's father, Henry I.

The document removed John's hated administrators, guaranteed the privileges of the church, introduced checks and balances into government, returned the king's mercenary troops to the Continent, protected the rights of widows, limited the amount of inheritance required of a baron's heir, prohibited the confiscation of land belonging to Jews and debtors, reduced the extent of the king's forest, and instituted trial by peers to prevent the king from arbitrarily confiscating someone's property. In addition, many of the rights granted to the barons by the king were also to be granted to the tenants of the barons. Perhaps most importantly, by declaring that taxes may not be levied without the consent of leading churchmen and barons, the document paved the way for Parliament.

John signed the document under duress, as the principles it embodied were contrary to everything he stood for. True to form, John had no intention of keeping this agreement any more than his earlier ones. The excuse for renouncing the charter arose later in the same year when John and the barons met to discuss how it should be enforced. When the convention broke up in quarreling, John appealed to the pope, asking him to squelch the charter.

Pope Innocent was only too willing to help his ally and annulled the document, denouncing it as "not only shameful and demeaning but also illegal and unjust." He went even further, forbidding John to obey it or the nobles to enforce it. The pope excommunicated all the rebel barons, as well as the citizens of London and the coastal towns in Kent and Sussex. When Langton refused to publish news of the excommunications, the pope removed him from all his duties.

John now looked upon the excommunicated rebel barons as enemies, not just of himself, but of the church. He therefore took the vows of a crusader and prepared to fight against them. The barons, who had once played the part of holy crusaders against an excommunicated king, found that the tables had turned.

DEATH OF KING JOHN

With the Magna Carta set aside, the rebellious barons believed there was no recourse left other than armed revolt. They appealed to the French for assistance, and the French prince Louis (son of Philip) was dispatched to help. It was during this war with Louis and the barons that John contracted dysentery and died, aged forty-nine. He was buried at Worcester at the shrine of his favorite saint, Wulfstan.

After his death, the rebel barons were defeated by the royalist army and Louis was forced to return to France. John's son, Henry III (r. 1216–1272), helped to bring stability to the land, although he continued to dispute with the barons over the Magna Carta. However, by this time the barons had become powerful enough that they forced Henry to call the first parliament in 1265, enabling many of the charter's provisions to be implemented.

THE LEGACY OF BAD KING JOHN

Rightly considered to be one of the most disastrous kings in English history, John earned himself the nickname "Bad King John." Yet despite all of this, John's legacy is not altogether negative.

Prior to John, the English monarchy's ties to France had been weakening, and by the days of John it had become very expensive to maintain the ancestral lands in Aquitaine and Normandy. Although John was looked upon as a failure for losing these domains, it did enable the sovereigns that followed him to focus exclusively on England. No longer merely an adjunct of France, England became free to develop a distinct identity and language.

By far the greatest monument of John's reign was the Magna Carta. Modern historians have downplayed the document's significance, pointing out that little changed for the people of England in the wake of its signing. They are also quick to point out that the charter caused the civil war it was designed to prevent. Nonetheless, the importance of the Magna Carta cannot be denied. In many respects it has defined the landscape of British politics over the centuries. In the hundred years following the meeting at Runnymede, the document was reissued thirty-eight times, with only a few alterations. Its emphasis on checks and balances, together with its assertion that the monarch is subservient to the law, has seeped into the very bloodstream of how English-speaking people think about government and law.

The charter also set an abiding precedent for the way in which political disputes would be treated in the future. In his book *The Offshore Islanders,* historian Paul Johnson points out that after the Magna Carta "the English came to see compromise, consultation, the settlement of dispute by argument as opposed to force as their outstanding national characteristics; and in time shaped their habits to conform with this image."[5] This way of doing politics would eventually reach fruition in the modern English parliament and, through Britain's influence, the rest of the Western world.

LESSONS FROM THE LIFE OF KING JOHN

The story of John's life teaches us the importance of conservatism. Contrary to the misguided notion that Magna Carta was a forward-looking piece of proto-democracy, the barons who signed it were actually looking *back* to liberties they had lost. The Magna Carta sought to restore many of the terms reflected in an earlier charter of freedoms that Henry I had issued, which itself was based on freedoms stretching back to King Alfred the Great (r. 871–899). John was the one pressing for "progressive reform," while the barons were the true "conservatives" of the day, claiming the restoration of freedoms that had historically been the heritage of the English people.

Another lesson we learn from John's life is that "[a] man's heart plans his way, but the LORD directs his steps" (Prov. 16:9). The churchmen who suffered from John's evil plans had no way of knowing the remarkable way God was actually directing events. From our vantage point nearly a thousand years later, it is easy to see how God

5. Paul Johnson, *The Offshore Islanders; England's People from Roman Occupation to the Present* (New York: Holt, Rinehart and Winston, 1972), 123.

brought good out of John's foolishness. As Winston Churchill put it in *History of the English-Speaking Peoples*:

> When the long tally is added, it will be seen that the British nation and the English-speaking world owe far more to the vices of John than to the labours of virtuous sovereigns; for it was through the union of many forces against him that the most famous milestone of our rights and freedom was in fact set up.[6]

QUESTIONS FOR DISCUSSION

1. Was John responsible for his sin even though his wickedness was the product of a family culture stretching back many generations? What is the relationship between one's environment and one's free will?

2. What were the strengths of the feudal system? What were its weaknesses?

3. When is it right to let a family member face the consequences of his or her wrong decisions? When is it right to show mercy by protecting such from those consequences? What can we learn about this from Richard's treatment of his brother John?

4. What standards determine whether a tax is just or unjust?

5. Since the Bible says we should be subject to the governing authorities, was it wrong of the barons to rebel against King John?

6. The Norman kings acted as though they owned all the land they ruled. Do some contemporary governments also act like this? Is such a position biblical?

7. Could there be situations where an interdict (suspending all activities of the national church) is biblically justified? Do you think it was justified during the reign of King John?

6. Churchill, *The Birth of Britain*, 190.

8. Did Pope Innocent III make the right decision when he excommunicated King John?

9. Did King John have the right to offer England as a gift to the pope?

10. How should we respond to a person's repentance if we suspect that the person is not being genuine?

11. What provisions within the Magna Carta have become features of America's judicial system?

12. Should kings always be subject to the rule of law or are there times when it is appropriate for the king be above the law? If the former, then how should it be determined which parts of the law the king must submit to?

PERSONAL CHALLENGE

We saw that God brought good out of John's foolishness. What are some ways that the Lord has brought good out of foolish decisions that you have made?

CHAPTER 6

A CLOSE ALLIANCE WITH GOD

The Justice of William of Orange (1533–1584)

CHURCH AND STATE IN MEDIEVAL EUROPE

The relationship between popes and kings had been tenuous throughout Western Europe during the Middle Ages. On one side of the debate, there were many who advocated a view known as **Caesaropapism** or **Erastianism**. According to this position, the church was under the authority of the king in any given land because the king derived his authority from God Himself. This view found expression in a large body of political literature written throughout the Middle Ages to rebuff the political claims of the papacy.

On the other side of the debate was the **theocratic** view. This position held that because the pope is the "Vicar of Christ" on earth, he has the right to wield Christ's totalizing authority in matters civil and **ecclesiastical**.

Between these two positions were numerous combinations and compromises, including the idea that the authority of the church and that of the state should regulate different jurisdictions. According to this doctrine, while the king held authority over the civil law of a nation, the pope exercised authority over the churches of the land. But even this position was not without its difficulties, for what happened should the king find it necessary to arrest a bishop, or if the pope decided to excommunicate a king?

None of these questions were resolved during the Middle Ages, leading to continual power tussles between church and state.

CHARLES V AND THE HOLY ROMAN EMPIRE

These tensions reached their peak beginning in 1519, when the Habsburg emperor Charles V—also known as Charles I of Spain— acquired the title of Holy Roman Emperor. He assumed control of an area covering modern-day Austria, the Netherlands, Switzerland, Germany, Naples, and Sicily, including Spain and her possessions in the New World.

No European king had controlled such a vast territory since Charlemagne. And like Charlemagne, Charles V was an outspoken champion of the papacy. Also like Charlemagne, he endeavored to use Roman Catholicism as a tool for uniting his own dominions.

Charles' accession to the throne of the Holy Roman Empire did not mean that the hundreds of principalities over which he ruled suddenly became part of Spain. Holy Roman Emperors ruled with the consent of regional overlords, many of whom governed small kingdoms themselves. In return for electing the emperor, these overlords expected to be allowed autonomy, as well a degree of influence over the larger empire. The resulting political balance was further complicated by the fact that central Europe contained hundreds of free imperial cities, in theory subject to the emperor, but in practice virtually independent. Each of these cities stood in a unique relation to the larger administration of which they were a part; the exact nature of these relations depended on a complex network of precedents that were hundreds of years old. Central Europe in the sixteenth century was thus awash in a kind of controlled chaos, with various overlapping levels of jurisdictions, tax laws, and trading regulations, all compounded by different regional customs and dialects.

As the most powerful man in Europe, Charles hoped to create more solidarity for the Holy Roman Empire than his predecessors had enjoyed. However, many of the German princes looked askance at the type of **hegemony** that Emperor Charles wished to create. Consequently, when the Lutheran Reformation began to sweep through

Europe, German princes in the North and East saw it as an opportunity to break free, not merely from the Roman Catholic Church, but from the Holy Roman Empire.

The Reformation likewise presented Charles with a unique opportunity. Because he viewed Protestantism as a political as well as a theological threat, it created the perfect occasion for showing the princes who was boss. He did this by banning Protestantism and mercilessly killing those that refused to embrace the Roman Catholic faith. During his entire reign, it is estimated that as many as one hundred thousand Protestants perished.

LIFE AT DILLENBURG

You would not have known that Europe was in a state of turmoil at this time had you visited the castle of Dillenburg, in the small principality of Nassau, located in what is now the Rhineland of modern Germany. William, the Count of Nassau-Dillenburg, was gifted with both tenacity and caution, and he employed these joint virtues towards insulating his estate from the religious conflicts abounding throughout the rest of Europe.

But William was not irreligious. In 1534 he officially changed his faith from Roman Catholic to Protestant. He then reformed the churches on his estate, but gently so as not to provoke protest.

William and his second wife, Juliana, had seventeen surviving children between them both. The Dillenburg castle was thus a hive of constant activity. While her husband, the count, busied himself with the welfare of the farmers on his estate, Juliana presided over a lively household full of children, governesses, tutors, grooms, and riding masters. The parents oversaw a school in the castle where their children and the children of friends could be educated by the many excellent tutors they employed.

William and Juliana were not wealthy, but they used what money they had to create a rich environment for their children, full of family games, country festivities, dancing, music, joy, and spiritual piety. Above all, the Nassau children were taught to love justice, to put the needs of others above their own, and to treat all people with love, kindness, and dignity.

This was the happy environment into which their eldest son, William, was born in 1533, and where he spent the early years of his life.

In 1544, when William was eleven, he came into an unexpected inheritance. A cousin of William's had been killed in France without any heir. By an apparent fluke, William had become heir to all his estates. The land he inherited included vast swaths of territory throughout France, Italy, and what is now Belgium and the Netherlands. One of these lands was a small principality in Southern France with the title "prince of Orange" attached to whoever owned it.

PRINCE WILLIAM

Overnight William had become one of the wealthiest and most important people in all Europe. But there was a condition attached to his new position: he would have to leave Dillenburg and be brought up at Charles V's court in Brussels, where he would receive a Roman Catholic education.

Despite the fact that William's parents were Lutheran converts, they agreed to release their son, praying he would never forget the lessons they had taught him.

William was sad to leave his family and friends, especially his brothers John and Louis, with whom he enjoyed riding, hunting, and playing. But William was a good-natured boy and greeted the change courageously.

His cheerful personality was well-suited to the elegant life at court. He quickly won the hearts of his new guardians, especially Charles V, who became like a second father to him. Charles V became so fond of young William that the emperor always kept him by his side when he was at court. As the boy grew older, this fondness increased and Charles eventually made William governor of three provinces and commander-in-chief of his army. William gained even more land and titles when the emperor chose a rich heiress to be William's bride.

Everyone loved William. He became a leader in fashion, commissioned new palaces, and enjoyed hosting extravagant parties at which he was the center of attention. In all the pomp and grandeur of his position, however, William never forgot what his gentle mother had taught him about treating all people with love, justice, and charity.

Little did William realize that his fortunes were about to dramatically change.

WAR WITH FRANCE

In those days, the Netherlands consisted of seventeen provinces covering the territory that is now Belgium, Luxembourg, and Holland. Within these provinces there were more than two hundred towns, most of them walled and semi-independent. It was in one of these cities, Brussels, where the court of Charles V was held.

From his court Charles continually schemed how he might augment his vast empire. When he decided it was time to bring France under his rule, he sent William at the head of his army to wage war on the country. The soldiers soon found that William was no ordinary general. He did everything he could to ease the hardships of his soldiers. Moreover, he hated the common practice of looting captured towns and constantly pleaded with the emperor to pay the soldiers who would otherwise be forced to steal to keep from starving.

During the campaign in France, William began to witness first-hand the atrocities committed against Protestants by the agents of his adoptive father. The hideous public executions in which Protestants were burned alive were almost too much for William to endure and left a deep impression on him. He would later write to his brother Louis that "to see a man burnt for doing as he thought right, harms the people, for this is a matter of conscience."[1]

PHILIP II AGAINST THE PROTESTANTS

Things changed for William in 1555 when Charles V suddenly decided to abdicate and live out the rest of his days in a monastery. His lands in Spain, the Netherlands, and Italy were handed over to his son, Philip II (king of Spain), while Charles' brother Ferdinand inherited the imperial title and the Austrian lands.

Upon taking power, Philip's first major goal was to strengthen the monarchy, centralize the government, and consolidate the lands he inherited. This was no easy task since many of these lands had historically been semi-autonomous.

In order to achieve his aims, Philip enforced the Roman Catholic religion with even more tenacity than his father had done. Catholics

1. Dawn Langley Simmons, *William, Father of The Netherlands* (Chicago: Rand McNally, 1969), 99.

throughout the Continent rallied behind him, regarding him as divinely chosen to save Europe from the growing Protestant movement. With crusading fervor, he used the Spanish army to persecute Protestants throughout his empire, burning, drowning, and torturing all who refused to acknowledge papal authority.

William, now taking orders from Philip, was dispatched to Paris to negotiate a treaty with the king of France, Henry II (r. 1547–1559). While there, he went on a hunting party with the French king. In the course of the hunt, the two men found themselves alone in the woods. Assuming that William was of one mind with Philip, King Henry began to speak to him of their secret plans to use Spanish soldiers to massacre the Protestants (whom Henry referred to as "accursed vermin") in the Netherlands and France.

Shocked by the news and feeling defensive of the people in his adopted homeland, William gave no sign of disapprobation but continued to converse courteously with the French king. This was one of the many incidents that helped to earn him the nickname "the Silent."

William would later write that he had felt overcome "with pity and compassion for all these good people doomed to destruction."[2] Yet he did nothing immediately, biding his time. He still was not certain where his duty lay, nor how to reconcile his many political commitments with his sense of justice.

THE SPANISH INQUISITION COMES TO HOLLAND

The Dutch provinces had been jealously guarding their long medieval tradition of self-government and resented the encroachments of Philip II. Antipathy against Philip grew when the Dutch learned that their taxes were being used to finance the Spanish army. It also didn't help that in 1554 Philip married the hated Mary I of England, known as "Bloody Mary" for her merciless persecution of Protestants.

Tension tightened in 1564 when Philip declared that all the decrees of the **Council of Trent** were to be promulgated as law, prompting a series of anti-Catholic riots in the Netherlands. "Tell the king," wrote William at this time,

---

2. Cicely Veronica Wedgwood, *William the Silent: William of Nassau, Prince of Orange 1533–1584* (London: Cassell, 1989), 29.

that whole cities are in open revolt against the prosecutions, and that it is impossible to enforce the decrees here. As for myself, I shall continue to hold by the Catholic faith; but I will never give any color to the tyrannical claim of kings to dictate to the consciences of their people, and to prescribe the form of religion that they choose to impose. Call the King's attention to the corruption that has crept into the administration of justice. Let the Government be reformed, the Privy Council and the Council of Finance, and increase the authority of the Council of State.[3]

At this point, William still hoped to appeal to Philip's better nature. Yet for many years the two men had been growing in different directions. Philip lacked the self-confidence to modify his opinions by experience, while William possessed a quiet assurance that translated itself into subtlety and political savvy. While Philip ignored the realities of the wider world and governed his life by a fanatical adherence to abstract principles, William judged every situation individually, making it often difficult to discern what he was thinking (another reason he was nicknamed "the Silent").

In 1567, Philip decided that the time had finally come to put into action the Protestant massacre. In deciding to crush Protestants in the Netherlands, Philip was motivated by more than a concern for theology. Rather, control of the provinces in the Netherlands was crucial for the success of his imperial ambitions. Situated at the commercial crossroads of northwestern Europe, these provinces were a rich source of commerce and industry. Having failed to efficiently manage Spain's potentially lucrative acquisitions in the New World, Philip looked to the Netherlands as an alternative source of revenue. The fact that much of the Netherlands had embraced Protestantism gave him the perfect excuse for invading the land and imposing a heavy tribute.

Philip sent the duke of Alva into the Netherlands at the head of an army of ten thousand Spanish soldiers. The duke made it illegal for the Dutch to discuss the Scriptures, while persons suspected of heresy could be tortured or put to death without trial. The duke

3. Frederic Harrison, *William the Silent* (London: Macmillan, 1897), 41–42.

began a six-year governorship in which eighteen thousand people were brutally slaughtered.

FROM ROMAN CATHOLIC TO PROTESTANT CHAMPION

Wishing to avoid open conflict with Philip II, William had withdrawn from his provincial governorship in the Netherlands and returned to his boyhood home of Dillenburg, where his mother Juliana still exercised her gentle rule. Though he had hoped the move would signal his neutrality, the duke of Alva responded by confiscating William's Dutch properties and the revenues attached to them. The duke also kidnapped William's eldest son, who was attending university in Louvain, and took him to Spain where he was forced to be an obedient Catholic servant of the Habsburgs.

During his four years of exile, William recovered the Protestant faith of his boyhood. Realizing that neutrality was no longer an option, he began to think of ways to defend the Netherlands. After four years of writing letters, gathering contacts, and organizing opposition, he managed to raise a small force of refugees and hired soldiers.

With his ragtag army, William went to war against the Spanish duke. Being no match for the well-trained Spanish forces, however, William and his men suffered several defeats. Eventually reduced to seventy men, his troops were forced to hide amid the canals and islands of the northern provinces. With no one to stand in his way, the duke of Alva proceeded to butcher the residents of those towns that defied him, even putting women and children to the sword.

During those dark days, William never lost his hope that God would deliver him and his people. Once, when he was asked if there was any hope of an alliance with a foreign power, he replied, "I have entered into a close alliance with the King of kings, and I am firmly convinced that all who put their trust in Him shall be saved by His almighty hand."[4]

God did send help from an unlikely quarter. A fleet of fishing-boats, manned by the seafaring folk of the Northern provinces, began to wage surprise attacks along the coast, disrupting the supply

---

4. John Lothrop Motley, *History of the Netherlands*, vol. 1 (Charleston: Forgotten Books, 2008), 447.

lines and destroying Spanish ships. Meanwhile, Queen Elizabeth of England sent supplies to William and his men, now growing again in number. Key towns were liberated from Spanish control, but at enormous cost.

The battles that followed were among the most violent conflicts in the history of European warfare. However, William and his men eventually forced the duke of Alva to resign in 1573. Even still, William had only managed to free the provinces of Holland and Zeeland. He knew that in order to be successful in completely ousting the Spanish from the Netherlands, he must accomplish the seemingly impossible task of uniting all the provinces. This was no easy job, since they were divided between Protestants in the North and Roman Catholics in the South. Yet his efforts reached fruition in 1576 with the Pacification of Ghent, an agreement that all the provinces would stand together until all Spanish troops had gone and an assembly could safely meet to discuss how best to preserve their ancient rights.

Not to be deterred, Philip responded to the agreement by sending a fresh army of twenty thousand Spanish troops. He managed to regain control of the southern provinces, but was unsuccessful in taking the North.

Many began to feel that in order for the provinces to successfully defend themselves, they needed more than a mere agreement uniting them: they needed to have a king. Though William was the obvious candidate, he refused, desiring to serve rather than rule. He suggested that Queen Elizabeth of England be appointed monarch of the Netherlands, but she also refused. William then persuaded the provinces to ask a French prince, the duke of Anjou, to accept the position. However, within a year the duke proved treacherous and had to be removed.

FATHER WILLIAM

William spent the later years of his life urging the northern provinces to remain united for purposes of defense. He knew that none of the provinces alone had the strength to counter another Spanish onslaught. They must group together and fight as one. To achieve this, many of the Dutch Calvinists wished to impose their faith on the nation. Though sympathetic with Calvinism, William wished to foster an environment in which Christians of different theological persuasions could live together in peace. In the words of biographer Cicely Wedgwood, he labored for "freedom from foreign control and liberty of conscience for all the people of the Netherlands of whatever creed."[5]

Ultimately, it was through love and service that William won the hearts of his people and caused them to listen to him. Though they did not always follow his wishes, particularly when he urged them not to repay cruelty with cruelty, they respected him and called him "Father."

ASSASSINATION

But there was one man who hated William to the core, and that was Philip II. Outraged that William had liberated part of the Netherlands, Philip declared him an outlaw and put a bounty of 25,000 crowns on his head.

In 1581, a man named Balthasar Gérard learned of this reward and made it his personal mission to assassinate William. For three years Gérard waited for the right moment to enact his dark plan. The opportunity presented itself on July 10, 1584, when Gérard succeeded in inveigling his way into William's residence in Delft, masquerading as the son of a murdered Protestant. As William was climbing the stairs after dinner, Gérard advanced upon him, pulled out a shotgun, and fired at point-blank range. William was immediately carried to a couch where his sister and wife tried unsuccessfully to staunch the wounds.

Gérard quickly fled to collect his reward but was caught on the way out of the royal lodgings. Furious at what he had done, William's men subjected Gérard to an unimaginable series of tortures. This is clearly not what William would have wished, for after a previous attempt on his life he had written, "I most willingly pardon them. If they are thought deserving of a signal and severe penalty, I beg the magistrates not to put them to torture, but to give them a speedy death, if they have merited this."[6]

5. Wedgwood, *William the Silent*, 127.
6. Harrison, *William the Silent*, 224.

THE LEGACY OF WILLIAM OF ORANGE

William of Orange is looked upon as the father of Holland since his efforts helped give birth to a united Netherlands. The love that the people of Holland still bear towards "Father William" can be seen in their many national symbols which originated with him. These include the flag of the Netherlands, derived from the red, white, and blue flag flown by the princes of Orange, the coat of arms of the Netherlands, derived from William's own coat of arms, and orange as the country's national color, worn today by Dutch athletes in the Olympics.

William's descendants continued to be great leaders. His sons won victories against the Spanish and further solidified the fledgling nation. William's grandson, William III of Orange (r. 1689–1702) and his wife Mary were even given the throne of Great Britain in an effort to preserve England's Protestant faith

Despite his manifold accomplishments, William's most important legacy was spiritual. In freeing the Netherlands from Philip's oppression, he helped to lay the foundation for Dutch Protestantism, which gave rise to a great number of incredibly vibrant Christian thinkers, artists, and statesmen. Protestants such as Rembrandt (1606–1669), Vermeer (1632–1675), Guilaumme Groen van Prinsterer (1801–1876), Abraham Kuyper (1837–1920), and many others may never have existed had not William of Orange freed the provinces from Spanish tyranny.

LESSONS FROM THE LIFE OF WILLIAM OF ORANGE

Many valuable lessons can be learned from the life of William of Orange. Chief of these is that authority flows through rulers who seek to serve the people they would lead. While Philip II believed that a leader must establish his strength through displays of force, power and might, William followed Christ by establishing strength through sacrifice and love.

Another lesson we learn from William is the importance of kindness and mercy. Though the Spanish committed heinous war crimes, William was remarkably merciful to his enemies. He lived by the rule his mother had taught him—that one should never repay evil for evil. Though William knew that during war it was often necessary to kill one's enemies, he eschewed the cruel treatment of prisoners that was commonplace at the time.

William also followed Jesus in being willing to lay down his life for his people. When he was finally murdered, it came as no surprise, for he knew that Philip II had a network of spies and assassins throughout Europe. Yet William was prepared to lay down his life for those he loved. Always thinking of his people, his last words were, "My God, have pity on my soul; my God, have pity on this poor people."[7]

William's life also teaches us that liberties are precious and are worth fighting for. Proverbs 22:28 says, "Do not move the ancient boundary which your fathers have set," and Proverbs 24:21 urges us to "not associate with those who are given to change" (NASB). In his pride, Philip II ignored the wisdom in these injunctions when he sought to strip the provinces of liberties stretching back hundreds of years.

William believed that another liberty worth defending was the right of a person to choose his own religion without government interference. In his letter to Philip he criticized the right of rulers to dictate the consciences of their people or to prescribe the form of religion they must follow.

William was criticized by his contemporaries for lacking principle since he often based his decisions on political utility, even if it meant playing a double game. Whether it is true that he lacked principle or not, William's life teaches us that it is not enough for a ruler to simply be in the right; a good ruler must also know how to be sly, when to hold his cards close to his chest and how to balance idealism with diplomatic adroitness.

The final lesson that William teaches us is that the battle belongs to the Lord. In fighting to defend the liberties of his people, William looked to God alone for deliverance, confident that He would listen to the cries of His people. This gave William a confidence that was infectious. He wrote to his brother John that

> We may see how miraculously God defends our people, and makes us hope that, in spite of the malice of our enemies, He will bring our cause to a good and happy end, to the advancement

7. Simmons, *William, Father of the Netherlands*, 225.

of His glory and the deliverance of so many Christians from unjust oppression.[8]

The trust that William placed in God was constant, even in the midst of apparent defeat. When writing an agonizing letter to his brother John after the news that their other brothers had been massacred, he said,

> If they be dead, as I can no longer doubt, we must submit to the will of God and trust in His divine Providence, that He who has given the blood of His only Son to maintain His Church will do nothing but what will redound to the advancement of His glory and the preservation of His Church—however impossible it may appear. And though we all were to die, and all this poor people were massacred and driven out, we still must trust that God will not abandon his own.[9]

QUESTIONS FOR DISCUSSION

1. What does the Bible teach about the relationship between church and state?

2. In territorial disputes, how much weight should be attached to precedent?

3. Did William's parents do the right thing in letting him leave them at the age of eleven to be raised as a Roman Catholic?

4. William believed that people should be free to choose their own religion without government interference. Is such freedom always a good thing? Along these lines, how do you think William would deal with the influx of Islam into present-day Holland?

5. What makes a war just?

8. Ibid., 126.
9. Ibid., 156.

6. To what extent has Philip II's ideal of a united Europe been realized through the contemporary European Union? Is this a good thing?

7. One of the reasons William was such an effective leader was that he was likable. How important is it that a leader be liked? Should a leader try to be popular?

8. It was suggested that one of William's virtues was that he knew how to be sly. But might this have actually been a weakness since it kept him from acting sooner to stop the Protestant slaughter?

9. While Philip II was blindly following abstract principles, William carefully weighed every situation on its own merits. From a biblical perspective, are there strengths and weakness in both these approaches?

10. In his darkest hours William trusted God to deliver him and his people. Can we always trust God to deliver us from evil?

11. How should the rule "Do not repay evil for evil" apply during times of war?

12. Most of the small kingdoms and city-states that existed in sixteenth-century Europe have become subsumed into larger nation-states. Is this a good thing or a bad thing?

13. Does trusting God involve a general spiritual attitude, or does it involve specific confidence that God will perform X (any specific event) in space and time?

PERSONAL CHALLENGE

William trusted God in the midst of the most trying and uncertain times. What can this teach you about your attitude to difficult circumstances in your own life?

CHAPTER 7

MERE CHRISTIAN

The Vision of Richard Baxter (1615–1691)

BACKGROUND TO THE ENGLISH PURITANS

When the English Parliament decided to break with the Roman Catholic Church in 1534 with the Act of Supremacy, there were many who felt that the resulting Church of England wasn't reformed enough. This included many Englishmen who later escaped to the Continent during the subsequent persecution of Bloody Mary. When Mary's sister, Elizabeth, inherited the throne in 1558 and the exiles were able to return, they brought with them ideas and practices they had encountered at such places as Geneva, Switzerland, where John Calvin and the exiled John Knox preached a stronger and more extreme form of reformation.

Thus it was that as the sixteenth century progressed, a growing number of English Protestants came to believe that the Anglican Church was compromised. The Book of Common Prayer contained remnants of Roman Catholicism, they argued, and the Anglican Church ought to purge itself of Roman practices such as wearing clerical vestments, using wedding rings as part of the marriage ceremony, baptizing with the sign of the cross, kneeling to receive the Lord's Supper, and so on.

Originally, the English Puritans had not intended to start a movement or even to break away from the established church. Rather, the movement emerged organically as like-minded people gathered together to seek a purer form of religion. As their ideas were rejected by the Church of England, the Puritans were spurred to become increasingly nonconformist in their ideology.

Although the term "Puritan," and especially the adjective "puritanical," has come to have pejorative connotations, the original English Puritans could not have been more unlike the contemporary stereotype. They were robust, joyful men and women who lived full and colorful lives. They had a strong sense of duty without being legalistic (something that could not always be said of their American counterparts) and a keen desire to pursue holiness without losing humility.

In setting themselves against in the Church of England, the Puritans were considered to be subversive. Though the Puritans were law-abiding and loyal to the crown, James I of England (r. 1603–1625) feared that because many of them rejected Anglican bishops, they might eventually reject the monarch. Consequently, he tried to force them to follow those bits of the prayer book with which they disagreed. When he encountered a stubborn Puritan resistance, the king promised to "harry them out of the land, or else do worse." The king turned England into such a miserable place for the Puritans that many of them emigrated to Holland and, later, America.

RICHARD BAXTER

It was into the rich—if sometimes over-reactionary—environment of English Puritanism that Richard Baxter was born in 1615. Beset with a number of illnesses, he assumed his life would be short and therefore endeavored to make the most of it by entering the ministry. At the age of twenty-three Richard was ordained, and three years later he accepted a post in the town of Kidderminster, in Worcestershire. He had not been ministering there long when civil war erupted.

The English Civil War (1642–1646, 1648) was the result of tensions between the Puritans and the crown that had been fomenting ever since the start of the Puritan movement. These tensions were exacerbated when Charles I (r. 1625–1649) married a Catholic wife and introduced a series of reforms aimed at strengthening the Church of England and ensuring religious unity throughout the land. These measures included dismissing nonconformist clergymen, closing Puritan organizations, and using the dreaded Court of High Commission and Court of Star Chamber to punish those who dissented. This served only to alienate Charles from a Puritan population that was growing in numbers and power.

Trouble increased after Charles mismanaged England's finances, closed Parliament for eleven years, reopened it, and then later marched into Parliament with an armed force to arrest his political rivals. The people revolted, leading to a civil war against the king and his supporters. Led by the fiery Puritan Oliver Cromwell (1599–1658) and his force of "Roundheads," the Puritan army attempted to overcome the king and his royalist army.

During the war Baxter took a break from his parish to serve as chaplain in Cromwell's army, playing an important role as a voice of moderation. This was not an easy time for Baxter since he and Cromwell clashed on a number of issues, including liberty of conscience and the legitimacy of the monarchy. Moreover, he was uncomfortable with the way many of his fellow Puritans were quick to sacrifice the unity of the church for the sake of perfectionism.

The Cromwellians finally overcame the royalists and, following protracted but unsuccessful attempts to negotiate with the king, executed him in 1649. The new government was run by Parliament, but when this proved inefficient, Cromwell himself marched into Parliament with an army, closed Parliament, and ruled by decree. For the next five years, Cromwell governed the country as a military dictator. Baxter's ministry, in spite of his ongoing disagreements with Cromwell, thrived under the new Puritan state.

MINISTRY AT KIDDERMINSTER

Returning to Kidderminster after the war, Baxter developed a style of ministry that would go down in history as a model for pastors to follow. On his arrival at this parish of about eight hundred homes, only about one family in every street attended worship services. When he left nineteen years later, there were some streets in which every single family loved Jesus. Visitors to the town would remark how on the

Lord's Day one could walk down the street and hear families singing psalms together or discussing that day's sermon.

Though a remarkable preacher, Baxter believed his greatest work lay in personal contact with his parishioners. Like Thomas Chalmers two centuries later, Baxter took a very hands-on approach to pastoral shepherding. Every Monday and Thursday he would start at one end of town, while his assistant would start at the other, each systematically visiting every home. By the end of the year, when their courses met in the middle of the town, they would have interviewed all eight hundred families.

During these visits Baxter and his assistant would spend about an hour with each household, instructing them and gauging the spiritual condition of each individual. They would offer counsel to those who were confused, comfort to those who were suffering and correction to those living in sin. Baxter would later attribute his success in Kidderminster to these visits, which he believed to be even more crucial than his preaching.

A prolific writer, Baxter used much of the income from his books to purchase Bibles for the poor in his parish. He made an arrangement with his publishers that every tenth copy would be given to him free, so that he could pass it on to those that could not afford to buy books.

God blessed Baxter's tireless labors. The town which formerly had a reputation for ignorance and debauchery became almost entirely converted to Christianity. It was also at Kidderminster, when he was forty-seven years old, that the Lord blessed Baxter with a wife. Though Margaret was twenty-one years younger and the couple had their struggles, their marriage blossomed. The Baxter home was permeated with the love and joy characteristic of so many Puritan families.

Although Baxter's energies were directly to his flock at Kidderminster, his vision was worldwide. G. F. Nuttall has suggested that Richard Baxter was unusual among seventeenth-century Puritans in his eagerness for the conversion of the nations.

TIME IN PRISON

After Parliament restored the monarchy in 1660, the Puritans were subjected to another wave of fierce persecution. Conscious of what had happened to his father, the new king, Charles II (r. 1660–1685), viewed the Puritans as a threat and ejected many of them from their pulpits. Though Baxter was a political moderate, he was caught in the legal backlash and sentenced to a week in prison in 1669.

Persecution of the Puritans intensified when Charles sought retaliation for what he regarded as Puritan pressure to exclude his brother James, duke of York, from succession to the throne. In 1685 Baxter was sent to prison again for eighteen months. This was a travesty since Baxter, unlike other leading Puritans, had been willing to accept the authority of bishops and worked to convince many of his fellow Puritans to remain in communion with the Church of England.

THE LEGACY OF RICHARD BAXTER

Toward the end of his life, Baxter was seen by many Puritans as the figurehead of their movement. Baxter himself avoided the label Puritan, referring to himself as a "mere Christian"—a term that would later influence the writer C. S. Lewis.

Baxter's writing, like his preaching, embodied the robust and grateful vision of life that characterized the English Puritan movement. By the time he died in 1691, at the age of seventy-six, he left behind over 130 books. These books sold better than those of any other English writer at the time. His works stress the importance of one's duty before God and man, as well as the need for humility, generosity, joy and gratitude. His book *The Reformed Pastor* left a deep impact on many other influential pastors, including the Wesleys, Charles Spurgeon, and George Whitefield, and continues to be a classic to this day. Many of his other works continued as devotional classics well into the nineteenth century, before they were superseded by the more sentimental devotional literature that has dominated ever since.

By far Baxter's greatest work was his ministry among the people of Kidderminster. Fifty years after his death, George Whitefield visited the city and commented, "I was greatly refreshed to find what a sweet savour of good Mr. Baxter's doctrine, works and disciplined remained unto this day."[1]

LESSONS FROM THE LIFE OF RICHARD BAXTER

Richard Baxter was a man of vision, able to look beyond short-term setbacks to the goals God had inspired him to reach. His long-term vision as he considered the effect his ministry would have after he was gone gave his ministry a generational focus. This inevitably found expression in Baxter's work with children. "In the place where God most blessed my labours at Kidderminster," Baxter would later reflect, "my first and greatest success was upon the youth."[2]

Believing that "the work of educating youth aright [was] one half of the great business of man's life,"[3] Baxter developed a vigorous youth ministry. This ministry had three aspects. First, he organized a "youth group" where he would meet for three hours on Saturday evenings in various homes, preparing the youth for the following Lord's Day. Second, he used weekly family conferences as a way to reach the children. During these conferences he would speak in turn to both adults and children. Third, every month he set aside one of his Thursday lectures to give a message aimed specifically at the youth and those responsible for their training.

Baxter knew that in order to have spiritually healthy children, there needed to be strong marriages. His advice to husbands and wives was characteristically practical. Husbands and wives, he taught, ought to stir up what is best in each other by not dwelling on each other's faults. If a husband spends too much time thinking about his wife's weaknesses, then his annoyance at her will be amplified. On the other hand, if he focuses his attention on her positive attributes,

1. Richard Baxter, *The Practical Works of Richard Baxter: With a Preface, Giving Some Account of the Author, and of This Edition of his Practical Works; an Essay on his Genius, Works and Times; and a Portrait : in Four Volumes* (London: George Virtue, 1838), xxvii.

2. William Orme, *The Life & Times of the Rev. Richard Baxter* (Boston: Crocker & Brewster, 1831), 147.

3. Baxter, *The Practical Works of Richard Baxter*, 3.

then "the good will most appear, and the evil will be as buried, and you will more easily maintain your love."[4]

Another lesson Baxter teaches us is the importance of church unity. Here again, he had extraordinary vision and spent much of his public career urging the various Protestant factions to stop bickering and work together towards personal holiness. Putting into practice the motto, "In necessary things, unity; in doubtful things, liberty; in all things, charity," Baxter threw himself into an impressive array of **ecumenical** work alongside Anglicans, Presbyterians, Congregationalists, and Baptists. Many of these other groups picked up his successful ideas and implemented them in their own parishes.

While church unity and interdenominational peace were always precious to his heart, Baxter's combative personality sometimes made him a difficult agent for achieving these goals. In his writing he was exceedingly gracious and diplomatic, seeking to build bridges between different factions. (He even developed a new theory of justification in an attempt to bridge the gap between Calvinism and Arminianism.) In person, however, the plain dealing and outspokenness that won the heart of his parishioners tended to alienate his peers. At the same time, many of his fellow Puritans were at odds with him for taking what they deemed too moderate an approach to many issues. For example, unlike other nonconformists, Baxter did not hold that it was a sin to participate in Anglican services.

To his dying day, Baxter never ceased to urge the Christian community to higher levels of unity and peace. "Is it not enough," he once wrote, "that all the world is against us, but we must also be against one another? O happy days of persecution, which drove us together in love, whom the sunshine of liberty and prosperity crumbles into dust by our contentions!"[5]

QUESTIONS FOR DISCUSSION

1. What do you think Richard Baxter would have thought of modern youth ministry?

4. Richard Baxter, *The Godly Home* (Wheaton: Crossway, 2010), 129.
5. Richard Baxter, *The Saints' Everlasting Rest* (Glasgow: W. Collins, 1831), 110.

2. What might be some of the reasons that Richard Baxter's ministry proved so productive and successful?

3. The fruit of Richard Baxter's ministry was still apparent some fifty years later when Whitefield visited Kidderminster. Are we able to see the effects today of ministry that was done two generations ago? Do contemporary approaches to Christian ministry aim at impacting future generations?

4. The reason the Puritans objected to such things as clerical vestments, baptizing with the sign of the cross, the use of wedding rings as part of the marriage ceremony, etc., is because of a belief called the "regulative principle." The regulative principle stated that all practices which scripture has not explicitly commanded for worship are therefore forbidden. Is the regulative principle itself biblical?

5. Was Oliver Cromwell a hypocrite when he objected to the king overthrowing Parliament, only to later do the same thing himself?

6. Richard Baxter worked to achieve unity between the various Protestant factions. If he could visit the church today, would he be pleased or grieved at the relationship between the different denominations?

7. Were Cromwell and his army of "Roundheads" rebelling against God's appointed authority when they fought to overthrow the king?

8. Can unity among different Christian groups ever be a bad thing?

PERSONAL CHALLENGE

In your own relationships, how are you doing at following the motto: "In necessary things, unity; in doubtful things, liberty; in all things, charity"?

CHAPTER 8

GLORIFYING GOD
AND REFRESHING THE HUMAN SPIRIT

The Devotion of J. S. Bach (1685–1750)

In April 2009, British atheist A. N. Wilson shocked the world by an-nouncing that he was returning to the Christian faith. When asked in an interview what was the worst thing about being faithless, the writer and newspaper columnist replied:

> When I thought I was an atheist I would listen to the music of Bach and realize that his perception of life was deeper, wiser, more rounded than my own. . . . The Resurrection, which pro-claims that matter and spirit are mysteriously conjoined, is the ultimate key to who we are. It confronts us with an extraor-dinarily haunting story. J. S. Bach believed the story, and set it to music.[1]

A. N. Wilson is not alone. In his introduction to the book *Does God Exist?*, Peter Kreeft noted that he personally knows three ex-atheists that were swayed by the argument, "There is the music of

---

1. A.N. Wilson, "Can you love god and agree with Darwin?: AN Wilson on his return to faith after a period of atheism," *New Statesman*, http://www.newstates-man.com/religion/2009/04/returning-to-religion (accessed January 6, 2012).

Bach, therefore there must be a God."[2] Of these, Kreeft informed his readers, two are now philosophy professors and one is a monk.

Even the God-hater Friedrich Nietzsche (1844–1900), upon hearing a performance of the St. Matthew Passion, was compelled to admit that "one who has completely forgotten Christianity truly hears it here as gospel."[3]

Bach would certainly approve, for he once remarked that "the aim and final end of all music should be none other than the glory of God and the refreshment of the soul."[4] To underscore this point, he wrote the initials SDG (*Soli Deo Gloria*—To God Alone the Glory) at the end of most of his scores.

But who was this man whose music reaches down through time to touch people in such powerful ways?

To answer this question, we must travel back to the early seventeenth century where, in the Saxon province of Thuringia (modern Germany), there lived a miller by the name of Veit.

THERE ONCE WAS A MILLER

Native to Hungary, Veit had fled to Thuringia to escape persecutions against him and his fellow Lutherans. In the Protestant protectorate in the heart of Germany, Veit found the environment he sought for raising his son in accordance with Lutheran principles. Defended by the Elector of Saxony, this was the same province that had offered Luther a haven following the judgment against him at the **Diet of Worms**.

Next to his faith and family, Veit's greatest joy came from making music on a cittern, an ancient predecessor to the mandolin. Although his work as a miller was demanding, Veit did find time to play on the instrument while the flour was grinding.

Veit died in 1619, but not before passing on both his love of music and his strong faith to his son, Johannes Bach. The love of music and

2. J.P. Moreland and Kai Nielsen, *Does God Exist?: The Great Debate* (Nashville: Thomas Nelson, 1990), 27.

3. Ernst Bertram and Robert Edward Norton, *Nietzsche: attempt at a mythology* (Urbana: University of Illinois Press, 2009), 52.

4. Gregory Wilbur and David Vaughan, *Glory and Honor: The Musical and Artistic Legacy of Johann Sebastian Bach* (Nashville: Cumberland House Publishing, 2005), 1.

the love of Christ lived on in the generations that followed. Indeed, towards the close of the seventeenth century, Veit's many descendants had come to dominate the German musical scene. Eventually over seventy Bachs occupied posts as professional musicians in the surrounding area. In fact, the word "Bach" even became a synonymous term for musician in that region.

THE MUSICAL BACHS

Veit Bach was the great-great-grandfather of Johann Sebastian Bach, who became one of the most renowned composers the world has ever known. As a child, Johann Sebastian recalled hearing his father recount with pride the accomplishments of their remote ancestor, who had brought both music and Lutheranism to the family.

Johann Sebastian was not only born into a family of musicians: he was also born into a family of Johanns. His parents, Johann Ambrosius and Elisabetha, had seven sons and they named all of them Johann. (The penchant for the name seems to have been almost as much of a family tradition as music: all of Ambrosius' twin brother's four sons were also given the name.)

The senior Johann occupied the position of *Stadtpfeifer*, or town musician, for the Eisenach council. This meant that he was responsible for providing daily music for the town's market, as well as playing for special civic and ecclesiastical functions.

Sebastian (as he was called to distinguish him from his brothers) learned two things from his father that helped to define the person he later became. First, his father's example taught him the importance of caring for others, especially relatives, who were in need. His father looked after his handicapped younger sister, his wife's widowed mother, the son of a cousin who had died in the Plague, and the orphaned son of another cousin.

Sebastian also learned from his father a love of music. He was taught this in the best possible way: **enculturation**. By being saturated in what was good, true, and beautiful from an early age, he learned to appreciate and enjoy fine art long before he could understand it.

Life changed dramatically for nine-year-old Sebastian when his mother died suddenly in May 1694. In February of the following year, his father died, leaving Sebastian an orphan.

His older brother, Johann Christoph (1671–1721), had recently married and settled down in the town of Ohrdruf. When their parents died, Christoph invited Sebastian to live with him, and he raised the boy as his own.

MOONLIGHT AND MUSIC

Sebastian continued his musical studies with his brother, who was an accomplished musician and held the post of organist at St. Michael's Church in Ohrdruf. By his early teens, Sebastian had positively devoured all the music that he had been shown, and he was hungry for more.

It was not just the joy of playing music that spurred Sebastian to lay his hands on all the music he could find. In every piece he surveyed, the boy learned something more about the techniques of harmony, counterpoint, form, genre, and **invention**. Even when he had grown to be a fully mature composer in his own right, Bach retained an insatiable curiosity to analyze other people's works and incorporate their ideas into his own.

Christoph had studied under Pachelbel (1653–1706) and owned a volume of music he had obtained from the composer. When Sebastian asked his brother for permission to transcribe the manuscript, Christoph refused. This was probably because the value of the music depended on its scarcity and Christoph feared lest any copies be made and circulated.

But Sebastian was positively determined to see the music. One night, when he had made sure that Christoph and his wife were safely in bed, Sebastian sneaked into the room where the music was locked in a cabinet. Because the doors of the cabinet were made of grillwork, he found he was able to pass his small hands through the openings and touch the coveted volume. As the parchment was too large to fit through the holes in the grillwork, Sebastian rolled it into a coil until it was small enough to carefully extract through the small holes.

Once he held the music in his hands, Sebastian faced a new problem: how was he to copy the music without his brother knowing?

Not allowed to have his own candle, he was forced to copy the book entirely by moonlight. Since his nights of productivity were limited to those when the moon was full, it took him six months to copy all of the music.

Despite the precautions that Sebastian took, his brother eventually came upon him playing from the copy he had made. Furious, Christoph punished Sebastian and took away the music.

FROM LÜNEBURG TO LEIPZIG

By the time Bach was fifteen, he was an accomplished soprano, violinist, and composer, as well as being proficient at the organ and all the other keyboard instruments of the day. He had also excelled in his academic studies, including Latin and theology.

When they had reached Sebastian's age, all his brothers had already left school to pursue positions in music. Sebastian could easily have followed this pattern but was eager for more schooling. Through the help of his choral instructor, Bach was able to secure a scholarship to continue his education at St. Michael's School in Lüneburg.

Although the music library at Lüneburg had at least eleven hundred volumes, Sebastian's thirst for music could not be quenched. During his time at Lüneburg he would often walk thirty miles to hear the organist John Reinken in Hamburg, before turning around and walking thirty miles back. Perhaps because of his excursions (which must have placed a strain on his finances), and also because his scholarship didn't cover all the expenses, Sebastian was forced to terminate his formal education in 1702.

In the period that followed, Bach occupied a succession of posts: violinist in the small chamber orchestra of Duke Johann Ernst of Weimar, church organist for the town of Arnstadt, church organist for the town of Mühlhausen (during which time he married his cousin Maria Barbara), again a member of the chamber orchestra at Weimar and organist to the Court there, and finally, Capellmeister for the court of prince Leopold of Anhalt-Cöthen.

A Capellmeister was the highest rank a musician could achieve during the **baroque** period. This meant that Bach was in charge of all the music at Prince Leopold's court. Leopold was himself an enthusiastic musician and handpicked the finest musicians to work for him. He and Bach struck up a close friendship and enjoyed many hours making music together.

Despite the absence of an organ at the Cöthen, these were happy days for Bach. He had plenty of time to compose, competent musicians on which to test out his pieces, and a growing family. Moreover, he was given invaluable opportunities to tour new places and learn new musical styles, for whenever Prince Leopold travelled around Europe, he took his musicians along.

Returning from one of the prince's tours, Bach received heartbreaking news: his beloved wife, Maria Barbara, had died, leaving their four children motherless.

The following year, when he was thirty-six, Bach met twenty-year old Anna Magdalena, a court singer. Needing a wife to help with his children, Bach proposed to Anna and she accepted. The marriage proved to be a great source of happiness to Bach, and also a blessing to his children, whom Anna loved as her own.

Within a week of the wedding, Prince Leopold also married. Unfortunately for Bach, the new princess took little interest in music and also discouraged Leopold from his musical activities. This, together with Bach's desire to live near a good Lutheran school that his children could attend, compelled him to seek another position. The opportunity presented itself when the post of cantor to the town of Leipzig fell vacant. Bach applied for the position and was accepted. In 1723 he moved his wife and children (now ages eight, nine, twelve and fourteen) to the city where he would spend the rest of his life.

THE FAITHFUL CANTOR

As musical director for all of Leipzig, Bach's duties were vast. He had to organize (though not necessarily compose) weekly music for the city's four main churches, as well as special music for ceremonial occasions. His job also required him to give private lessons in singing and instrumental performance, to teach Latin (a duty he delegated), and to serve as hall monitor for the school one week every month, calling boys to morning prayer, supervising meals, and enforcing curfew.

The transition from the easy life at court—where he could compose and make music as he pleased—to the strenuous and demanding responsibilities of a town cantor must have been quite a challenge for a creative genius like Bach. Yet he embraced his duties with characteristic faithfulness, seeking to fulfill the needs of his employers to the best of his ability. This was not always easy, for Bach was frequently frustrated by the petty bureaucracy of the town council.

The controversies with the municipal authorities were sometimes ideological, as many city officials wished to modernize the city (and its music) according to Enlightenment principles. The modernists believed Bach was clinging to obsolete forms of music. Other officials looked upon the composer as a regretted necessity, since their first two choices of town cantor—Telemann and Kauffmann—had not been available. They kept Bach on a meager salary, barely sufficient to meet the needs of his growing family. Throughout the rest of his life, Bach had to deal with personal attacks, including a series of newspaper articles written against him.

Despite this lack of support, Bach composed his most splendid music in Leipzig. During the first five years, he went through a frantic period in which he wrote hundreds of sacred cantatas, even though this was not required by his job description, and despite the fact that the Leipzig authorities were not always supportive of the projects. Cantatas were multi-movement works, sung by a choir and solo voices, to be used in worship on Sunday morning or feast days. They incorporated both the gospel reading and the Lutheran hymn for the day, the latter of which formed a thematic background to the entire work. By the time Bach finished, he had given the church three complete annual cantata cycles, to be used according to the liturgical calendar.

In addition to being great musical achievements, many of the cantatas articulate the exquisite sweetness of a relationship with Jesus. In one of his best-loved cantatas, "Awake, A Voice is Calling," the following passionate duets occur between Jesus and the Soul:

The Soul: When are you coming, my Savior?
Jesus: I am coming, your portion.
The Soul: I am waiting with burning oil. Open the hall for the heavenly banquet.
Jesus: I am opening the hall for the heavenly banquet.

The Soul: Come, Jesus!

Jesus: I am coming; come, sweet soul![5]

Then, a little later in the work, Jesus and the soul are united and celebrate with an even more intimate exchange:

The Soul: My friend is mine,

Jesus: And I am his.

Jesus and the Soul: Nothing shall separate this love.

The Soul: I will feed on heaven's roses with you,

Jesus: You shall feed with me on heaven's roses

Jesus and the Soul: Where abundant joy and bliss will be found.[6]

THE FAITHFUL TEACHER

During the twenty-seven years he spent in Leipzig, Bach taught between sixty and one hundred students. In fact, he seems to have spent almost as much time training the next generation of musicians as he did composing. Many of these students became close personal friends with the Bach family and even lived in their home over the years. Bach's method of teaching was described by in 1802 as follows:

> as long as his scholars were under his musical direction, he did not allow them to study or become acquainted (besides his own compositions) with any but classical works. The understanding, by which alone what is really good is apprehended, develops itself later than the feeling, not to mention that even this may be misled and spoiled by being frequently engaged on inferior productions of art. The best method of instructing youth, therefore, is to accustom them to what is excellent. The right understanding of it follows in time, and can then still farther confirm their attachment to none but genuine works of art.[7]

5. Ron Jeffers and Gordon Paine, *Translations and Annotations of Choral Repertoire: German Texts* (Corvallis: Earthsongs, 2000), 51.

6. Ibid., 53.

7. Johann Nikolaus Forkel, "On Johann Sebastian Bach's Life, Genius, and Works," in *The Bach Reader: A Life of Johann Sebastian Bach in Letters and Documents,* ed.

LATER LIFE AND DEATH

In Leipzig, Anna bore Bach thirteen more children, although seven of these died at a young age. Those that survived gave their father much joy. In his later years, Bach withdrew as much as possible from public life, finding fulfillment in his faith, family, and music.

Also during his later years, Bach experimented with perfecting various musical forms as well as reworking a number of his earlier compositions in light of his increased musical knowledge. These works have been termed his summation works and have been described by biographer Greg Wilbur as "compositions of such beauty, erudition, achievement and comprehensiveness that they approach musical perfection and rival any intellectual accomplishment in the history of man."[8]

By the time Bach died on July 28, 1750, he left behind a collection of compositions staggering in its proportions. It has been said that it would take a present-day copyist seventy years just to copy out all the pieces and parts that Bach wrote, and yet Bach composed this music while fulfilling many other duties.

Unfortunately, after his death the Leipzig authorities defrauded Anna of her rightful inheritance. She was forced to sell many of her husband's unpublished manuscripts. Some people at Leipzig even reportedly used his manuscripts to wrap garbage in.

THE NEGLECT AND REDISCOVERY OF BACH

Though Bach's music was admired by his students and musicians throughout Europe, his music never achieved the following of other baroque composers like Vivaldi, Telemann, and Handel. In Leipzig he was remembered more as an organ virtuoso than a great composer.

Significantly, the date of his death has traditionally marked the end of the baroque period and the beginning of the classical era. Instead of the elaborate, complex, and often dissonant music of composers like Bach and Handel, people began to prefer the simplicity and classical elegance of composers such as Mozart and Haydn. Consequently, Bach's music fell into disuse and much of it, especially the

Hans David and Arthur Mendel (New York: W.W. Norton, 1945), 330.

8. Wilbur and Vaughan, *Glory and Honor,* 90.

vocal works, was forgotten. While individual composers (including Mozart and Beethoven) were greatly influenced by him, it was not until Felix Mendelssohn staged a performance of the St. Matthew's Passion in 1829 that Bach's compositions were once again appreciated by a wider audience. This jumpstarted an enormous interest in Bach studies and a search to recover and publish as much of his music as possible. Unfortunately, by then much of his music, including around one hundred cantatas, had either been lost or destroyed. What remains today is only a small portion of his total output.

THE LEGACY OF J. S. BACH

It is impossible to describe Bach's musical legacy in a few words. His compositions are incredibly varied and defy categorization. From works that reach dizzying heights of mathematical complexity (*The Art of Fugue*), to lush melodies like his "Air on the G String," to works such as the *Chromatic Fantasy* that approach a jazzy dissonance, his music is of astonishing range and variety. Though his music has sometimes been caricatured as being dry and academic, his compositions actually explore the full range of human emotions from deep sadness (*Passacaglia and Fugue for Organ in C Minor*) to playful joy (the Brandenburg concertos).

But by far Bach's greatest legacy remains his Sunday morning worship music. "His conscious life-long purpose," wrote Edward Dickinson in *Music in the History of the Western Church*, "was to enrich the musical treasury of the Church he loved, to strengthen and signalize every feature of her worship which his genius could reach: and to this lofty aim he devoted an intellectual force and an energy of loyal enthusiasm unsurpassed in the annals of art."[9]

The theological underpinning behind Bach's church music was drawn from 1 Chronicles 25 where David and the captains of his army separated out certain individuals for praising God through music. In the marginal notes of his Calov Bible commentary (drawn from Luther's writings, which Bach used to study Scripture), Bach commented that 1 Chronicles 25 formed "the true foundation of all

9. Edward Dickinson, *Music in the History of the Western Church: With an Introduction on Religious Music Among the Primitive and Ancient Peoples* (New York: Charles Scribner's Sons, 1902), 283.

God-pleasing music."[10] Elsewhere he scribbled the marginal observation, "Where there is devotional [or reverent] music, God with His grace is always present."[11]

In Bach's church music one can feel that gracious presence. This is especially true of the music he composed for the Passion narratives of Matthew and John. The St. Matthew Passion centers mainly on the sacrificial nature of Christ's death. In this dark but rich musical setting, the agony of Christ is almost palpable.

Bach's work with the Passion narratives emerged out of the extreme importance he attached to the finished work of Christ on the cross. It is no coincidence that in his Bible commentary, Bach underlined Luther's comments on John 19:30, where the reformer writes that "Christ's suffering is the fulfillment of Scripture and the accomplishment of the redemption of the human race."[12] Bach clung to this redemption, which gave him a quiet confidence in God in the midst of life's many difficulties.

Even though his genius reached the pinnacle of perfection in his church music, Bach is remembered today mainly for his instrumental works. Yet even these compositions preach to us and are a musical expression of the dynamic harmony of differences that lie at the heart of Trinitarian life. He was able, like no other composer before or since, to present a number of independent melodies, all unique in themselves, but which weave together to form a single texture that is itself complete without compromising the diversity of the parts.

LESSONS FROM THE LIFE OF J. S. BACH

In his book *Outliers,* Malcolm Gladwell asks what makes some people so successful. The usual answer has been that it is all comes down to a combination of innate talent and hard work. While both of these factors play an important role, Gladwell argues convincingly that the ingredients which separate the genius from the ordinary person have

10. Robin A. Leaver, *J.S. Bach and Scripture: Glosses from the Calov Bible Commentary* (St. Louis: Concordia Publishing House, 1985), 93.

11. Ibid., 97.

12. Calvin Stapert, *My Only Comfort: Death, Deliverance, and Discipleship in the Music of Bach* (Grand Rapids: W.B. Eerdmans, 2000), 122.

as much to do with the family, heritage, and community in which a person has grown up.[13]

Nowhere is this more evident than in the life of J.S. Bach. One of the reasons that the Bach clan was able to become so influential in eighteenth-century Germany was because they looked after each other through an informal network of mutual support, loyalty, and love. Uncles took on nephews as apprentices, widows were supported by in-laws, and other relatives took in one another's children when disaster struck, as it often did in that age of high mortality. Always on the alert for ways to assist each other, the older Bachs used their influence to help the younger relatives secure lucrative jobs, while each was careful to pass on to the next generation the musical knowledge he had acquired during his life.

A lesson that Bach's life teaches us, therefore, is the importance of culture. Geniuses like Bach do not arise out of a vacuum. They are the product of years—often centuries—of collective input from dozens of individuals. Most of these individuals will probably be unaware of the heritage they are contributing to, yet their collective efforts help to foster and sustain a culture in which greatness can thrive. Sometimes this can be the culture of a family (such as Ambrosius Bach's family before his death in 1695), the culture of an extended family (the Bach clan), the culture of a nation (Protestant Germany in the early eighteenth century), or the culture of an entire civilization (Christendom). When there is such a confluence of these types of overlapping cultures, and when they are all favorable to personal industry, rationality, and creativity, then the opportunities for greatness are manifold.

The network of charity, self-giving, and musical enjoyment that characterized the culture into which Bach was born, began five generations earlier with Veit. The life of Veit Bach, no less than J.S. Bach, shows us that faithfulness in the small things, particularly when it comes to investing in posterity, can leave a generational footprint beyond reckoning.

Bach realized this. He understood the importance of having a multi-generational vision and invested an enormous amount of

---

13. Malcolm Gladwell, *Outliers: The Story of Success* (New York: Little, Brown and Co., 2008).

energy in his own children. "What is amazing," wrote Bach's biographer Otto Bettmann, "is the zeal and endless devotion with which he devoted himself to the upbringing of his children, musically and otherwise."[14] Bach viewed his work with his family as essentially no different than his music, believing that God calls a man to faithfulness in whatever sphere he finds himself. Significantly, in his Calov Bible commentary, he underlined Luther's comments on Psalm 127, where the reformer had written that we should pray, "Lord, I accept my calling and do what you have commanded, and will in all my work surely do what You will have done; only help me to govern my home, help me to regulate my affairs, etc."[15]

Despite his faithfulness as a father and the attention he gave to the spiritual training of his children, one of his sons rejected his father's wisdom and incurred large debts, having to leave town twice to escape his creditors. Although this was a cause of great sorrow to Bach, he never ceased to love and pray for his wayward son, as the following letter he wrote on his son's behalf reveals:

> What can I do or say more, my warnings having failed, and my loving care and help having proved unavailing? I can only bear my cross in patience and commend my undutiful boy to God's mercy, never doubting that He will hear my sorrow-stricken prayer and in His good time bring my son to understand that the path of conversion leads to Him.[16]

Bach's work preparing the next generation was not limited to his family. No other composer taught so many students who themselves went on to become great composers. One reason Bach is still remembered today is because he was such a devoted teacher. Were it not for his students, who disseminated copies of his music throughout Europe, much of his solo keyboard work would now be lost.

Another lesson we learn from Bach is the importance of humility. Bach's first biographer, Johann Forkel (1749–1818), noted that "if he

14. Wilbur, *Glory and Honor,* 193.

15. Leaver, *J.S. Bach and Scripture,* 147.

16. Patrick Kavanaugh, *Spiritual Lives of the Great Composers* (Grand Rapids: Zondervan, 1996), 20.

had thought fit to travel, he would (as even one of his enemies has said) have drawn upon himself the admiration of the whole world. But he loved a quiet domestic life, constant and uninterrupted occupation with his art, and was . . . a man of few wants."[17]

Bach was incredibly gracious to other composers whose music was clearly inferior to his own. He never thought of himself as a genius and would frequently make light of his ability, which he attributed more to hard work than talent. When asked by someone how he had mastered music to such a high degree, he replied: "I was obliged to be industrious; whoever is equally industrious will succeed equally well."[18]

POSTSCRIPT

Nearly a hundred years after Bach's death, a monument to his memory was raised in Leipzig. Before the unveiling ceremony, Mendelssohn tried to find some of Bach's descendants. He followed every trace but found nothing.

Despite the strength of the Bach clan during the eighteenth century, it is not surprising that by the nineteenth century they had fragmented. In the years following Bach's death, the cultural landscape of Europe underwent a dramatic shift. As the church and the aristocracy (Europe's two largest music patrons) both declined, the types of positions that had been filled by musical Bachs became obsolete. As a consequence, the Bach clan ceased to remain intact and by 1843 Mendelssohn could find no family descendants to honor.

On the day of the ceremony, however, a curious old man of eighty-four, still full of energy, hobbled into sight, seemingly from nowhere. He claimed to be the grandson of Johann Sebastian Bach.

"No one knew of his existence," wrote the composer Robert Schumann, "not even Mendelssohn, who had lived so long in Berlin and, he supposed, had followed every trace of Bach he could discover. Yet his grandson had resided there for over forty years."[19]

17. Hans T. David, Arthur Mendel, and Christoph Wolff, *The New Bach Reader: A Life of Johann Sebastian Bach in Letters and Documents* (New York: W. W. Norton & Company, 1999), 461.

18. Ibid., 459.

19. Charles Sanford Terry, *Bach: A Biography* (Whitefish: Kessinger Publishing, 2003), 278.

Upon investigation, it was discovered that this mysterious figure was not only a musician, but "had filled the office of Capellmeister to the consort of Friedrich Wilhelm III, and enjoys a pension which maintains him in comfort."[20]

This lone figure, apparently the last in Veit's long line of musical descendants, was himself a stark reminder of the way Johann Sebastian, like his ancestor, had taken care to pass on his love of music to the next generation.

QUESTIONS FOR DISCUSSION

1. Because of his Protestant work ethic, Bach did not recognize the distinction between the sacred and the secular, but rather believed that all things should be done for the glory of God. He was just as comfortable writing non-religious music as church music. What can we learn from this about our own approach to music?

2. What are some ways parents can pass on a love of beauty to their children?

3. During most of his career, Bach was employed by the city council of Leipzig. Is it right that a city should use the taxpayers' money to support the arts? Should our government do this?

4. Is it possible, or preferable, for extended families today to remain as intact as the Bach clan? What are some factors in our world that make this a difficult ideal?

5. Peter Kreeft refers to ex-atheists that were converted by the argument, "There is the music of Bach, therefore there must be a God." Is this a legitimate argument?

6. Right up to the end of his life, Bach was hungry to learn from other composers and to incorporate their ideas into his own works. Beethoven, on the other hand, would often intentionally avoid studying the music of others so as not to pollute his own originality. Do both these approaches have equal merit, or is one better than the other?

20. Ibid.

7. Is Bach's music objectively beautiful, or is beauty just a matter of personal taste?

8. If Bach had promoted himself more, he might have been more widely appreciated and consequently, much of his music would not have been lost. Should he have done more to "toot his own horn"?

9. When writing church music, Bach beautified tunes and conventions that were already part of the larger culture, even as Luther had done for his generation. Is this something church musicians should still strive to do?

10. Discuss the quotation on page 136 about Bach's teaching methods. How might his approach to musical education be applied to other subjects, including literature, visual art, and the appreciation of movies?

11. How does a person that has achieved greatness, and knows he or she is great, remain humble?

12. Towards the end of Bach's life the aristocracy and the church (Europe's two main music patrons) were in decline. As a consequence, composers had to write music that would appeal to a wider audience. How might this have affected musical style? Does this help to explain the huge difference between music of the baroque period (roughly 1600–1750) and music of the classical period (roughly 1750–1820)?

13. How does Bach's music display the glories of the blessed Trinity?

14. Is there anything we can learn from Bach's approach to worship? How does the music of your own church compare to the type of Sunday morning worship music that Bach endeavored to promote?

PERSONAL CHALLENGE

What can you be doing now to help cultivate a love of beauty in your family?

CHAPTER 9

ABSOLVED FROM
BEING GOOD-MANNERED

The Romantic Totalitarianism of
Jean-Jacques Rousseau (1712–1778)

In her 1910 publication, *Euthenics, the Science of Controllable Environment*, Ellen H. Richards wrote that

> The control of man's environment for his own good as a function of government is a comparatively new idea in republican democracy. . . . It is part of the urban trend that the will of the man, of the head of the family, should be superseded by that of the community, city, state, nation. . . . In the social republic, the child as a future citizen is an asset of the state, not the property of its parents. Hence its welfare is a direct concern of the state.[1]

Richards' idea was a simple one: children do not belong to their parents, but are the property of that Great Parent known as the state.

The idea that parents should stop thinking of their children as belonging to them was echoed more recently in 1996, when Hillary

---

1. Ellen Henrietta Richards, *Euthenics, the Science of Controllable Environment: A Plea for Better Living Conditions as a First Step Toward Higher Human Efficiency* (Boston: Whitcomb & Barrows, 1910), 131–133.

Clinton addressed the United Methodist General Conference. "As adults," she said, "we have to start thinking and believing that there isn't really any such thing as someone else's child. My child, your child, all children everywhere, must live and make their ways in society, and now, in the increasingly shrinking world we live in, in the larger globe as well."

Such ideas are not limited to the United States. In 2007, the UK's Institute for Public Policy Research put forward a proposal for increasing "identity, citizenship and community cohesion" in Britain. The report urged christening services to be replaced by "birth ceremonies" in which the parents agree to "work in partnership" with the state to raise their children.[2]

The idea that we should think of the state as a parent is actually nothing new but is as old as sin itself. When the emperor Diocletian published his Edict of 301, mandating the persecution of Christians, he justified the move by referring to himself and his associates as "the watchful parents of the whole human race."[3] Similar examples abound throughout the history of the ancient world.

But while the idea of the parental state may be nothing new, its modern manifestation can be traced back to one notorious French villain: Jean-Jacques Rousseau.

ROUSSEAU AND THE ENLIGHTENMENT

Jean-Jacques Rousseau (1712–1778) was the product of the European Enlightenment—a movement which tended to downplay reliance on inherited forms of authority and instead emphasized the virtues of autonomous reason. This often led to a questioning of Christianity and, ironically, the unthinking acceptance of certain radically secularist presuppositions. Moreover, as the eighteenth century wore on, there was an increase in the type of antagonism towards institutional Christianity that we find in philosophers such as Voltaire (1694–1778), David Hume (1711–1776), and Denis Diderot (1713–1784).

2. Hal G.P. Colebatch, "Britain's Escalating War on Christianity," *The American Spectator* (November 8, 2007), http://spectator.org/archives/2007/11/08/britains-escalating-war-on-chr/1 (accessed April 27, 2012).

3. Herbert Schlossberg, *Idols for Destruction* (Wheaton: Crossway Books, 1990), 183.

The Enlightenment movement was also **utopian**. On the eve of the Industrial Revolution, many Enlightenment writers eagerly anticipated the bright future that invention, efficiency, and utilitarianism would make possible in a society unhampered by spiritual superstition.

Although Rousseau was a key figure in this movement, he was also one of the Enlightenment's harshest critics. At the beginning of the 1700s, to be "enlightened" meant that you were a rationalist in the broader sense of the term: that is, you ordered your life according to the dictates of reason, and you looked back to the order, poise, and elegance of the classical world for inspiration. The perfectly balanced couplets of Alexander Pope's poetry or the idealized portraiture of Joshua Reynolds' paintings embodied this early Enlightenment emphasis. Yet by the end of the eighteenth century, being "enlightened" came to be associated not so much with classical Greece and Rome, but with the new savage societies that were being discovered by explorers like Captain Cook. The "good life" gradually began to be seen as having less to do with reason than with feeling, less with the mind and more with the heart, less with order and more with disorder, asymmetry, and flux. The full impact of this metamorphosis would not be seen until the Romantic movement of the nineteenth century, though the rumblings of this change were felt in the late 1700's in the changes in landscape architecture, the paintings of William Turner, or the neo-pagan spirituality of Mozart's opera *The Magic Flute* (1791).

Rousseau was a key link in the chain of this fascinating shift. He bridges the gap between the reason-based Enlightenment of the eighteenth century and the emotion-based Romantic movement of the nineteenth, even as Beethoven's music bridged the gap between the classical order of Mozart and the romantic expressiveness of Chopin.

One of the ways Rousseau did this was through a heightened emphasis on feeling. Instead of appealing to first principles of reason as philosophers like Hume were doing, he appealed to the "internal sentiment," constantly telling his readers to "consult your own hearts while I speak: that is all I ask."[4]

---

4. Jean-Jacques Rousseau, *Emile, or On Education* (Sioux Falls: NuVision Publications, 2007), 241.

This shift from reason to feeling can be traced to the exact center of the eighteenth century. In 1750, when Rousseau was thirty-nine, he entered an essay competition on "Whether the rebirth of the sciences and the arts has contributed to the improvement of morals." He argued that they did not. He contended that the progress of the civilized world, as epitomized in the rise of arts and sciences, had been moving mankind farther away from his natural condition. The uncivilized, primitive condition was actually morally superior, since to be "civilized" was to be a slave. By creating "more refined taste" and the uniformity demanded by "politeness" and "propriety," civilization results in "people follow[ing] customary usage, never their own inclinations. One does not dare to appear as what one is." The solution, Rousseau argued, was a return to habits "rustic but natural." His prayer is "Almighty God…deliver us from the enlightenment and the fatal arts of our fathers, and give us back ignorance, innocence, and poverty, the only goods which can make our happiness and which are precious in Your sight."[5]

Rousseau won the prize and was immediately catapulted into a career as one of the most distinguished intellectuals in France. Through his writings he began to shift the focus of the entire Enlightenment movement away from civilization and onto "nature," away from urban sophistication and onto rustic simplicity. A new cult of "being natural" was about to emerge, with the artist rather than the logician as the principle guru.

NO ORDINARY MAN

How could Rousseau know that his feelings were a reliable guide to truth? If Rousseau's *Confessions* are anything to go by, the answer seems to be that his feelings were self-evidently correct *because they were his.* If this seems like an arbitrary, even arrogant, valuation on his part, the answer is that Rousseau believed that he was no ordinary person. "I am not made like any of those I have seen," he remarked in the beginning of his tedious autobiography. "I venture

5. Jean-Jacques Rousseau, "Jean-Jacques Rousseau, Discourse on the Arts and Sciences, [The First Discourse]," Vancouver Island University, http://records.viu.ca/~johnstoi/rousseau/firstdiscourse.htm (accessed January 6, 2012)

to believe that I am not made like any of those who are in existence. If I am not better, at least I am different. Whether Nature has acted rightly or wrongly in destroying the mould in which she cast me, can only be decided after I have been read."[6] He dares any on the Day of Judgment to stand before God and say, "I was better than that man!" Elsewhere in the book he mused, "My situation is unique, unheard of since the beginning of time and, I am sure, never to be paralleled."[7]

But just how was Rousseau so unique? One of the areas he believed he differed from everyone else was in the uprightness of his character. He once wrote, "Never have I known the hateful passions, never did jealousy, wickedness, vengeance enter my heart. I get carried away by anger sometimes but am never crafty, never bear grudges."[8] Rousseau apparently achieved this virtuous condition through his great love for himself and for mankind. "I love myself too much to hate anybody," he once noted.[9]

Those that had the misfortune of living in close proximity to him may well have doubted the veracity of Rousseau's self-assessment. The hateful passions did seem to come quite naturally to this embittered Frenchman, who believed that life owed him something. Those that tried to help him, including those that gave him money, learned the lesson only too quickly. The verdict of his former friend and fellow philosopher, David Hume, was a typical reaction of anyone that spent extended time with him. Hume contended that Rousseau was "a monster who saw himself as the only important being in the universe."[10]

Rousseau knew there were people out there that thought of him in this way, but he assures his readers that only lack of enlightenment could cause people to think ill of such a worthy and noble character as himself. "I say it without fear," he remarked, "if there were a single

6. Jean-Jacques Rousseau, *The Confessions of Jean Jacques Rousseau* (New York: Modern Library, 1945), 3.

7. Jakob Herman Huizinga, *The Making of a Saint: The Tragi-Comedy of Jean-Jacques Rousseau* (London: H. Hamilton, 1976), 15.

8. Jakob Herman Huizinga, *Rousseau: The Self-made Saint* (New York: Grossman Publishers, 1976), 73.

9. Ibid.

10. Paul M. Johnson, *Intellectuals: From Marx and Tolstoy to Sartre and Chomsky,* 1st ed. (New York: Harper Perennial, 1990), 26.

enlightened government in Europe, it would have erected statues to me."[11] Rousseau looked to posterity for the adulation to which he felt entitled, and he proclaimed the day would come when "it will then be no empty honor to have been a friend of Jean-Jacques Rousseau."[12]

Since Rousseau represented all that was best in the human race, anyone who took offense at him inadvertently became an enemy of mankind in the process. And there were many who did take offence at him; not surprising, considering that he was stingy with money, autocratic, and a hypochondriac, to say nothing of being excessively quarrelsome, calculating, self-pitying beyond the bounds of sanity, and egotistical almost to the point of madness.

Rousseau was also a grumbler, but not in the ordinary sense. He attached dramatic significance to his physical discomforts, and this gave him the notion that life owed him special treatment. "As a sick man, I have a right to the indulgence humanity owes to a man who suffers," he once remarked.[13] And again: "I am poor and it seems to me that on this account too I merit special consideration."[14]

Rousseau was also tremendously lazy. It is true that in the first half of his life he tried his hand at a number of honest professions, but he failed at almost every one. According to the French Ambassador in Venice, the Comte de Montaigu, this was due to his "vile disposition," his "unspeakable insolence," and his "high opinion of himself."[15] However, like Socrates before him and Ralph Waldo Emerson after him, Rousseau believed he was above doing ordinary labor. He once said, "my idea of happiness is . . . never to have to do anything I don't wish to do."[16] After winning the essay contest, Rousseau was finally able to attain his ideal. Because of his writings, he was in popular demand among the wealthy intellectual elite, many of whom gave him generous support. He particularly liked forming relationships with women who were independently wealthy.

11. Huizinga, *The Making of a Saint*, 182.
12. Johnson, *Intellectuals*, 19.
13. Huizinga, *The Making of a Saint*, 58.
14. Ibid.
15. Johnson, *Intellectuals*, 6.
16. Ibid., 13.

Although constantly in debt to his many aristocratic benefactors, Rousseau never reciprocated their generosity. Possessing what he termed "a certain resentment against the rich and successful as if their wealth and happiness had been gained at my expense,"[17] he was deliberately rude to his patrons. Yet he also had an incredible knack for so manipulating circumstances that his benefactors felt indebted *to him*. He remarked that "friendship does not reckon services and the one who has loved the most is the real benefactor."[18] Since Rousseau axiomatically assumed that he always exercised the most love, it followed that he was always the real benefactor. It is doubtful, however, if Rousseau ever felt any love that was disinterested, as he seems to have valued all his friendships only by what he could get out of them for himself. He admitted as much, saying, "I want to love my friends for the pleasure I get out of doing so . . . the moment they demand gratitude for services rendered . . . pleasure vanished."[19] Rousseau believed he was doing his benefactors a favor by displaying ingratitude, thus signifying that they were the recipients of *his* friendship, and "gratitude and friendship cannot coexist in my heart."[20]

Being himself untrustworthy, Rousseau trusted no one, ever convinced that conspiracies against him were in the works. On one occasion when he was in England, visiting Hume, he came to believe that the Scottish philosopher was plotting his downfall, in league with dozens of assistants. Hume's guilt had been established beyond any reasonable doubt one evening after Rousseau had jumped on Hume's knee and bathed his host's face in kisses and tears. (Rousseau conceived friendship as a reciprocal "unburdening" of "loving hearts," accompanied by "delight of weeping together.") When the stoical Hume responded with less-than-adequate gush, Rousseau took this as proof of his treachery. At the height of these delusions, Rousseau even went so far as to write to Lord Camden, the Lord Chancellor of England, asking for his help against this imagined conspiracy.

17. Johnson, *Intellectuals*, 24.
18. Huizinga, *The Making of a Saint*, 57.
19. Ibid.
20. Ibid.

"RUDE ON PRINCIPLE"

Not only was Rousseau unapologetic for his abominable behavior, but he had a knack for being able to convert his vices into virtues. His rudeness was sanctified by an appeal to the cult of Nature and the revolt against convention that was becoming a feature of high French society. "I have things in my heart which absolve me from being good-mannered," he once said.[21]

Putting into practice what he had written for the essay contest, Rousseau dared to appear as he really was. He thus took great pride in being "uncouth, unpleasant and rude on principle"[22] and once remarked with satisfaction, "I am a barbarian."[23]

Rousseau said that "even the most trifling social duties are unbearable to me" and decided instead "to adopt manners of my own."[24] We may well question if Rousseau had any manners at all when he began to display before polite French society the details of his toilet troubles. Indeed, his biographical *Confessions* do not hide the disastrous results of being unable to find somewhere to urinate while in the company of high-society ladies. "In short," he confessed, "I can urinate only in full view of everybody and on some noble white-stockinged leg."[25]

One might think that such candor would have damaged Rousseau's reputation. In fact, it did the opposite. It helped to solidify the impression that he was a what-you-see-is-what-you-get kind of guy. Rousseau never seemed to practice subterfuge nor to possess multiple layers to his personality. He was prepared to reveal everything about himself—including painfully embarrassing truths—even though it might cause others to think ill of him. Everything about the man seemed to be on the surface. This forthrightness endeared Rousseau to his audience, especially women. His contemporaries testified that there was something endearing about him when he told his "story." All his words seemed to be bathed in an air of candor, and he exuded a

21. Jonas E. Alexis, *In the Name of Education* (Longwood: Xulon Press, 2007), 103.
22. Johnson, *Intellectuals*, 11.
23. Ibid., 23.
24. Huizinga, *The Making of a Saint*, 49.
25. Ibid., 50.

childlike simplicity and innocence—a genuineness that drew people to him on the first meeting.

Those who got to know Rousseau a little better learned that this transparent guilelessness was a façade. Behind the air of childlike spontaneity lay an exceptionally calculating and deceptive mind. Beneath the exterior of false humility was one of the greatest egotists that ever existed. Behind the smokescreen of truthfulness lurked a man willing to manipulate, twist, and distort the truth as part of the publicity stunt that was his life. It is even possible that many of the apparently damaging admissions in his *Confessions* were fabricated in order to create the impression of a man who had nothing to hide.[26] When he began to stage seventeen-hour-long readings of his *Confessions* in fashionable houses, there were many who could contradict the veracity of his accounts. His response: "[Whoever] examines with his own eyes my nature, my character, morals, inclinations, pleasures, habits, and can believe me to be a dishonest man, is himself a man who deserves to be strangled."[27]

Many of his contemporaries, and an astonishing number of his subsequent devotees, have taken Rousseau's self-assessment at face value. He had and continues to have an uncanny ability to persuade people that he was honest merely because he appeared to be frank; to convince them he was inwardly sincere only because he acted outwardly naïve; to deceive others about his character because he first managed to deceive himself.

MANKIND'S BEST FRIEND

Rousseau did not believe in original sin but held that man is inherently good. But although we are born in a condition of innocence, we quickly fall when exposed to the corrupting influences of civilization.

---

26. Paul Johnson writes, "The 'facts' Rousseau so frankly admits often emerge, in the light of modern scholarship, to be inaccurate, distorted or non-existent. This is sometimes clear even from internal evidence. . . . It gradually emerges that no statement in the *Confessions* can be trusted if unsupported by external evidence. . . . What makes Rousseau's dishonesty so dangerous—what made his inventions so rightly feared by his ex-friends—was the diabolical skill and brilliance with which they were presented" (*Intellectuals*, 18).

27. Ibid., 16.

As Rousseau put it in the famous opening line of *The Social Contract*, "Man was born free, and he is everywhere in chains."[28]

If the corrupting influences of society constitute the fall of man, redemption lay in escaping these influences through being "natural." Yet when Rousseau wrote his parenting manual *Emile* to show what a return to nature looked like, it hardly resembled an uncivilized primitivism. It is true that Rousseau advocated vegetarianism, cold baths, loose clothing, and breastfeeding, but in many respects the utopian upbringing he gives to the fictional *Emile* is not unlike that given to the children of rich Frenchmen in the eighteenth century. Rousseau tended to cherry-pick the aspects of society he liked and called these "natural," while those aspects of society he didn't fancy were dismissed as "unnatural."

But how was Rousseau himself able to escape the widespread corrupting influences of society in order to become a reliable guide to others? What gave him the right to pontificate what was natural and what was not? The answer could have something to do with the fact that Rousseau considered himself a reliable guide because of the special relationship he harbored with mankind. He saw himself as a kind of steward of humanity, carefully nurturing mankind to maturity even when the human race, like a spoiled child, was prone to turn on its guardian. Yet to the end he remained mankind's best friend, a prophet of the brotherly love that spontaneously overflowed from his bosom towards the human race. As Rousseau himself put it, "I was born to be the best friend that has ever existed . . . I have a very loving heart. . . . The person who could love me as I can love is still to be born. . . . Show me a better man than me, a heart more loving, more tender, more sensitive, more captivated by the delights of friendship, more susceptible to the good and the beautiful."[29] Elsewhere he writes, "If my soul were not immortal God would be unjust."[30] "I would leave this life with apprehension if I knew a better

28. Jean-Jacques Rousseau, *The Social Contract* (London: Penguin Classics, 1968), 49.

29. Huizinga, *The Making of a Saint*, 55.

30. Maurice William Cranston, *The Noble Savage: Jean-Jacques Rousseau, 1754–1762* (Chicago: University of Chicago Press, 1991), 122.

man than me." "Posterity will honor me . . . because it is my due." "I rejoice in myself." "[M]y consolation lies in my self-esteem."[31]

Had Rousseau spared even a fraction of his love of mankind for those real people nearest him, then the course of his life might have been very different. Although he presents himself as one who reveled in the company of children, eyewitness accounts show that he was mean-spirited toward them. But his greatest malice, cruelty, and heartlessness was reserved for his own offspring. His mistress Thérèse bore five children. In each case Rousseau insisted that they be sent, unnamed, to almost certain death at Paris's dreaded Foundling Hospital. (With over five thousand abandoned infants to care for every year, it is not surprising that two-thirds of the babies in the hospital died within the first year. Only fourteen out of one hundred even made it to the age of seven. Those who did survive had to eke out a miserable existence on the street.)

What could have possessed Rousseau to abandon his children to such a fate? He later reflected that the children would have been "an inconvenience," and that to support them he would have had to stoop to a labor beneath his dignity, including "all those infamous acts which fill me with such justified horror."[32] In short, the great Rousseau was not a man to change dirty diapers.

Rousseau expected his readers to instinctively understand the predicament that children would have created for him. "How could I achieve the tranquility of mind necessary for my work," he asks, "my garret filled with domestic cares and the noise of children?"[33] The irony, of course, is that among the "work" he refers to was the writing of his parenting manual, *Emile*. The needs of *real* children would have interfered with Rousseau's ability to set himself up as the greatest parenting guru of all time. Even so, he shows no hesitation in assuring his readers that he would have made a splendid father, given his great love for mankind:

> [M]y ardent love of the great, the true, the beautiful and the just; my horror of evil of every kind, my utter inability to hate

31. Huizinga, *The Making of a Saint*, 182–183.
32. Johnson, *Intellectuals*, 22.
33. Ibid.

or injure or even to think of it; the sweet and lively emotion which I feel at the sight of all that is virtuous, generous and amiable; is it possible, I ask, that all these can ever agree in the same heart with the depravity which, without the least scruple, tramples underfoot the sweetest of obligations? No! I feel, and loudly assert—it is impossible! Never, for a single moment in his life, could Jean-Jacques have been a man without feeling, without compassion, or an unnatural father.[34]

"FORCED TO BE FREE"

In *Emile,* Rousseau shows how to produce the perfect person by tinkering with the child's external environment. Where he becomes really dangerous is when he attempts to apply this utopian principle on a larger scale. Just as the problems faced by the individual find their solution in the perfect upbringing, so the solutions faced by mankind as a whole find their solution in the perfect state. This was the basis of his political tract, *The Social Contract.*

Rousseau was as gifted a polemicist as he was a self-publicist, but clarity was not among his virtues. Since he contradicted himself many times, an entire Rousseau industry has developed around the question of what he actually meant in *The Social Contract.* Despite its incoherence, however, certain tenets of his political thought remain clear. The first of these is that private property is among the first curses of "civilization," contributing to our alienation from "nature." As Rousseau put it in his *Discourse on the Origin of Inequality:*

The first man who, having enclosed a piece of land, thought of saying "This is mine" and found people simple enough to believe him, was the true founder of civil society. How many crimes, wars, murders; how much misery and horror the human race would have been spared if someone had pulled up the stakes and filled in the ditch and cried out to his fellow men: "Beware of listening to this impostor. You are lost if you

---

34. Ibid.

forget the fruits of the earth belong to everyone and that the earth itself belongs to no one."[35]

Rousseau's antipathy to private property would reach such a pitch of fanaticism that, three years before his death, he denied the legitimacy of commerce: "I am so fully convinced that any system of commerce is destructive to agriculture that I do not even make an exception for trade in agricultural products."[36]

Just as no one could ultimately claim ownership of any object, so no man has a natural authority over his fellows. The only legitimate authority comes when people consent voluntarily to be governed. This is the basic view of government outlined in *The Social Contract*: all legitimate authority exists by the will of the people.

Delving deeper, however, it becomes evident that Rousseau is saying a lot more than just the fact that rulers govern with the consent of the people. The "general will" of the people not only gives rulers the mandate to govern, it is also the ultimate source of freedom and moral values. Furthermore, it is also the ultimate proprietor of all property. Rousseau could thus remark that "the right of any individual over his own estate is always subordinate to the right of the community over everything."[37]

If this seems like an inordinate amount of power being invested in the civil community, Rousseau assures his readers that we need have no fear, for the general will that controls the state can never err: "the general will is always rightful and always tends to the public good."[38] Thus Rousseau simply made the general will infallible by definition.

How is the general will mediated to society? It is when we ask this question that the totalitarian implications of Rousseau's theory start to really become apparent. In short, the general will is forced

---

35. Jean-Jacques Rousseau, "A Discourse On a Subject Proposed by the Academy of Dijon: What is the Origin of Inequality Among Men And Is it Authorised by Natural Law?," The Constitution Society, http://www.constitution.org/jjr/ineq.htm (accessed January 9, 2012).

36. Jean-Jacques Rousseau, 'Constitutional Project for Corsica', The Constitution Society, http://www.constitution.org/jjr/corsica.htm (accessed January 9, 2012).

37. Rousseau, *The Social Contract*, 68.

38. Ibid., 72.

upon the people through the political machinery of the state. Since the state is a mirror of what the people really want, "the laws are but registers of what we ourselves desire."[39] While Rousseau provides no signs by which the general will can be correctly identified, nor the specific mechanisms for government by which it can be preserved, he does assume that rulers at the helm of the state will always know what the people really want—that is, what is really in the public's best interest. The result is not democracy, but its opposite, since the multitudes cannot be trusted to understand what they really want. "By themselves," he wrote, "the people always will what is good, but by themselves they do not always discern it. The general will is always rightful, but the judgment which guides it is not always enlightened. It must be brought to see things as they are, and sometimes as they should be seen."[40]

What from a distance looks like a democratic government run by the people appears, upon closer inspection, to be a form of **oligarchy** or dictatorship run ostensibly in the name of the people. Yet it is in name only, for when one person's opinion conflicts with what the rulers determine is in the best interest for him, then the ruler's decision is what stands. "If my particular opinion had prevailed against the general will, I should have done something other that what I had willed, and then I should not have been free."[41]

It is here that Rousseau's utopia becomes rather spooky. The state can force us to be free even if *we* think freedom looks very different, and even if "freedom" must be forced on us at the point of the sword. As Rousseau puts it, "Whoever refuses to obey the general will shall be constrained to do so by the whole body, which means nothing other than that he shall be forced to be free."[42] In short, it means that anything the ruler chooses to do is automatically just: "For the rulers well know that the general will is always on the side which is most favorable to the public interest, that is to say, the most equitable; so that it is needful only to act justly to be certain of following

39. Ibid., 82.
40. Ibid., 83.
41. Rousseau, *The Social Contract,* 153–154.
42. Ibid., 64.

the general will."[43] In this way, the state that Rousseau presents is functionally infallible.

The problem, of course, is that an infallible state is one that can aspire to omnipotence. Such a state might demand that its citizens surrender to it their individuality, property, and lives, which is exactly what Rousseau urges: "Each one of us puts into the community his person and all his powers under the supreme direction of the general will; and as a body, we incorporate every member as an indivisible part of the whole."[44] Moreover, since individual liberties are always defined in terms of what benefits the whole, the state has the right to dispose of individual members when it deems that it is necessary:

> If the state, or the nation, is nothing other than an artificial person the life of which consists in the union of its members and if the most important of its cares is its preservation, it needs to have a universal and compelling power to move and dispose of each part in whatever manner is beneficial to the whole.[45]

THE STATE AS PARENT

One potential interpretation of his political theory is that Rousseau, who never had a good relationship with his own parents, had an inner need to ascribe parental characteristics to the state. In a document he wrote for a proposed reformation of Poland, he spoke about the country in explicitly parental terms:

> When first he opens his eyes, an infant ought to see the fatherland, and up to the day of his death he ought never to see anything else. Every true republican has drunk in love of country . . . along with his mother's milk. This love is his whole exis-

---

43. Jonah Goldberg, *Liberal Fascism: The Secret History of the American Left, From Mussolini to the Politics of Meaning,* 1st ed. (New York: Doubleday, 2008), 39.

44. Rousseau, *The Social Contract,* 61.

45. Ibid., 74.

tence . . . when he has ceased to have a fatherland, he no longer exists; and if he is not dead, he is worse than dead.[46]

As this quote seems to suggest, Rousseau looks to the state as the supreme Parent—one who has a right to the earth and the fullness thereof. Rousseau's state gives us life and nurtures us to maturity in her bosom. We owe our very existence to her, and for this very reason we must be willing to surrender to her our property and our lives at a moment's notice:

> Now, as citizen, no man is judge any longer of the danger to which the law requires him to expose himself, and when the prince says to him: "it is expedient for the state that you should die," then he should die . . . his life is no longer the bounty of nature but a gift he has received conditionally from the state.[47]

Because all life is a gift that we receive conditionally from the state, private property does not exist. All property belongs to Father State. "Every member of the community gives himself to it at the moment it is brought into being just as he is—he himself, with all his recourses, including all his goods."[48] And again, "For being nothing except by it, they will be nothing except for it. It will have all they have and will be all they are."[49]

Rousseau came close to applying this dangerous idea in the real world in 1765, when he had the opportunity to write a potential constitution for the island of Corsica. Had Corsica adopted Rousseau's proposals, the people would have been subjected to an early form of communism. "Far from wanting the state to be poor," wrote Rousseau in the draft, "I should like, on the contrary, for it to own everything, and for each individual to share in the common property only in proportion to his services." The document has the Corsicans saying, "I join myself, body, goods, will and all my powers, to the

---

46. Emilio Gentile, *Politics As Religion* (Princeton: Princeton University Press, 2006), 19.
47. Rousseau, *The Social Contract*, 78–79.
48. Ibid., 65.
49. Johnson, *Intellectuals*, 25.

Corsican nation, granting her ownership of me, of myself and all who depend on me."[50]

Of course, Rousseau had a strong personal incentive to dislike private property, since he spent his life sponging off the property of others. Like Karl Marx, whose tirade against capitalism grew out of his own envy of those that could support themselves when he could not (or would not), Rousseau's antipathy for private ownership may be the result of his own inability (and unwillingness) to support himself through honest labor. He developed a vitriolic hatred of those who had more than he, having once confessed to "a certain resentment against the rich and successful, as if their wealth and happiness had been gained at my expense."[51] By giving all wealth over to his imagined state, Rousseau may have been satiating this resentment and the deep-seated hatred he felt against the wealthy.

By the time Rousseau died on July 2, 1778 at the age of sixty-six, he had set the trajectory for the modern totalitarian movement. When Benito Mussolini famously quipped, "All within the state, nothing outside the state, nothing against the state," he was working within the template given by Rousseau, who once wrote, "Everything is at root dependent on politics."[52] This seems to have included morality. As the Enlightenment scholar Norman Hampson has observed in a discussion of Rousseau,

> Since obligation did not exist in the state of nature, but was created with society, the community was therefore the source, not merely of law, but of moral values also. There could be no appeal, in the name of the individual conscience, to any standard beyond the collective interests of the society of which he was a member.[53]

These notions lay behind the contemporary assumption that the vocation of the state is to create liberty, property, and human rights,

50. Ibid.

51. Ibid., 24.

52. Marvin N. Olasky, *Central Ideas in the Development of American Journalism: A Narrative History* (Hillsdale: L. Erlbaum Associates, 1991), 56.

53. Norman Hampson, *Enlightenment: An Evaluation of Its Assumptions Attitudes and Values* (Harmondsworth: Penguin, 1968), 246–247.

rather than to preserve the liberty, property, and rights which exist independently of it. This distinction is crucial, as it forms the chief difference between the older, classical liberalism and modern liberalism or progressivism.

Ultimately, Rousseau's state is more than merely a parody of human parents: it is a parody of our Heavenly Father, being fundamentally messianic in nature. Salvation comes as the totalitarian state brings to man the wholeness that he lost through "civilization." As Rousseau puts it, "Make man one, and you will make him as happy as he can be. Give him all to the state, or leave him all to himself. But if you divide his heart, you tear him in two." By giving "all to the State" we receive back from it true happiness and goodness: "they will be one, they will be good, they will be happy, and their happiness will be that of the Republic."[54]

ROUSSEAU'S LEGACY: FROM THE FRENCH REVOLUTION TO FASCISM

History is scattered throughout with egotists like Rousseau (though admittedly few have sunk to such extremes of narcissism, self-deception and arrogance), but what is truly extraordinary is the way he has been honored by posterity as a paragon of virtue.

Though he abdicated the fathering of his own illegitimate offspring, Rousseau remains the father of innumerable gurus, ideologues, and *isms*. He is the father of modern introspective biography, of Romanticism, of utopian education, of revolution, of socialism, and of modern totalitarianism.

Even in his own day, Rousseau was regarded as something of a secular patriarch. He developed a cult following that continued to grow in the years following his death. His claims about his own moral excellence and wisdom were accepted with such seriousness that by the 1790s the French had practically deified him. In his book *Rousseau: The Self-Made Saint*, J.F. Huizinga tells how European intellectuals began flocking to Rousseau's tomb to do reverence to his memory. One incident Huizinga recounts involved a French curate and a Prussian baron, who began their journey by paying their respects

54. Johnson, *Intellectuals,* 25.

to Rousseau's tobacco-pouch. One of them records that "my fingers touched this box, my heart trembled, and my soul became purer."[55] As the pair approached the island where their idol was buried, they were "agitated as Apollo's high priestess at the approach of the god." When they actually arrived on the spot they were ecstatic, and performed a liturgical ritual involving prayers, vows and a burnt sacrifice offered up to Rousseau. The sacrifice consisted in incinerating an essay written by one of Rousseau's critics, while proclaiming in a loud voice: "We offer this expiatory sacrifice on the tomb of the great man, handing over to the flames a libel which the lie claims its own and truth disavows."[56]

What is so astonishing is that the list of those who paid Rousseau super-human reverence reads like a *Who's Who* of nineteenth-century literature. In his book *Intellectuals,* Paul Johnson presents a smattering of the praise that has been heaped upon him by literary notables:

> To Kant he had "a sensibility of soul of unequalled perfection." To Shelley he was "a sublime genius." For Schiller he was "a Christlike soul for whom only Heaven's angels are fit company." John Stuart Mill and Goerge Eliot, Hugo and Flaubert, paid deep homage. Tolstoy said that Rousseau and the gospel had been "the two great and healthy influences of my life." One of the most influential intellectuals of our own times, Claude Lévi-Strauss, in his principal work, *Tristes Tropiques,* hails him as "our master and our brother . . . every page of this book could have been dedicated to him, had it not been unworthy of his great memory."[57]

In revolutionary France Rousseau's ashes became a sacred relic, and Edmund Burke noted with disgust that the revolutionaries engaged in great disputes over which one of them best resembled Rousseau. And Robespierre, the architect of the French Revolution's reign of terror, reflected the public mood when he declared that Rousseau

55. Huizinga, *The Making of a Saint,* xvi.
56. Ibid.
57. Johnson, *Intellectuals,* 27.

was "one man who, through the loftiness of his soul and the grandeur of his character, showed himself worthy of the role of teaching of mankind."[58]

When Robespierre launched his reign of terror against the people of France, he was able to appeal to the type of collectivism that Rousseau had championed: the good of the whole always trumps the freedom of the individual. As Robespierre put it, "The people is always worth more than individuals. . . . The people is sublime, but individuals are weak."[59]

It is true that *The Social Contract* had little direct influence on the initial outbreak of the French revolution, which was launched largely by the illiterate classes. It is also true that Rousseau would likely have disapproved of the way Robespierre and the **Jacobins** used his ideas to justify terror. Nevertheless, Rousseau did provide the philosophical scaffolding, not only for the reign of terror, but for the nationalistic and centralized states that emerged out of the chaos of revolutionary Europe. He did so by making the story of the modern state the story of man's redemption. In his book *Theopolitical Imagination*, William Cavanaugh articulates the main tenets of this story: "The modern state is founded on certain stories of nature and human nature, the origins of human conflict, and the remedies for such conflict in the enactment of the state itself."[60]

But it is Rousseau's indirect relationship to fascism that is perhaps the most fascinating aspect of his legacy. Jonah Goldberg hardly exaggerated when he called Rousseau "the father of modern fascism."[61] Following the path charted by Rousseau, the Romantics of the nineteenth century believed that the modern world, epitomized by the industrialism, modernism, and scientism of the Enlightenment, had left mankind out of touch with nature and its true feelings. The salvation story they told was one of man finding redemption in a fresh assertion of the self, releasing his basic instincts, emotions, and impulses to find true expression. It was this story that the German

58. Stephen R. C. Hicks, *Explaining Postmodernism: Skepticism and Socialism From Rousseau to Foucault* (Phoenix: Scholargy Publishing, 2004), 101.

59. Goldberg, *Liberal Fascism*, 38.

60. William T. Cavanaugh, *Theopolitical Imagination: Christian Practices of Space and Time* (Edinburgh: T & T Clark International, 2003), 9.

61. Goldberg, *Liberal Fascism*, 38.

fascists adopted. During the interwar era, many Germans had experienced a sense of angst, concerned that their identity and folk traditions were being absorbed into an increasingly homogeneous and impersonal modern world. German fascists absorbed the story the Romantics told about the Self, but appropriated it to their *volk*. Echoing Rousseau, fascism sought to recover a pre-Enlightenment sense of spirituality and transcendence, but within a neo-primitive framework. Hitler's fascination with the occult, Norse mythology, and relics of ancient Egypt would never have been tolerated by Enlightenment rationalists or by twentieth-century Marxists, but was welcomed by the spiritually starved and disillusioned society of inter-war Germany.

To stave off this spiritual starvation, fascism also drew on the idea of the "noble savage" that had been given legitimacy by Rousseau's attack on civilization (although the term "noble savage" actually originated with Dryden, not Rousseau). The description that Gene Edward Veith gives fascists might be equally applied to Rousseau:

> Fascists made a point of distinguishing between *culture* and *civilization*. *Culture* was organic and ethnic, calling to mind the rural, agrarian life that was close to nature. *Civilization,* on the other hand, was mechanical and rational, calling to mind the city with its machines and its alienation. Culture was good; civilization was bad. Culture created a sense of ethnic identity. . . . Fascists sought to undermine the sophisticated rationalism of Western civilization with its Enlightenment politics and its Judeo-Christian values. In its place, they sought to resurrect the more primitive and communal ideals of the pre-Christian Greeks, Romans, and Germanic tribes.[62]

Fascism also echoed Rousseau's communal emphasis, especially the stress that the individual is expendable to the goals of the whole. The following statement from the 1920 Nazi Party Platform sounds as though it could have been lifted directly out of *The Social Contract*: "The first obligation of every citizen must be to work both spiritually

---

62. Gene Edward Veith, *Modern Fascism: Liquidating the Judeo-Christian Worldview,* 1st ed. (St. Louis: Concordia College, 1993), 37–38.

and physically. The activity of individuals is not to counteract the interests of the universality, but must have its result within the framework of the whole for the benefit of all."[63]

The French Revolution and fascism are long gone, but unfortunately Rousseau's legacy is not. His writings provide the ideological gloss for romanticizing the primitive and demonizing the civilized—both of which have become salient features of our age. The cult of being "natural" that found expression in the "free love" movement, the antagonism to Western civilization that came to fruition in the Frankfurt movement (see Chapter Sixteen), and the quest for "the noble savage" that has energized everything from nudist colonies to neo-paganism, can all look back to Rousseau as their spiritual progenitor.

The fact that Rousseau has been eulogized by our own society speaks volumes about ourselves and our (perhaps unconscious) approach to civil government.

LESSONS FROM THE LIFE OF ROUSSEAU

Some scholars have suggested that one of the reasons Rousseau may have been motivated to describe the state in parental terms is because it helped palliate the guilt he felt for handing his five children over to the state-sponsored workhouse. Though he sometimes refers to the decision as wrong, he also notes that he was actually doing his babies a service. He goes so far as to say, "If only I could have had the same good fortune."[64] Elsewhere he defended his actions by musing, "I thought I was performing the act of a citizen and a father and I looked on myself as a member of Plato's Republic."[65] As he reflected deeper on this, his thoughts seemed to have taken shape in *Emile* and *Social Contract,* which grant to the state the authority of ultimate parent. Thus, we might say with some truth that Rousseau's abdication of his own fatherhood was the egg out of which the ideology of the modern state was hatched. Paul Johnson has made this important connection, observing that "by a curious chain of

63. Goldberg, *Liberal Fascism,* 411.
64. Johnson, *Intellectuals,* 23.
65. Ibid.

JEAN-JACQUES ROUSSEAU   169

infamous moral logic, Rousseau's iniquity as a parent was linked to his ideological offspring, the future totalitarian state."[66]

This lesson teaches us that those men who have failed to properly manage their own families are often the ones most tempted to fix other people's problems. As the Apostle Paul told Timothy that those who could not rule their own household should not be trusted with ruling the household of God (1 Tim. 3:5), we should also beware of those who neglect (or in Rousseau's case, completely abandon) members of their own families in order to solve the world's problems.

Another lesson we learn from Rousseau is that those who have never learned to be responsible and self-regulating have difficulty conceiving solutions to life's problems apart from the extremes of complete **antinomianism**, on the one hand, or complete totalitarianism on the other. In Rousseau's thought we find both these extremes competing for mastery. The arbitrary **despotism** towards which his theory of government inevitably tends was born out of his inability to imagine a society in which individuals were self-regulating. ("If government, based on the rule of law, is not possible—and I candidly avow I do not think it is—we must go to the other extreme . . . and establish the most arbitrary despotism conceivable."[67])

If this teaches us anything, it is that freedom apart from Christ always leads to bondage. Rousseau and the fascists had almost schizophrenic tendencies: both wanted to free the individual from all external restraints, all the while attempting to squeeze him into a communal mold. They viewed civilization as the problem and also saw it (invested with the appropriate political mechanisms) as the solution. They desired both to liberate human nature and to control it, and strove to escape the slavery of society while imposing uniformity on those in their power. The contradictory relationship of these extremes is alluded to in 2 Peter 2:19: "While they promise them liberty, they themselves are slaves of corruption; for by whom a person is overcome, by him also he is brought into bondage."

66. Ibid.
67. Huizinga, *The Making of a Saint*, 220.

QUESTIONS FOR DISCUSSION

1. What are some ways that the state is treated like a parent in America today?

2. Rousseau advocated an ideology (called communitarianism) in which the good of the whole always trumps the freedom of the individual. Are there ever situations in which the good of the individual should be sacrificed for the good of the whole? Can you think of any examples from the Bible? If so, what is the difference between them and Rousseau's model?

3. How does our public education system reflect Rousseau-type assumptions about the nature of the state?

4. In *The Social Contract* Rousseau wrote, "Since no man has any natural authority over his fellows, and since force alone bestows no right, all legitimate authority among men must be based on covenants."[68] Is this a true statement? According to the Bible, where does authority gain its legitimacy?

5. Compare and contrast Rousseau's view of freedom with that taught in the Bible.

6. What are some ways that the story of the modern state, as summarized by Cavanaugh on page 166, are reflected in contemporary political discourse, especially at election time?

7. Rousseau was rude on principle because he did not want to conform to the conventions of society. Since many of the conventions of society are merely relative to a particular social context, how much weight should we put on them? How important is it to conform to social good form?

8. Why do you suppose that many people have taken Rousseau's boasts at face value and assumed that he was as virtuous as he claimed?

68. Rousseau, *The Social Contract*, 53.

9. Compare the biblical critique of sinful civilization with Rousseau's critique of civilization itself. Compare the biblical teaching of "natural man" with Rousseau's views on "natural man."

10. Rousseau considered himself to be a Christian, even though his "Christianity" amounted to little more than **deism**. How ought we to define a Christian? Should we consider anyone a Christian who claims to be?

11. The rationalists of the early Enlightenment sought to find truth through reason while Rousseau and the Romantics sought to find truth through feelings. Does the Bible give us any help in navigating between these two extremes?

12. Had he lived long enough, what do you think Rousseau would have thought of the French Revolution?

13. The Bible tells us to submit to the governing authorities (Rom. 13:1). What form should such submission take when the state asserts ownership of our property, whether explicitly or implicitly? When should we defy the government in order to defend our lentil patch, so to speak?

14. Rousseau wrote that "everything is at root dependent on politics."[69] What are some ways, if any, that this statement reflects the thinking of contemporary Americans?

15. What are the practical implications of saying that the state exists to create liberty, property, and human rights, rather than to *preserve* these things?

PERSONAL CHALLENGE

Are you ever tempted to resent those who have more than you? Why or why not?

69. Olasky, *Central Ideas in the Development of American Journalism*, 56.

CHAPTER 10

IDEAS HAVE CONSEQUENCES

The Wisdom of Edmund Burke (1729–1797)

The Anglo-Irish statesmen Edmund Burke couldn't have entered politics at a more critical point in history. As a member of the British Parliament during one of Europe's most tumultuous periods (1765–1794), Burke was uniquely poised to offer a restraining voice against the forces of radicalism and barbarism that threatened to sweep across all of Christian Europe.

After graduating from Trinity College, Dublin, Burke moved to London in 1750 to study law. He soon gave it up to travel in Continental Europe, while trying to support himself as a writer. When he returned to London, he published his famous treatise on aesthetics, *A Philosophical Enquiry into the Origin of Our Ideas of the Sublime and Beautiful.* In 1757 Burke married Jane Mary Nugent, the daughter of a physician who had once treated him.

His career in politics began as a result of his acquaintance with an Irish member of Parliament, William Gerard Hamilton. When Hamilton was appointed Chief Secretary for Ireland, Burke became his private secretary. In 1765 Burke took the position of private secretary to another statesman before finally entering Parliament himself as an MP for Wendover that same year. He remained in Parliament until 1797, a loyal member of the Whig party.

As an orator and writer, few have ever equaled Burke. One of the most engaging and captivating writers in the entire tradition of English prose, he has been compared to Cicero, Milton, and even Shakespeare. Yet it is not his eloquence alone that makes Burke relevant over two hundred years later. The Lord also gifted him with a Jeremiah-like ability to read the signs of the times and to bring his razor-sharp mind to bear on the problems of his day. With prophetic insight he was able to penetrate the surface of things and discern undercurrents and implications that would only later be clear to everyone else.

LIBERTY AND THE RULE OF LAW

Burke's political career was largely unsuccessful because of his unpopular, though uncompromising, commitment to liberty and the rule of law. At a time when these two concepts were often pitted against each other, Burke argued that neither freedom nor law could exist at the exclusion of the other. Liberty, he believed, is meaningless if it is not rooted in responsibility—a responsibility derived from God and the laws He has written into creation.

For this reason, Burke never advocated liberty in an unqualified sense. He knew that unrestricted liberty for fallen man could only mean anarchy, followed by tyranny. As he once remarked, "Liberty, when men act in bodies, is *power.*" Instead, Burke urged his readers to cling to "a manly, moral, regulated liberty," and to enlarge the bounds of that liberty "only gradually and with great caution."[1]

On many occasions he went against the grain of popular politics to defend these twin pillars of law and freedom. When the king's party sought to increase the royal prerogative, he resisted. When the Whigs attempted to use government to enrich their own class, he resisted. He defended the American colonists living under the arbitrary will of George III's ministers, the people of India under Hasting's tyrannical oligarchy, Irish Catholics suffering from unjust trade conditions, and the Africans oppressed by Britain's merciless slave trade. Burke's defense of liberty could simultaneously set itself against the tyranny of despotism as well as the tyranny of mass

1. Edmund Burke, *The Best of Burke: Selected Writings and Speeches of Edmund Burke* (Washington: Regnery Publishing, 1963), 515.

democracy. Whether he was defending the king and queen of France or the rights of the least important person in the realm, Burke's principles remained constant. He once wrote,

> When, indeed, the smallest rights of the poorest people in the kingdom are in question, I would set my face against any act of pride and power countenanced by the highest that are in it; and if it should come to the last extremity, and to a contest of blood, God forbid! God forbid!—my part is taken; I would take my fate with the poor, and low, and feeble. But if these people came to turn their liberty into a cloak for maliciousness, and to seek a privilege of exemption, not from power, but from the rules of morality and virtuous discipline, then I would join my hand to make them feel the force which a few, united in a good cause, have over a multitude of the profligate and ferocious.[2]

FROM REVOLUTION TO TERROR

In 1789, when Burke was sixty years old and considering retirement, revolution erupted in France. The floodgates had broken loose when King Louis XVI's government called a meeting of the Estates-General in May of that year. This was a parliamentary-type body made up of representatives from the three social classes: the clergy, the nobility, and the population. The convocation was an attempt to solve the financial crisis threatening the nation. However, it quickly became apparent that the people had other plans. This "third estate" was bitter over the fact that, though comprising ninety-seven percent of the population, they could always be out-voted by a consensus of the other two groups. Now they seized the opportunity to form a new body, which they called the "National Assembly." Though the Assembly had no legal standing, it produced an alternative constitution and set out to win popular support.

The king attempted to suppress the Assembly but was hampered by urban and rural uprisings. The people of France, long embittered by a monarchy that had been out of touch with their needs, were

---

2. Edmund Burke, *The Works of The Right Honourable Edmund Burke* (London: Rivington, 1812), 139.

whipped up into a mob by revolutionary politicians, who appealed to the ideas of the "Enlightenment." Building on the notion that all authority—whether of the church or of the monarchy—was a vestige of an unenlightened, superstitious past, the revolutionaries demanded a new society structured around the trinity of "liberty, equality, and fraternity." Revolutionaries also drew on the utopian theories of men like Rousseau, who believed that human nature could be remade through political action. (Burke had little time for Rousseau and said that "Vanity was the vice he possessed to a degree little short of madness."[3])

On July 14, 1789 the Bastille prison—a hated symbol of the old regime—was stormed by a rioting mob looking for gunpowder. From that point on, civil unrest worsened, and on October 6 throngs of discontented peasants broke into the palace at Versailles and forced the royal family to march to Paris, paraded behind the heads of decapitated palace guards. Though ostensibly under the protection of the National Assembly, the king and queen were really the prisoners of an increasingly unstable public.

Four months after the revolutionaries had declared France to be a republic, and following a thwarted attempt by the royal family to escape to Austria, the king was executed. From there, the Revolution began to spiral out of control. By the summer, state power had become concentrated in a twelve-man war dictatorship known, ironically, as the "Committee of Public Safety." Led by Maximilien de Robespierre, the committee formally suspended the Revolution's own constitution and instituted a "Reign of Terror," under which anyone suspected of being a royalist was arrested and executed on the guillotine.

Robespierre and his committee members then began a dechristianization policy in a desperate attempt to purge all memory of the Christian faith from French society. Their measures included:

· The dispossession, deportation, or killing of the clergy.

· Implementing a calendar to replace the Christian one. The new calendar, adopted in 1793 and used for twelve years, employed

---

3. Burke, *The Best of Burke*, 616.

a ten-day week, thereby eliminating Sunday. The year 1792 (when Louis XVI was taken into custody) was declared to be Year 1—"the Year of Liberty."

· The criminalization of all religious education.

· The elimination of all Christian symbols from the public sphere, including removing the word "Saint" from street names and destroying or defacing churches and religious monuments.

· The supplanting of Christian holidays and symbols with civic and revolutionary monuments, such as those which venerated the "Cult of Reason" and "Cult of the Supreme Being." A statue to the goddess Reason was even erected and worshiped in Notre Dame Cathedral on November 10, 1793.

It was not just Christians that suffered under the Reign of Terror: supporters of the monarchy were also persecuted. Even supporters of the Revolution could be brought to the guillotine and executed without trial if someone accused them of not expressing enough enthusiasm for the changes. Freedom of the press, freedom of religion, and freedom of speech were all abolished and replaced with a totalitarianism unseen since the days of the Caesars. Under the banner of liberty, justice, equality, and human rights for all, over 40,000 French citizens were decapitated, while more than 350,000 Parisians spent time in jail.

In 1793 Queen Marie Antoinette followed her husband to the "national razor," while revolutionary France, now intent on world domination, declared war on Britain, Holland, and Spain.

The French Revolution left a legacy of civil war and international conflict in its wake that would last for the next twenty-five years, lending credibility to Madame Roland's words "Oh, Liberty, what crimes are committed in thy name!"[4]

4. Irving A. Taylor, *Life of Madame Roland* (Whitefish: Kessinger Publishing, 2005), 319.

BRITAIN AND THE FRENCH REVOLUTION

France's old regime was hated by the English. Not only had monarchical France been rivals with Britain in the scramble for colonial domination, but they had helped the American colonies gain independence. Thus, it was not without some appreciation that Britain watched as their old nemesis was overthrown.

Naturally, British approval was quickly extinguished once the massacres began. However, in the critical time between the advent of the Revolution and the outbreak of the Reign of Terror, many of England's leading intellectuals believed the French were emancipating themselves. Prime Minister William Pitt and his colleague, Charles Fox, even went so far as to praise the Revolution in Parliament. Still others held up the National Assembly as a model that England would do well to copy.

So great was public sympathy among the English that many historians believe England came perilously close to entering a similar debacle. It was during this decisive period, with England teetering in the balance, that Edmund Burke delivered his penetrating critique of the revolutionary mentality, warning England not to follow France down the slippery slope of destructive folly.

Burke argued that the French Revolution was first and foremost a revolution of ideas. Because ideas have consequences, Burke aimed to correct people's thinking before correcting their policies.

Burke's assessment of the Revolution occupied the form of an extended letter to the young man Charles DePont, who had written to Burke asking for his opinion on events in France. Titled *Reflections on the Revolution in France,* the letter first appeared in print in 1790 and sold twelve thousand copies in the first month alone. In less than a year there were eleven editions. By 1796 over thirty thousand copies had been sold, making it one of the most influential political books ever published.

Written before the Reign of Terror revealed the true nature of the Revolution, Burke's *Reflections* predicted with remarkable accuracy what the result of the revolution would be. He knew that when principles such as liberty, equality, and human rights are emulated as ends in themselves, stripped of all connection with circumstance, the result must inevitably be dictatorship and terror.

"They have wrought under-ground a mine," he wrote, "that will blow up, at one grand explosion, all examples of antiquity, all precedents, charters, and acts of parliament."[5] Burke believed that this underground mine, if left unchecked, could explode throughout all of Europe, replacing Christendom with an atheistic tyranny. Here again he showed an uncanny discernment, for all of the great European revolutions of the nineteenth century, which themselves set the template for the turmoil of the twentieth century, self-consciously followed in the wake of revolutionary France.

IDEAS HAVE CONSEQUENCES

If anyone understood the maxim that ideas have consequences, it was Burke. His writings show the pivotal role that worldviews play in shaping the affairs of men. Speaking of the French Revolution in his *Letter on a Regicide Peace,* he observed that "a silent revolution in the moral world preceded the political, and prepared it," while his *Reflections* states that the revolution in France was first and foremost "a revolution in sentiments, manners, and moral opinions."[6]

Burke minced no words in identifying the worldview behind the French revolution as none other than pure atheism:

> But if, in the moment of riot, and in a drunken delirium from the hot spirit drawn out of the alembic of hell, which in France is now so furiously boiling, we should uncover our nakedness, by throwing off that Christian religion which has hitherto been our boast and comfort, and one great source of civilization amongst us, and amongst many other nations, we are apprehensive (being well aware that the mind will not endure a void) that some uncouth, pernicious, and degrading superstition might take [the] place of it.[7]

5. Burke, *The Best of Burke*, 543.
6. Ibid., 25.
7. Ibid., 560.

THE LEGACY OF EDMUND BURKE

Burke's *Reflections* had a remarkable effect in turning English public opinion against the revolutionary impulse. Moreover, his writings have been useful sources of wisdom for those who followed in his footsteps and who have had to continually oppose the philosophy of the Revolution.

Although Burke is remembered as one of the greatest statesmen in the history of the English-speaking world, his legacy was not particularly appreciated by his contemporaries. His life thus demonstrates the fact that God does not judge success and failure in the same way as man.

"By the vulgar standards of immediate success and external appearances," wrote Peter Stanlis in his introduction to *The Best of Burke,* "it would seem that Burke's political career was largely wasted in serving lost causes. But in his constant efforts to establish an orderly, just, and free society, under constitutional and moral law, he set forth the vital ideas and principles of his political philosophy, which has continued to influence men throughout history long after the partisan causes which triumphed over him were buried in the graveyard of dead politics."[8]

LESSONS FROM THE LIFE OF EDMUND BURKE

The life and teachings of Edmund Burke continue to offer lessons of remarkable relevance to our own day and age.

Firstly, Burke teaches us that atheism, for all its transitory pomp, is always doomed to failure because it goes against our instincts as men and women created in the image of God. "We know, and it is our pride to know," he wrote, "that man is by his constitution a religious animal; that atheism is against, not only our reason, but our instincts; and that it cannot prevail long."[9]

Secondly, Burke teaches us the necessity of listening to our ancestors. It was Burke who first declared, "People will not look forward to posterity, who never look backward to their ancestors." He believed that only by revering our ancestors could freedom be preserved.

8. Ibid., 22.
9. Ibid., 560.

This is because liberty is not a natural right of man (as Rousseau had claimed), but the product of tradition, family, and faith. It is passed on in much the same way as property is transmitted, from one generation to another, namely, through inheritance. To support this notion of liberty as an inheritance, Burke pointed to the great freedoms of the British tradition, showing that they had accumulated over a period stretching back to the Magna Carta, the Declaration of Rights, and the entire network of common law freedoms which the hereditary succession of the monarchy helped to preserve. The legacy of these liberties would not long abide a generation that was willing to cast off the heritage of their ancestors. Because of this, whenever Burke wished to reform, it was in order to conserve. He was sympathetic to the American struggle (it is not true that he actually supported their war for independence, as many history books have claimed) for the same reason that he looked positively on England's so-called "Glorious Revolution" of 1688: both of these struggles were aimed at preserving an existing network of charters, customs, and liberties.

Thirdly, Burke teaches us the folly of revolutionary solutions to social problems. Burke did not advocate a static traditionalism. On the contrary, he taught that "A state without the means of some change is without the means of its conservation."[10] The question is *how* does change occur? Burke's answer was that change must be sought through slow, organic reform based on constitutional precedent. If we must repair the walls, he asserted, we should do so on the old foundations. In this Burke echoed the words that Solomon had written thousands of years earlier:

> My son, fear the LORD and the king; Do not associate with those given to change; for their calamity will rise suddenly, and who knows the ruin those two can bring? (Prov. 24:21–22)

10. Burke, *The Best of Burke*, 552.

QUESTIONS FOR DISCUSSION

1. Burke believed that neither law nor liberty could exist without the other. Was Burke correct? What does the New Testament teach about the relationship between law and liberty?

2. The French revolutionaries championed "liberty, equality, and fraternity." Are any or all of these values good in and of themselves?

3. Burke opposed those who would try to use liberty to get rid of law (anarchy or antinomianism), as well as those who sought to use the law to remove liberties (**statism** and totalitarianism). Do either of these extremes manifest themselves in today's society? If so, what would be Burke's solution?

4. Burke advocated gradual reform instead of sudden revolution as a means for dealing with social problems. Do we find examples of either of these approaches in the Bible? What can we learn from the biblical examples?

5. Burke called for "a jealous, ever-waking vigilance, to guard the treasure of our liberty, not only from invasion, but from decay and corruption."[11] What are some ways in which liberty could decay and become corrupt in a "free" country?

6. The French Revolution ostensibly began as a movement of the people, yet turned against the very people it promised to liberate. Why do you think that was? What lessons can we learn for our own society?

7. Burke could often predict what would happen in the future by studying the principles being followed in the present. If Burke were alive to observe our own society, what would be some predictions he might make?

8. Burke was writing at a time when it was still generally acknowledged that philosophy has practical ramifications. What does the general

---

11. Edmund Burke, *Reflections on the Revolution in France* (New York: P.F. Collier & Son, 1937), 192.

public think about philosophy today? If Burke was writing now, do you think he would have the same impact on public opinion?

PERSONAL CHALLENGE

What would be a revolutionary solution to a problem you are currently facing? What would be a reformational solution to the same problem?

CHAPTER 11

LIGHT IN A TIME OF DARKNESS

The Faithfulness of William Wilberforce (1759–1833)

Britain was the commercial and military capital of eighteenth-century Europe. However, national success had been purchased at a heavy price. The utilitarianism of the Enlightenment had made England resourceful but cruel, productive but heartless, industrial but inhuman. In the crowded cities, efficient factories worked both adults and children to exhaustion with sixteen-hour days and unsafe conditions. In England's colonies, production was achieved through the forced labor of millions of slaves captured from Africa.

Between one-fourth and one-third of all slaves shipped from Africa to the Western Hemisphere never made it there alive. This is hardly surprising when we consider what life was like aboard the slave ships. "Often, the slaves found themselves jammed into small cubbyholes on the slave ships' lower decks, body on top of body, unable to move," explains John Dwyer in his book *The War Between the States*. He continues,

> Their journey across the Atlantic lasted anywhere from four days to three weeks. They had little food or water, and sometimes no toilet facilities except where they lay atop one another. In these unsanitary conditions, disease ran rampant. Weaker

slaves often died early in the voyage, only to lie rotting in the cargo holds. Those still alive could not get away from them and often lay atop or beneath them, day after day. The slaves faced dehumanization, brutality, and sometimes the merciless, sadistic beatings of the slave ships' crews.[1]

Slavery had been accepted as a basic fact of life for Britain since the sixteenth century. Even though the Bible clearly forbade the slave trade (Exod. 21:16), both the state and the church refused to acknowledge that it was a problem. Historian Adam Hochschild noted, "If pressed, some Britons might have conceded that the institution was unpleasant—but where else would sugar for your tea come from?"[2] Some evangelicals even went so far as to justify the slave trade based on erroneous appeals to alleged practices in Old Testament Israel and the New Testament church. Part of the reason for this moral ambivalence was that the aristocracy, who controlled both the government and the church, were the ones who most directly benefited from the colonial revenues wrought by this trade in human lives.

That was the England of 1759, when William Wilberforce was born into a wealthy mercantile family in the port town of Kingston upon Hull.

EARLY LIFE AND COLLEGE

When William was nine his father died, and he was sent to live with his aunt and uncle. It was while living with his uncle that Wilberforce met John Newton, a former slave ship sailor and author of the hymns "Amazing Grace" and "Glorious Things of Thee are Spoken." Though it would be many years before William's own conversion, Newton no doubt had an influence on his young mind.

Although he was a sickly child, the young Wilberforce excelled at his studies, entering St. John's College, Cambridge when he was seventeen. His uncle died in 1777, leaving William independently

1. John Dwyer, *The War Between the States: America's Uncivil War,* 1st ed. (Denton: American Vision Press, 2007), 69.

2. Adam Hochschild, *Bury the Chains: Prophets and Rebels in the Fight to Free an Empire's Slaves* (Boston: Mariner Books, 2006), 85.

wealthy. With so much money on his hands, the young man turned from serious study to the lively university social life, pursuing the pleasures of cards, gambling, and late-night drinking.

But William's life was not solely devoted to pleasure. He also took a keen interest in politics. With a personality that could easily rally people to his side, a wit that few could match, and a voice well-crafted for eloquent speeches, William was a born politician. At that time he made many important friends, including William Pitt, the future Prime Minister. Pitt urged Wilberforce to enter politics with him and William, who required little persuading, agreed.

PARLIAMENT

At the age of twenty-one, while still a student, Wilberforce ran successfully as a Member of Parliament for Hull. The two major parties at the time were the Whigs and the Tories. Rather than identify himself with either group, Wilberforce preferred to be a "no party man." He voted according to his conscience, while working closely with whichever party happened to be in power.

In December 1783 Pitt became the youngest prime minister in British history, at the age of twenty-four. In the following year Wilberforce stood as Parliamentary candidate for the county of Yorkshire and won. This was an important political move for Wilberforce, increasing his influence in Parliament since Yorkshire was one of the biggest and richest counties in England.

CONVERSION

Later in the same year, Wilberforce traveled around Europe with his mother, his sister, and Isaac Milner, a long-time friend. The trip would prove to be instrumental in William's spiritual transformation.

Though he had been brought up in the faith, Wilberforce was only a nominal Christian, whose habits and thinking mirrored the prevailing culture around him. As a result of long discussions and study with Isaac this began to change, and William decided to fully embrace the Christian faith. Repenting of his sinful habits, he began to rise early in the morning to pray and study the Scriptures.

On his return to England, Wilberforce faced a dilemma: should he continue to pursue a life of politics or enter church ministry? At the time, "religious enthusiasm" could spell the end to one's political career, since it was looked down upon by "polite society." Wilberforce also struggled to discern how his faith should inform his public life. Was religion separate from politics and culture, or did the two realms somehow coincide?

He sought the advice of John Newton. Newton, like Pitt, urged Wilberforce to remain in politics as a force for good. "It is hoped," Newton told him, "that the Lord has raised you up to the good of His church and for the good of the nation."[3]

Heeding the guidance of his friends, Wilberforce decided to remain in politics as a Christian voice. "It is evident," he wrote, reflecting on his decision, "that we are to consider our peculiar situations, and in these to do all the good we can. Some are thrown into public, some have their lot in private life. It would merit no better name than desertion if I were thus to fly from the post where Providence has placed me."[4]

From then on Wilberforce began to practice politics differently. Prior to his conversion, he had been known as the Prime Minister's "pit bull," because of the way he was used to launch attacks on the opposition. But now he was gentle, without losing any of his firmness, eloquence, and political savvy. Significantly, he earned a new nickname: "the Conscience of Parliament."

AGAINST THE SLAVE TRADE

Prior to his conversion, Wilberforce had been exposed to the problems of the slave trade while having dinner with the Reverend James Ramsay. A former ship's surgeon and medical supervisor of plantations in the West Indies, Ramsay offered firsthand details of the horrific conditions endured by slaves on the ships and on the plantations.

---

3. Eric Metaxas, *Amazing Grace: William Wilberforce and the Heroic Campaign to End Slavery* (New York: HarperOne, 2007), 68.

4. Robert Isaac Wilberforce and Samuel Wilberforce, *The Life of William Wilberforce* (London: J. Murray, 1939), 106.

His descriptions gave teeth to the anti-slavery movement already underway in England during the 1780s.

It was only after his conversion that Wilberforce followed up on his meeting with Ramsay. At first his involvement in the anti-slavery movement was tentative, as he felt himself unequal to the monumental task. But at the continual urging of various anti-slavery campaigners and because of his own desire to put his Christian principles into practice, Wilberforce began to pay close attention to the issue. In May 1787, Prime Minister Pitt persuaded the hesitating William to set the matter before Parliament. Though Parliament refused to take the problem seriously, Wilberforce intensified his campaign.

While an increasing number of Christians began to support the cause, Wilberforce also attracted many enemies. The pro-slavery lobby was extremely powerful and well-funded. As much as 80 percent of Britain's foreign income was derived from ships sailing the "triangular route," in which merchants would carry British goods to sell to African traders in exchange for slaves, then travel on to the West Indies to trade the slaves for slave-grown products such as sugar, tobacco, and cotton, and finally return to Britain to sell those products for a handsome profit.

REFORMATION OF MANNERS

Slavery was not Wilberforce's only concern. Around this time he wrote in his diary, "God Almighty has set before me two great objects, the suppression of the Slave Trade and the Reformation of Manners."[5] By "manners" he meant moral values. William believed that morality could flourish only in a society where the principles of Christianity were applied to every area of public and private life. If society was not undergirded by Christian morality, then even if slavery were abolished, there would be no long-term effect and other injustices would rise up in its place.

These realizations had led Wilberforce in 1773 to begin writing his book *Practical View of the Prevailing Religious System of Professed Christians, in the Higher and Middle Classes of This Country, Contrasted With Real Christianity.* In it, he countered the idea—as

5. Metaxas, *Amazing Grace,* 85.

popular in his day as in our own—that there is a political solution to all of society's ills. He argued, instead, that a nation founded on human wisdom is a nation that will eventually end in tyranny even if it has all the correct laws. As he put it in his *Practical View,*

> I must confess equally boldly that my own solid hopes for the well-being of my country depend, not so much on her navies and armies, nor on the wisdom of her rulers, or on the spirit of her people, as on the persuasion that she still contains many who love and obey the Gospel of Christ.[6]

When the book was finally completed and published in 1797, it became a bestseller and remained so for the next fifty years. The book points out that where true Christianity has flourished, it has raised the moral standards of society, to the particular benefit of the poor and the weak. In contrast to that is a cultural landscape scarred by the "fatal and widespread effects of . . . not considering [Christianity] as a principle of universal application and command for all of life."[7] Although the book did not mention slavery, one of its side effects was to encourage Christians to become involved in the abolitionist movement.

MARRIAGE AND FAMILY

Though William showed no particular interest in women, his friends were anxious for him to marry. When he was in his late thirties and his health was declining, Wilberforce's friend Thomas Babington urged him to meet twenty-year-old Barbara Ann Spooner. William immediately fell in love with her. He proposed eight days later and they were married in May 1797. Barbara was a devoted wife, attending to her husband's needs, though she showed little interest in her husband's political activities.

---

6. William Wilberforce, "A Practical View of the Prevailing Religious System of Professed Christians, In the Higher and Middle Classes in This Country, Contrasted With Real Christianity," Project Gutenberg, http://www.gutenberg.org/files/25709/25709-h/25709-h.htm (accessed January 9, 2012).

7. Ibid.

William and Barbara had four sons and two daughters. Given the breathtaking array of his political and religious duties, it is surprising how much time Wilberforce had to spend with his children. Yet he devoted himself as much to his children's welfare as he did to the welfare of the nation. When they were young, he always found time to play with them, and even when they moved away to school, Wilberforce showered them with letters. These letters, which have been collected together by Stephanie Byrd in her book *Amazing Dad: Letters from William Wilberforce to His Children,* reveal a father who was loving, kind, and encouraging, but above all anxious for the spiritual welfare of his children.[8]

SUCCESS

A **deft** tactician, Wilberforce formed a coalition with former political rivals (including Charles Fox, the opposition party leader), in addition to gathering to himself other Christians committed to bringing their faith into the public square. In this way, the anti-slavery movement continued to gain momentum.

Without the modern benefits of photographs or television, few people could know of the horrific conditions aboard the slave ships. Nor could they know what life was like on the plantations of the West Indies, where men, women, and children were worked to death like animals. Those who did know often had vested interests in keeping quiet about the horrors of the system. Wilberforce and his colleagues set out to dispel this general ignorance, educating the public on the realities of slave life.

Year after year Wilberforce put anti-slavery legislation before Parliament, and year after year it failed. However, his base of support within Parliament and the general populace was gradually expanding. Wilberforce and his supporters canvassed the country with pamphlets, petitions, and rallies. One petition contained eight hundred thousand signatures on a scroll that Wilberforce dramatically rolled out across the floor of the Parliamentary chamber.

---

8. Stephanie Byrd, *Amazing Dad: Letters from William Wilberforce to His Children,* (Longwood: Xulon Press, 2010).

For twenty years he doggedly pressed Parliament to outlaw the slave trade. Each year, he came a little closer to success but never had enough votes. Finally, in 1807, he succeeded through the help of the government that Lord Granville and Charles Fox formed. Parliament passed the "Abolition of the Slave Trade Act," outlawing the transatlantic traffic. The Royal Navy enforced the ban under a policy of stop and search. This set an example to other nations, and the following year the United States enacted its own legislation against the Atlantic trade in slaves, while allowing domestic traffic to continue.

EMANCIPATION

For Wilberforce, abolishing the trade was just the beginning. While it was now illegal to acquire any new slaves from Africa, those who were already enslaved, as well as any children those slaves might bear, remained locked in a life of unspeakable suffering.

Although the stress of his political battles had taken its toll on his health, Wilberforce began campaigning to emancipate those still in slavery. However, he lacked his former energy.

When he was forced to retire from politics in 1825, Wilberforce's goal of emancipation was still unfulfilled. But eight years later, on July 26, 1833, Wilberforce received word that the Whig government had made a concession that would guarantee the passing of the emancipation bill. The slaves in the British territories would soon be free.

"Thank God," wrote an aged Wilberforce after receiving the news, "that I have lived to witness a day in which England is willing to give twenty millions sterling for the Abolition of Slavery."[9]

Three days later, at the age of seventy-four, Wilberforce died.

THE LEGACY OF WILLIAM WILBERFORCE

Although Wilberforce is most remembered today for his campaign to abolish the slave trade, he was far from being a single-issue politician. He campaigned against pornography, gambling, illegal

---

9. Eugene Stock, *The History of the Church Missionary Society: Its Environment, Its Men and Its Work* (London: Church Missionary Society, 1899), 344.

lotteries, prostitution, brutal treatment of animals, and dishonest business practices, in addition to many other injustices. He achieved hard-fought victories in prison reform and helped to improve factory conditions.

Nor were his efforts limited to the political arena. He worked to raise general Bible literacy and was a pioneer in the field of philanthropy. He organized the Society for the Suppression of Vices and was closely involved in sixty-nine charities, including the Bible Society, the Society for Bettering the Condition of the Poor, and the Society for the Prevention of Cruelty to Animals.

Wilberforce gave much of his own money to help the poor but did so anonymously because he sought no credit. From his pocket he paid for African children to come to England to be educated, to demonstrate that black people could be just as intelligent as anyone else.

In addition to his social activism, Wilberforce touched many lives through his writings. As Edmund Burke read Wilberforce's *Practical View* during the last few days of his life, he was greatly comforted by the work and sent a message to Wilberforce saying that if he lived, he should thank his friend for "having sent such a book into the world."[10]

LESSONS FROM THE LIFE OF WILBERFORCE

We remember Wilberforce for what he achieved. Yet the most valuable lesson from his life comes not from what he accomplished, but *how* he accomplished it. Unlike in America, where abolitionists were willing to use violent force to achieve their ends, in England abolition remained a peaceful movement. This was no accident, for Wilberforce steadfastly refused to pursue revolutionary means for achieving his goals. This is because he recognized that the slave trade was not itself the root problem but merely a symptom of a society that had rejected God's laws. It followed, he believed, that spiritual rather than revolutionary means were necessary in the fight for justice. As Regis Nicoll noted in a series of articles for the two hundredth anniversary of the abolition of the slave trade:

10. Sir James Prior, *A Life of Edmund Burke* (London: G. Bell & Sons, 1891), 457.

Wilberforce realized that the spiritual dimensions of a slave economy required spiritual weapons. He devoted himself to prayer, meditation, and Bible study and submitted himself to the counsel of brothers and sisters who shared his faith and vision.[11]

A second lesson Wilberforce teaches us is the importance of God's sovereignty. He believed that his efforts would be effective only to the degree that they were blessed by the hand of the Almighty God. This conviction comforted William during those periods of his life when he faced incredible discouragement.

The third and final lesson is that God calls us to be faithful in the jobs He has given us, but He does not guarantee the consequences of doing right. Faithfulness, not success, is what truly matters in the Lord's economy. As one of the characters in N. D. Wilson's book *Dandelion Fire* put it:

> Sometimes standing against evil is more important than defeating it. The greatest heroes stand because it is right to do so, not because they believe they will walk away with their lives. Such selfless courage is a victory in itself.[12]

QUESTIONS FOR DISCUSSION

1. After his conversion, Wilberforce was faced with having to decide whether to remain in politics or enter the church. What would you have decided, and why? What type of principles should guide us in making such a decision?

2. To what extent does a consideration of potential consequences help to determine whether an action is right in the first place?

3. At first Wilberforce felt unworthy for the monumental task of abolishing the slave trade. Are there some jobs we should take

11. Regis Nicoll, "The Legacy of Wilberforce, Part 3," Break Point, http://www.breakpoint.org/features-columns/breakpoint-columns/entry/2/18743 (accessed March 1, 2012).

12. N.D. Wilson, *Dandelion Fire* (New York: Random House, 2009), 173.

up even if we think ourselves unqualified? G. K. Chesterton once remarked that if a job is worth doing, it's worth doing badly.[13] Was Chesterton correct?

4. England overcame slavery through political reform while the United States overcame it through violence. Why do you think there was this difference? Was America's way wrong?

5. Throughout the eighteenth and early nineteenth centuries, many Christians in England and America did not have a problem with slavery. What might be some reasons for this?

6. Some people have argued that slavery is supported by the Bible, and the Old Testament in particular. Can a biblical argument be made to support certain types of slavery?

7. In 1 Corinthians 7:21, the apostle Paul told slaves to gain their freedom if they could. Can we infer from this suggestion that Paul would probably have supported the abolition movement?

8. Wilberforce opposed the idea that there is a political solution for every problem. In our own day, how does this idea manifest itself?

9. Was Wilberforce's job of raising godly children as important as his political victories?

PERSONAL CHALLENGE

Prayer and Bible study were the foundation of Wilberforce's achievement. How is your devotional life?

13. G. K. Chesterton, *What's Wrong with the World* (New York: Dover Publications, 2007), 192.

CHAPTER 12

REACHING THE WORLD
THROUGH THE NEIGHBORHOOD

The Ministry of Thomas Chalmers (1780–1847)

From the invention of the clock in the Middle Ages to the rise of the internet in the twentieth century, human beings have had a remarkable knack for adopting characteristics of the tools they employ. Technologies that offer to give man greater mastery over nature often end up exerting mastery over man.

The inventions that spawned the industrial revolution were no exception to this pattern. Following the perfection of the steam engine in the 1770s, industries in England and Scotland began to thrive. Work which previously required skilled laborers was taken over by machines. While these machines needed human operators, they required a certain *type* of human being, one that resembled the machines themselves: mindless, repetitious, and uncreative. If those who sought industrial jobs in the late eighteenth and early nineteenth centuries did not possess these characteristics, it was certain that after a lifetime in the factory they would. The unsafe conditions, smothering uniformity, and mind-numbing repetitions tended to suck the humanity out of the men, women, and children who worked the machines.

The amount of people caught up in this change was astronomical. At the beginning of the nineteenth century, approximately 85

SAINTS AND SCOUNDRELS

percent of those who lived in Britain worked on farms. At the end of century, 62 percent of Britain's population were city-dwellers, and most of these were industrial workers cramped in the main metropolitan centers, working long hours in what William Blake called the "dark Satanic mills."

The thousands of peasants who left their farms in the countryside for the cities had little choice. Forced privatization left entire populations of peasants exiled from common lands that had sustained them for centuries. A series of Inclosure Acts meant that even entire villages sometimes had to be deserted, prompting Oliver Goldsmith to write his moving poem *The Deserted Village* in 1770.

All those forced into the city began to experience changes in how they thought, perceived the world, and related to one another. Just as the invention of the clock had caused man to perceive the flow of time separate from the flow of events, so life in the factory oriented men and women to see their lives not only separate from nature but as separate from any transcendent purpose. Value and meaning shifted from the transcendent to the functional in a world where everything hinged on efficiency.

THOMAS CHALMERS' BOYHOOD

It was into this changing world that Thomas Chalmers was born on March 17, 1780, the sixth child of John and Elizabeth Chalmers. Thomas was born in a small fishing and trading village on the southeast coast of Fife, Scotland.

The Chalmers family owned a dye-and-thread works as well as a general merchant's business. The money provided by these businesses made it possible for John to give his children a good education. As important as education was, however, John's primary desire was that his children would excel in what he termed "practical Christianity."

The family home was a happy hub of activity as Thomas, along with his eight brothers and five sisters, was encouraged to read widely and to discuss the latest scientific advances with his parents.

From an early age it was evident that Thomas was an extremely gifted child. At the age of three he outstripped his parents' resources and was enrolled in the local school. When he was only ten he was ready to enter St. Andrews University but was too young and had to wait until he was twelve to begin.

When he entered the university in 1792, Thomas quickly outpaced the curriculum, showing particular aptitude at mathematics. While still a student he became one of the greatest theoretical mathematicians in the world.

Thomas hoped to become a professor at the university when he was old enough. However, at the age of fifteen he began to sense a call to the ministry. Thus, in 1795 Thomas entered the divinity school in order to prepare for a career in the church. Three years later he finished the course but took a post as a private tutor because he was too young to become ordained.

In 1799, Thomas Chalmers was able to be ordained, but there was still no opening in which to serve. Thus he continued to take courses at the university, eventually becoming an assistant professor. It was evident to the entire university that he was a man of exceptional intellectual gifting. Although he began teaching graduate courses to students older than himself, being an expert in everything from chemistry to moral philosophy to history to economics, he was still too young to be offered a permanent position.

On the side, Chalmers taught himself German. (He had already taught himself French in order to read French math books). He also began to dabble in the Nordic languages, ultimately inventing his own Nordic-based language in which to record his journal entries.

A RISING STAR

In the year 1803, two opportunities simultaneously presented themselves to Chalmers. He was simultaneously offered the rural parish of Kilmany and a position as a permanent faculty member at the university teaching mathematics. Since Kilmany was not far from St. Andrews, Chalmers simply accepted both posts.

An energetic orator, Chalmers quickly became the most popular preacher in the entire region and the most sought-after professor at the university. Transfixed by his magnificent intellect, students described being spellbound as they listened to him. Likewise in his church at Kilmany, his parishioners were transformed as they listened to his elegant sermons.

Thomas Chalmers was clearly a rising star, and his fame began to spread far and wide. It wasn't long before people were travelling from all over England and Scotland to meet this incredibly accomplished young man.

As popular as he was, however, the needs of Chalmers' parishioners were not being met. Stewart Brown noted that Chalmers treated his parish ministry as "little more than a sinecure while he pursued academic preferment" while "his congregation withered on the dry intellectualism passed down from the pulpit."[1]

FROM SELF-SUFFICIENCY TO CHRIST-SUFFICIENCY

When he was twenty-nine, Chalmers was struck by a series of bereavements. His older brother and sister were stricken with tuberculosis. During the long period of suffering prior to their deaths, Chalmers nursed them at their bedside.

During the bedside vigils, Chalmers encountered in his brother and sister a faith and love for God deeper than anything he had known. Chalmers found himself completely transformed by his dying brother's understanding of God's grace, and the peace in his eyes as he was ushered into Jesus' presence. Likewise with his sister, who asked her younger brother to sing the entire Psalter to her eight times as she withered away.

When Chalmers returned to the parish at Kilmany, he was a completely changed man. He now realized that his greatest abilities were actually his greatest liabilities. From then on, instead of drawing strength from his talents, Chalmers' ministry was marked by humility and utter dependence on Christ. Reflecting on this transformation, he would later write,

> In the death of my beloved I have discovered the one thing I never discovered at university, that I am at heart a fool. I have always been heralded as wise and I have now discovered the gospel truth of my dire need of Christ Jesus and of the gospel. I have discovered the fleeting nature of time. Should I ever

1. Stewart J. Brown, "Chalmers, Thomas (1780–1847)," Oxford Dictionary of National Biography, http://www.oxforddnb.com/view/article/5033 (accessed February 20, 2012).

resort to my pride and my strength again, O God, prune me quick. Prune me quick.[2]

Prior to this transformation, Chalmers had been deserting his parish during the week to teach at the university. He once even remarked that after discharging his duties "a minister may enjoy five days in the week of uninterrupted leisure."[3] But now Chalmers devoted himself full-time to the people of his church, committing to visit every home in the parish. He went out three times a week, thus visiting all the families in the course of time.

In 1812 Chalmers married Grace Pratt. It was a happy marriage, and their six daughters helped create a lively and hospitable atmosphere in the home.

TIME IN GLASGOW

The Lord blessed Chalmers' ministry amazingly, attracting the attention of the church leaders in Glasgow, who asked Chalmers to apply his gifts there. While loathe to leave his beloved Kilmany, in 1815 Chalmers decided to move to Glasgow to see if the biblical principles he had applied in the country would work in the city.

As has already been noted, the Industrial Revolution had radically altered the landscape of the cities, turning them into cruel wildernesses where swarms of human beings lived in isolation and poverty. Nowhere was this more true than in Glasgow.

Immediately upon arriving in the city, Chalmers applied himself to the needs of the twelve thousand families he was responsible for. Believing that it was the job of the church, not the state, to improve society and help the poor, he entered into an organizational frenzy to radically transform the region.

The Lord blessed Chalmers' work so amazingly that government social services spending in Glasgow was reduced by 80 percent in three years. This included all services from cleaning of streets to

---

2. James Moffat, *Chalmers: A Biography* (New York: Culbertson and Brothers, New York, 1854), 61.

3. James Dodds, *Thomas Chalmers, A Biographical Study* (Oxford: Oxford University Press, 1870), 44.

policing, helping the poor, hauling away rubbish, sewage management, and so forth.

When Chalmers had begun work in Glasgow, virtually the only people who went to school were children whose parents could afford to send them to expensive private academies. Eight years later virtually everyone in his parish could attend a parish school.

BESTSELLING AUTHOR

Chalmers was brought to the public eye again when he began giving Thursday afternoon lectures in astronomy as part of a businessman's lunch series at the church. By the second lecture the church where he was speaking was packed with twenty-one hundred people. At a time when there was increasing polarization between science and religion, Chalmers used these lectures as an opportunity to proclaim that astronomy, like all the sciences, declares the providence of God. He drew attention to the fact that astronomy's purpose is to capture that which is Christ's own and show it as His own.

Because Chalmers' lectures, like his sermons, were always written down, they were easily collected by one of Glasgow's small religious publishing houses and put into a book. Within twenty minutes of being published the entire inventory sold. The publishers printed more, only to have them outsell Sir Walter Scot's popular Waverly novels that were published on same day. Nine printings in the first year still could not meet the demand.

Chalmers quickly became the most popular author in the entire world.

THE ST. JOHN'S EXPERIMENT

In 1819, Chalmers transferred to the parish of St. John's, an even more difficult part of Glasgow. The parish contained twenty-one thousand people, which included some of the roughest and poorest people in the entire town.

Determined to keep poor-relief within the funds available from church offerings, he believed it was crucial that the poor learn how to responsibly manage the little they had. Thus, Chalmers and his deacons systematically visited every home in the parish, interviewing the families and giving them counsel on how they might be more effective in managing their money. Chalmers made sure that poor-relief was kept at a personal level, investigating every situation and circumstance individually.

Unlike some champions of the "War on Poverty," Chalmers did not believe that the solution to poverty was found in the liberality of the rich. Rather, he taught that the solution to poverty lay in the hearts and habits of the poor. To address that, the poor first needed the gospel. They also needed practical instruction to know how the gospel fleshed out into every area of the household.

At the same time, Chalmers taught the poor to think beyond themselves and their immediate needs. He established missionary societies so that the poor could support the work of foreign missions. (He believed the poor would be less apt to waste money if they were regularly giving a portion of their income to missions.)

PARISH LIFE

Because Chalmers believed that his model for parish life was biblical, he was convinced that it could be successfully copied in all of the cities. His plan for parish life sought to restore dignity to the vast population of paupers who had been victims of the Industrial Revolution. The transition from the agrarian life of the village to the industrial life of the city invoked a sense of disconnection from the rhythms of nature and from important social ties with each other. What was lost was a sense of place—that indeterminate sense of belonging somewhere and being rooted in the type of stabilizing social community that Chalmers had experienced at Kilmany. Could the parish life of the village neighborhood be implemented in the cities? Could the industrial centers be re-personalized? Chalmers believed that they could and worked tirelessly to make his vision a reality.

The first step was giving back to the poor the dignity they had lost in the factories and helping them to escape from the homogeneous mold they were being squeezed into. He started parental uplift programs to teach mothers basic skills so that they might better train and teach their own children. He designated a spiritual mother for each community to give housecraft schools once a week, so that the poor might learn to beautify their homes instead of simply surviving.

He established evening Sabbath schools so that the poor might learn to read. He started day schools for the children in the city, which taught trades as well as academics. He organized small groups and Bible studies for the poor. He emphasized the priority of family worship and encouraged orphans to join in the family worship at the houses of neighbors. He started wash-houses, where the poor could wash themselves, clean their teeth, and clean their clothes.

All of these projects were based on Chalmers' belief that the gospel needed to transform society by being woven into fabric of everyday life. He believed this was best achieved in communities of manageable sizes. Thus, within each of the large parishes he established smaller parishes. This enabled all the houses within a parish to be within walking distance, not only to allow his deacons to visit their flock but to allow a sense of village life for those who lives had previously been isolated in the smothering uniformity of the metropolis. The vision is best expressed in Chalmers' own words:

> Let next-door neighbours be supplied with one common object of reverence and regard, in the clergyman who treats them alike as members of the same parochial family; let his church be the place of common repair upon the Sabbaths; let his sermon, which told the same things to all, suggest the common topics, on which the similarly impressed might enter into conversations, that begin and strengthen more and more the friendship between them; let the intimacies of the parish children be formed and ripened together, at the same school—these all help as cementing influences by which to bind this aggregate of human beings into one comunity, and with a speed and certainty, not by many inconceivable, to set up a village or domestic economy, even in the heart of a crowded metropolis.[4]

4. Thomas Chalmers, *On the Sufficiency of the Parochial System: Without a Poor Rate, For the Right Management of the Poor* (Glasgow: William Collins, 1841), 275–276.

ST. ANDREWS

In 1823 an exhausted Chalmers was persuaded to go to St. Andrews to teach moral philosophy. In accepting this invitation, Chalmers hoped to use his position as a teacher to make more leaders like him. One of the main criticisms made against him is that his plans were unrealistic and required Chalmers' magnetic personality in order to make them work. But by teaching the principles of his work to others at St. Andrews, Chalmers hoped to train a new generation of Christians to continue the work he had started.

At the university, Chalmers instantly became a phenomenon again, as people flocked to listen to him. A year after moving to St. Andrews he published two volumes of one of the best pre-evolutionary natural histories of all time, titled *On the Power, Wisdom and Goodness of God as Manifested in the Adaptation of External Nature to the Moral and Intellectual Constitution of Man.*

Five years after coming to St. Andrews, Chalmers went to University of Edinburgh to take the divinity chair, with equal success. Right up until his death in 1847, he continued to teach, to work for social reform, and to be deeply involved in church matters.

THE LEGACY OF THOMAS CHALMERS

Chalmers left a remarkable legacy in his wake that included numerous missionary and Bible societies, sixty schools, organizations for supplying Bibles to soldiers, hundreds of organizations for helping the poor, forty libraries, fourteen publishing houses, and three art galleries. He funded a new edition of the Psalter and encouraged hymnists, composers, and artists to trumpet the claims of Christ in the arts.

Despite his titanic accomplishments, Chalmers is practically unheard of today. This is partly because after his conversion Chalmers self-consciously rejected the spotlight for himself. Though he was the most influential man in Christendom, Chalmers chose to spend his time among the poor, ministering to their most basic needs.

LESSONS FROM THE LIFE OF THOMAS CHALMERS

Thomas Chalmers teaches us the importance of having bold and out-rageous vision. He once remarked, "Regardless of how large, your vision is too small." Chalmers lived by these words, always seeking ways to expand his vision. His vision was so large that it went beyond the confines of his own country and was international in its scope. He was concerned, not just with Scotland, but with Christendom.

But although Chalmers' vision for God's kingdom was a vision for the whole world, it always started with the needs that lay closest to home. Unlike Rousseau, who neglected the needs of those closest to him in order to save the world, Chalmers' love for mankind always manifested itself in his love for the person next door. The key to changing the world was to change the neighborhood.

Secondly, Chalmers teaches us important lessons about the centrality of the church. He taught that it is the vocation of the church, not the state, to transform society. Although the government should cooperate with the church's goals, giving preferential treatment to the church's causes and removing legal obstructions to her work, the vision of bringing hope and prosperity to cities has been entrusted to the people of God. In his book *The Christian and Civic Economy of Large Towns*, Chalmers articulated the problems that would persist in large metropolitan cities if the church were not central to the life of the growing cities. If the church is not central to the economy of a town, he argued, cities will be sucked into the "servile status of the grand, glorious smothering state." The gospel is needed as a hedge on the growing power of the state. "It is only the gospel of Jesus Christ," he wrote, "which has the power to deter the effects of this looming disaster and all of the ministrations of the state will only portend to the undoing of the family, the rescinding of initiative and the recoiling from human dignity."[5]

5. F.A. Brittain, *Decadence and Reconstruction*, (London: H. Holt, 1923; Quest Reprints, 1991), 41.

QUESTIONS FOR DISCUSSION

1. Chalmers taught that the way to transform the world is to transform the neighborhood. Would Edmund Burke agree with this? Why or why not?

2. Although Chalmers was one of the most intellectually brilliant men of his time, he spent most of his life attending to the basic needs of the poor. What does this indicate about his character?

3. The Romantic movement in the mid-nineteenth century reacted against the dehumanizing impact of industrialization and urged a return to a more primitive and nature lifestyle. Is this a biblical alternative?

4. Compare and contrast Rousseau's critique of "civilization" with Chalmers' critique of the Industrial Revolution. Are there any points of commonality in their concerns?

5. Was the Industrial Revolution good or bad? Discuss in relation to the dominion mandate of Genesis 1.

6. Chalmers was aware of the smothering and dehumanizing influences wrought by the Industrial Revolution. Does this mean that the Industrial Revolution was bad? What should be a Christian's attitude towards technological inventions when those inventions have a dehumanizing effect?

7. Chalmers said, "Regardless of how large, your vision is too small." What are some ways that our vision can sometimes be too small?

8. Was Chalmers correct in his views on the role of the church and the state? What would be some things that would have to change if our society followed his teaching in this area?

PERSONAL CHALLENGE

Through the dying testimony of his siblings, Thomas Chalmers learned to become Christ-sufficient rather than self-sufficient. Has anything ever happened in your life that has helped you to learn that lesson?

CHAPTER 13

AMERICAN IDOL

The False Prophecies of Joseph Smith (1805–1844)

The year was 1844. A congregation of around ten thousand people had gathered in Nauvoo, Illinois to observe the funeral of King Follett, an elder in the movement called the Church of the Latter Day Saints (LDS).

The movement's founder, Joseph Smith, stood to address the assembly. From the moment Smith began to speak it was clear that this would be no ordinary funeral sermon. "We have imagined," Smith told the crowd, "and supposed that God was God from all eternity. I will refute that idea, and take away the veil, so that you may see." He continued:

> It is the first principle of the gospel to know for certainty . . . that he was once a man like us; yea, that God himself, the Father of us all, dwelt on an earth, the same as Jesus Christ himself did . . . Here then, is eternal life—to know the only wise and true God; and you have got to learn how to be Gods yourselves, and to be kings and priests to God, the same as all Gods have done before you.[1]

---

1. Joseph Smith, *Teachings of the Prophet Joseph Smith: Taken from his Sermons and Writings as They are Found in the Documentary History and Other*

Smith went on to explain that there had once been a time before Jesus Christ was God. And just as both Jesus and the Father had attained divinity, so Smith's disciples could also become divine by a similar process. As Joseph Fielding Smith, the tenth president of the Latter Day Saints, wrote in his *Origin of the Reorganized Church and the Question of Succession:*

> Joseph Smith the Prophet taught a plurality of Gods, and moreover, that man, by obeying the commandments of God and keeping the whole law will eventually reach the power and exaltation by which he also will become a God.[2]

The idea that there are many gods was not new to Smith's followers. As early as 1814, Smith had taught that "the doctrine of a plurality of gods is as prominent in the Bible as any other doctrine. It is all over the face of the Bible."[3]

Less than three months after King Follett's funeral, Smith was killed in a shootout at the Carthage jail. Shortly after that he is said to have attained the divinity he predicted. Brigham Young, one of the "Twelve Apostles" sanctioned by Smith, commented in 1859, "He reigns [in the Celestial Kingdom of God] as supreme, a being in his sphere, capacity, calling, as God does in Heaven."[4]

Today there are millions that cling to this promise of divinity offered by Smith. The denomination that he started is now the largest indigenous American church, while approximately eight hundred people *per day* convert to the Mormon faith. Even more astonishing, the Mormon church outperforms all other American religious traditions in successfully transmitting its beliefs to the next generation.

Publications of the Church and Written or Published in the Days of the Prophet's Ministry (Salt Lake City: Deseret Book Company, 1972), 345–346.

2. Joseph Fielding Smith, *Origin of the Reorganized Church and the Question of Succession* (Salt Lake City, The Deseret News, 1909), 99.

3. From Joseph Smith's sermon "The Christian Godhead—Plurality of Gods" in Joseph Fielding Smith, *Teachings of the Prophet Joseph Smith,* 370.

4. Brigham Young, *Journal of Discourses* (London: Published by Brigham Young, 1860), 289.

Who was Joseph Smith, and why did thousands of people flock to hear him preach that day in Nauvoo, Illinois? What were the origins of this man who still exercises such a hypnotic hold over so many?

To answer these pressing questions, we must travel back to the very inception of the American nation. Smith could never have been taken seriously in any other social context, but there was something in the very atmosphere of early America that favored spiritual innovators such as himself.

A PIONEER THEOLOGY

When colonization of the New World first began in the 1600s, it took a certain type of person to leave the established institutions and comforts of Europe to face the uncertainties and challenges ahead. If you were not cut from the rugged pioneer cloth, the new continent would not just be unappealing—it would break you.

By the middle of the eighteenth century, life in the colonial cities had become fairly domesticated, but by then the pragmatic, anti-institutional mentality of the original settlers had been etched deep into the consciousness of the colonists.

Related to this was the idea of the "self-made man." Whereas the old world had a social hierarchy determined largely by birth, the early settlers had no aristocracy and few inherited privileges that they wished to acknowledge. Operating on the idea that "all men are created equal," they generally assumed that it was by the sweat of one's brow, not by his pedigree, that a man earned a name for himself in the world. The **egalitarian** foundations for this idea not only found their way into the "self-evident truths" proclaimed in the opening of the Declaration of Independence, but created an atmosphere of entrepreneurship, independent thinking, and rugged individualism that helped to make America so successful.

It is not hard to see how the pioneer spirit manifested itself in westward expansion or how the idea of equality found expression in the gradual democratizing of American government. What is not so often appreciated is how these distinctive features carried over into the American approach to faith. As the nineteenth century progressed, the strong individualism and independent mentality of the pioneers became hallmarks of American spirituality.

Sometimes there were practical reasons for this. Since there were not enough ministers willing to travel and plant churches in all the outposts, many of the settlers in the frontiers of the American west were unchurched. To fill this gap, itinerant evangelists would travel the circuit, make converts, and then depart for the next town. Since conversion was occurring independent of the apparatus of any church and its ongoing ministry, it helped to solidify the individualistic and anti-institutional flavor of the religion of the western territories, while undermining the connection these Christians had with the larger historical church. As Sidney Mead has noted in his book *The Lively Experiment,* "the common sense of opportunity to begin all over again in the new land, which was so characteristic a feature of the mind of the early planters, also worked to erase the sense of continuity with the historic Church."[5]

Such individualism was not limited to the outposts of the frontier. In the early to mid-nineteenth century, the revivalist model that had been so successful during the First Great Awakening (1730s and 1740s) began to be employed throughout New England by evangelists such as Charles Finney (1792–1875). As part of the "Second Great Awakening," Finney distilled the do-it-yourself pragmatism of the American pioneer into a theology. For him, converting large crowds was just as simple as raising a barn or starting a farm: follow the right techniques, and you will have success; neglect them, and you will fail. Finney put this idea into practice by staging revival meetings in which he would employ the latest marketing techniques to manipulate the emotions of large crowds. Significantly, he tended to downplay the role of the Holy Spirit in the process.

Finney tended to downplay efforts to transform society, believing that such efforts might overshadow the work of conversion. As "inward spiritual progress began to be separated from Christian efforts to shape the entire society,"[6] and as this inward spiritual progress began to be measured in increasingly experiential terms[7] the institutions of

5. Sidney E. Mead, *The Lively Experiment: The Shaping of Christianity in America* (Eugene: Wipf & Stock Publishers, 2007), 110.

6. Mark Noll, *The Old Religion in a New World: A History of North American Christianity* (Grand Rapids: Eerdmans, 2002), 98.

7. Os Guinness, *Fit Bodies, Fat Minds: Why Evangelicals Don't Think and What to Do About It* (Grand Rapids: Hourglass Books, 1994), 58–59.

church, culture, and Christendom became largely displaced by the primacy of personal experience. This merely accentuated the strongly anti-institutional bias of American Christianity. But it also added fervor to American pragmatism, since personal experience became the most important spiritual barometer. The type of experience that Finney valued and tried to replicate in all his meetings was one in which the sinner feels—often acutely, with tears and groaning—the power of God, a conviction of sin, and the assurance of salvation. Only by such authentic experiences could you know that you were *truly* saved.

Joseph Smith rose to prominence precisely because he was able to draw upon all these elements of American Protestantism and incorporate them into his new religion. Mormonism was birthed out of the individualism of the self-made pioneer, the egalitarianism of American democracy, the autonomous personal experience of revivalists like Finney and the hostility to established institutions characteristic of nineteenth-century America. But before we are in a position to consider how Smith masterfully wove these familiar strains into the new melody of Mormonism, we must consider one more piece of the cultural puzzle: the urge towards revolutionary religion.

"UNRESTRAINED EXPERIMENTS OF INNOVATORS"

Revolutionaries throughout the ages have steered their ships by two guiding lights: the quest for utopia and a rejection of the past. Jettisoning the collective wisdom of his forefathers, a revolutionary will seek to bring heaven to earth through sudden and convulsive innovation.

Nineteenth-century New Englanders were particularly susceptible to the lure of revolutionary solutions. This did not escape the observation of America's French observer and social critic, de Tocqueville, who commented that "it appeared as if New England was a region given up to the dreams of fancy and the unrestrained experiments of innovators."[8]

---

8. Alexis de Tocqueville, *Democracy in America* (Cambridge: J. Allyn, 1862), 43.

In the political sphere, the revolutionary mentality manifested itself in the urge towards the type of statism[9] that has tinctured New
liberalism ever since. During the nineteenth century the revolutionary urge was strongly felt in the arena of religion, with various Christian groups self-consciously rejecting the need for creeds, catechisms,
and the wisdom of past practice. Taking the millennial fervor of the
American Puritans to a new stage of utopian expectation, many of
these groups claimed to be spearheading the "restoring of all things"
spoken of in Acts 3:21. They sought to restore a pure and pristine
Christianity which, purportedly, relied only on the Bible.[10] What
this really meant was that nearly two thousand years of Christian
tradition was substituted by the novel traditions and prejudices of
nineteenth-century America.

The revolutionary spirit was encapsulated in a hymn written by the
itinerant preacher Joseph Thomas early in the nineteenth century:

> Let Christians now unite and say,
> We'll throw all human rules away,
>   And take God's word to rule us;
> King Jesus shall our leader be,
> And in his name we will agree,
>   The priests no more shall fool us.[11]

In dismissing the need for creeds, clergy, and any system of authority other than the lone individual and his Bible, much of the New
World's Protestantism presented itself as a "people's movement." The
ideals of autonomy and popular sovereignty became hallmarks, not
only of American politics, but of American religion. Paradoxically,

---

9. See Robin Phillips, *"Evangelicalism and Nationalism,"* http://tinyurl.
com/7nnj6sz (accessed February 20, 2012); Richard M. Gamble, *The War for Righteousness: Progressive Christianity, the Great War, and the Rise of the Messianic
Nation* (Wilmington: ISI Books, 2003).

10. As such, these groups were "Biblicist" rather than Biblical. For a discus-
sion of the difference between these categories, see section 3 in my article "Why
Nouthetic Counseling is Unbiblical," at http://tinyurl.com/7op328n (accessed
February 20, 2012).

11. Mark A. Noll, *A History of Christianity in the United States and Canada*
(Grand Rapids: William B. Eerdmans Publishing Company, 1992), 143.

however, this people's movement became incredibly elitist, since it justified an almost endless number of schisms which existed in self-conscious opposition to the wider church.

Even as teachers routinely said to their students, "Any one of you can grow up to become the president," so preachers taught that anyone, guided only by the twin stars of Scripture and one's personal relationship with Jesus, could become another Moses, Jeremiah, or Paul. There thus emerged all manner of apostles, each claiming the vocation of "restoring" the faith. But unlike the biblical prophets, who built on the old foundations to repair the ruins, these modern prophets eschewed all wisdom from the past. D. G. Hart described the situation in his biography of John Williamson Nevin:

> [T]he new form of Christianity liberated the people from the oversight of clergy and the theological norms of creeds or confessions and . . . took the spiritual insights and longings of the laity at face value, imbuing them with a worth and significance previously unimagined in settings dominated by ministers and the creedal statements to which they subscribed.[12]

It was in New England, and particularly upstate New York, where this revolutionist spirituality attained a pitch of fanaticism unseen in the annals of church history.

The region was termed the "burnt-over district" by Finney to describe an area so heavily subject to revivals that there was no "fuel" left to burn. Not only had everyone been converted, but after experiencing the supernatural power of intense and repeated revivals, the people of the province had become spiritually exhausted and cynical. Consequently, it required more extreme measures to excite their once-combustible spiritual enthusiasm. The "burnt-over district" thus became a breeding ground for an array of cults and spiritual fanatics. By exploiting the climate of cynicism about traditional religion, these fanatics were able to find a ready audience for their revolutionary and utopian schemes.

12. D.G. Hart, *John Williamson Nevin: High-Church Calvinist* (Phillipsburg: P & R Publishing, 2005), 24.

It wasn't merely upstate New York, for throughout all of New England there was an explosion in the number of evangelical sects and schisms, each following the impulse of New England's original settlers to achieve a "pure" church, faithful only to the Bible. With Promethean bravado, each of these sects assumed the mantle of giving to man the divine fire, as it had steadily burnt before being snuffed out by creeds and tradition. For example, the "Disciples of Christ," a Protestant denomination that emerged out of the Second Great Awakening, claimed "that the revelations of God should be made to displace from their position all human creeds, confessions of faith, and formalities of doctrine and church government."[13] The "Church of God," a group that emerged from the **holiness movement**, boasted that it had "no authoritative constitution, ritual, creed, catechism, book of discipline or church standard, but the Bible."[14] The Millerites were even more succinct: "No other creed or form of discipline than the written word of God."[15]

Stripped of all foundations that might link these different groups to the larger church, the resulting void was filled by every person's own private interpretation of Scripture. Each group took it for granted that an autonomous **hermeneutic** would vindicate its own claims. In reality, all it produced was a confused cacophony.

It is not to be wondered at that many Americans felt deeply dissatisfied with the visible church by the middle of the nineteenth century. Those who had grown frustrated with the spirit of sect and schism tended either to abandon the institutional church altogether for a subjective spiritual individualism, or else to find solace in the claims of spiritual revolutionaries who held out the promise of uniting the people of God under one banner.

13. John Williamson Nevin, *The Mercersburg Review* (Mercersburg: Alumni Association of Marshall College, 1849), 491.

14. Israel Daniel Rupp, *Religious Denominations in the United States, Their Past History, Present Condition, and Doctrines, Accurately Set Forth in Fifty-three... Articles Written by Eminent Clerical and Lay Authors...Together With Complete and Well-digested Statistics. To Which is Added a Historical Summary of Religious Denominations in England and Scotland* (Philadelphia: C. Desilver, 1861), 176.

15. Ibid., 41.

ECHOING A FAMILIAR STRAIN

Smith's own series of revelations emerged out of this complex network of spiritual urges. Indeed, all the religious impulses of a New Englander reached their culmination in Joseph-Smith-style-religion.

Significantly, Smith's own autobiography describes how his first "revelation" grew out of his discontent with both revivalism and the sect system in New York State. In 1816, when Joseph was eleven, his family moved to Manchester, New York. This was a region that had been the scene of repeated revivals during the Second Great Awakening. In his own autobiography, published as part of *The Pearl of Great Price*, Smith recounted how his first vision was triggered by a revival that broke out in the spring of 1820:

> [I]ndeed, the whole district of [sic] country seemed affected by it, and great multitudes united themselves to the different religious parties, which created no small stir and division amongst the people, some crying, Lo here, and some, Lo there; some were contending for the Methodist faith, some for the Presbyterian, and some for the Baptists'.[16]

Fourteen-year-old Joseph went into the woods to pray about which one of these sects was the correct one. It was then that he received his first vision, in the form of a visitation from God the Father and Jesus.[17] The message Smith supposedly received echoed the rallying

16. Joseph Smith, *The Pearl of Great Price: Being a Choice Selection from the Revelations, Translations, and Narrations of Joseph Smith, First Prophet, Seer, and Revelator to the Church of Jesus Christ of Latter-Day Saints* (Salt Lake City: Latter-Day Saints' Printing and Publishing Establishment, 1878), 45.

17. At least, that is how Smith's contemporary followers generally interpret what is known as the "first vision." However, as George Mather and Larry Nichols point out, "In the earlier edition of *The Pearl of Great Price*, Smith identified one of the personages as being Moroni. In a later edition of the same book, Smith identifies the celestial visitor as being Nephi. Nephi and Moroni are two distinct characters in Mormon literature. Second, in the first edition of *The Pearl of Great Price*, Smith had mentioned having been visited by 'one personage.' The later edition(s) speak of 'two personages,' constituting a rather serious discrepancy, especially because the truth of Mormon revelation rests on the prophetic authority of its books" [Larry A. Nichols, George Mather, and Alvin J. Schmidt, *Encyclopedic*

cry of all the sects: "the personage . . . said all their creeds were an abomination in His sight; that those professors were all corrupt."[18]

Smith was on familiar territory here. His father claimed to have received seven visions, many of which vividly portrayed the barrenness of the institutional church. According to Smith's biographer, Richard Bushman, Joseph Sr. "could not embrace the institutional religion of his time," which he considered "empty and silent, or fiercely hostile to true wisdom and understanding." Joseph Jr.'s vision in the "Sacred Grove" simply confirmed his father's outlook.

Smith did not hesitate to take up the popular restorationist mantle. But whereas other restoration groups sought to strip away all creeds and traditions in order to ostensibly return to "just the Bible," Smith stripped away all creeds and traditions in order to give his followers a new collection of "creeds" substantially longer than the Bible itself.

The corpus of extra-biblical revelations did not arrive all at once. Smith claimed that three years after the "Sacred Grove" incident, he was visited by Moroni, a resurrected saint who had died about A.D. 400. Moroni had been the last of the Nephites, an ancient people who had migrated to the American continent before being crushed by the rival Lamanites. The entire story, Moroni said, was engraved in plates buried under the nearby Cumorah Hill.

Each September for the next four years, Moroni appeared on Cumorah Hill to prepare Smith to eventually possess and translate the plates. In the September of 1827, when Smith was twenty-one, Moroni gave him the long-awaited engravings, instructing him to show the plates to no one. Over the next two years Smith is said to have translated into English the unique writing that was a mixture of "Egyptian, Chaldaic, Assyriac, and Arabic."[19] Unable to read the text, Smith employed a Urim and Thummim (which Moroni had also helpfully provided) in addition to reading reflections in a Seer Stone at the bottom of his hat. Apparently, by gazing at the stone Smith could see the translated words. Smith then dictated the words to his secretary, Martin Harris, who stood on the other side of a curtain

---

Dictionary of Cults, Sects, and World Religions: Revised and Updated Edition (Grand Rapids: Zondervan, 2010), 188].

18. Smith, *The Pearl of Great Price*, 47.

19. Richard Lyman Bushman and Jed Woodworth, *Joseph Smith: Rough Stone Rolling* (New York: Vintage Books, 2007), 65.

and wrote down the words as the prophet spoke. (Harris was forbidden on pain of immediate death from looking at the tablets.) When the translation was complete, before anyone besides Smith had a chance to lay eyes on the engravings, he returned them to Moroni, who took them up to heaven.[20]

THE RISE OF THE LATTER DAY SAINTS

As Smith's base of followers began to expand, so did the body of revelation. By the end of his life he had produced three works, which his followers consider to be on par with Scripture: *The Book of Mormon*, *The Pearl of Great Price*, and *Doctrine and Covenants*. (The last book was added to by later generations to include revelations by Brigham Young and his successors.) Smith also issued a "translation" of the King James Version of the Bible, in which he claimed to "correct" many of its errors, although this has never been officially published by the Mormon church since it was never completed.

The three translated books became the basis for Smith's church, the Latter Day Saints, or the Mormon church, named after a native-American called "Mormon," who supposedly lived in the fourth century B.C.

Like so many other eighteenth- and nineteenth-century sects, the Mormons claimed to be the only pure church. But Smith took his restoration one step further, asserting that from the close of the apostolic age until 1820, no true church had ever existed. As Smith put it in his address, "Testimony Against the Dissenters at Nauvoo":

> I have more to boast of than ever any man had. I am the only man that has ever been able to keep a whole church together since the days of Adam. . . . Neither Paul, John, Peter, nor Jesus ever did it. I boast that no man ever did such a work as I. The followers of Jesus ran away from Him; but the Latter-day Saints never ran away from me yet.[21]

20. A number of Smith's supporters claimed to have seen the sacred tablets before they were returned to Moroni. However, they later admitted that they had only seen them in a spiritual rather than in a physical sense.

21. Joseph Smith, "History of Joseph Smith," *The Latter-Day Saints' Millennial Star* (Manchester: P.P. Pratt, 1861), 672.

Such boasts may sound incredible, but then Smith believed he was no ordinary man. The LDS publication *History of the Church, Volume 5* quotes him as saying,

> I combat the errors of ages; I meet the violence of mobs; I cope with illegal proceedings from executive authority; I cut the Gordian knot of powers; and I solve mathematical problems of Universities: with truth, diamond truth, and God is my "right hand man."[22]

Taking Smith's claims at face value, the Latter Day Saints followed him west, where they sought to establish a community based on his teachings. However, it was not always easy to keep up with Smith's ever-growing collection of revelations. On September 22 and 23, 1832, he claimed to have received inspired word that a temple would be built in western Missouri within his generation and that all Mormons would be gathered there. The next year the Mormons were driven out of Missouri by hostile "Gentiles." Once they settled in Illinois, Smith received word that God had considered the failed attempt to build the temple to be acceptable.[23] In 1832, he announced that an American civil war would trigger off a world war involving "all nations." Two years later he claimed to have received a vision that the coming of the Lord was fifty-six years away. In December 1832, he predicted that "not many days hence the earth would shake, the sun be darkened and the moon turn the color of blood."[24]

Smith's theology also kept pace with his changing morality. During his early career, Smith apparently did not believe it was proper for a man to take more than one wife, for the *Book of Mormon* calls

22. Joseph Smith and Heman C. Smith, *History of the Church of Jesus Christ of Latter Day Saints 1836 to 1844, Part Two* (Whitefish: Kessinger Publishing, 2004), 654.

23. Ibid., 68–69. Also in *Doctrine and Covenants 124,* available online at www. lds.org/scriptures/dc-testament/dc/124 (accessed March 1, 2012). Some Mormons have argued that the prophecy is still to be fulfilled. This is the approach taken by Orson Pratt.

24. Joseph Smith, *The Doctrines and Covenants 88:87,* The Church of Jesus Christ of Latter-Day Saints, www.lds.org/scriptures/dc-testament/dc/88 (accessed January 9, 2012).

the practice an "abomination" (Jacob 2:24, 27). However, around the same time that he made the spurious prediction about the temple in Missouri, Smith began quietly advocating both *polygamy* (one man, many wives) and *polyandry* (one woman, many husbands).

Smith had a keen eye for younger women, and by the end of his life he had been "sealed" to thirty-three different women. Ten of his wives were under twenty years of age. He kept many of these marriages secret, and this is hardly surprising given that one-third of Smith's women were married to other men at the same time.

How did Smith persuade so many women to be united to him? One effective way was to hold out to them the promise of eternal salvation. For example, in May 1843, a thirty-seven-year old Smith promised salvation to fifteen-year old Helen Mar Kimball if she would take the step. For others he offered even more, claiming that plural marriage would "ensure your eternal salvation and exaltation and that of your father's household and all your kindred."[25] In other cases, he told the women that God had threatened to slay him if he did not marry them. Joseph even received a "word" stating that his wife, Emma, must stand ready to receive the additional wives of her husband on pain of everlasting damnation. (This Word from the Lord made it into the sacred *Doctrine and Covenants,* section 132.)

Richard Bushman, a sympathetic Mormon biographer, has pointed out that

> in the first six months of 1843, Joseph married twelve women, two of them already married to other men, one single and fifty-eight years old. Five of the women boarded in Joseph's household when he married them. Emma probably knew nothing of these marriages at first and then temporarily accepted them before regretting her action and demanding that all five leave.[26]

Though Smith bowed to Emma's wishes and dismissed his harem, this did not stop him taking additional wives. The women now were expected to simply carry on with their lives as before, but with

25. Bushman and Woodworth, *Joseph Smith: Rough Stone Rolling,* 439.
26. Bushman and Woodworth, *Joseph Smith,* 490–491.

one difference: they might receive an occasional "visit" from their prophet husband.

Smith's successors developed an elaborate theology out of Smith's revelations about plural marriage. For the generation that followed, plural marriage became a way that both men and women could earn their salvation. Brigham Young had fifty-five wives, at least six of whom had living husbands. But Brigham was more public about his polygamy than Smith, pronouncing, "Now if any of you will deny the plurality of wives, and continue to do so, I promise that you will be damned."[27] And again, "The only men who become Gods, even the Sons of God, are those who enter into polygamy."[28] According to Young, even Christ was a good Mormon polygamist: "Jesus Christ was a practical polygamist; Mary and Martha, the sisters of Lazarus, were his plural wives, and Mary Magdalen was another."[29]

"AN AMERICAN RELIGION"

At the time of Smith's death on June 27, 1844, tens of thousands of Americans had lapped up his elitist and utopian message. They did this largely because Smith had skillfully tapped into the presupposition to which they already subscribed. In particular, he harnessed the spirit of sect and schism so popular among New Englanders, who were accustomed to starting new groups that self-consciously excluded the entire rest of the visible church. This important point is easily overlooked by contemporary Mormons, who have begun claiming that their religion allows for historic Christians to be saved, in addition to claiming that Joseph Smith fulfilled rather than completely overturned traditional Christianity. But Joseph Smith was once asked, "Will everybody be damned, but Mormons?" His answer was, "Yes, and a great portion of them, unless they repent, and work righteousness."[30] Here again he was on common territory with a myriad of other nineteenth century restorationist movements.

27. Brigham Young and Church of Jesus Christ of Latter-Day Saints, *Journal of Discourses* (Liverpool: F.D. and S.W. Richards, 1856), 266.
28. Young, *Journal of Discourses*, 269.
29. Ann Eliza Young, *Wife, No. 19* (Whitefish: Kessinger Publishing, 2003), 307.
30. Fielding Smith, *Teachings of the Prophet Joseph Smith*, 119.

By telling a narrative that effectively drew on all the popular religious themes of his day, Smith was able to give plausibility to his otherwise incredible story.

Smith's abiding legacy was that he gave Americans a religion tailor-made for them: a belief-system perfectly fitted to their prejudices, assumptions, and aspirations.[31] This has been a major reason for the success of the Latter Day Saints in the United States. (Even their success internationally has largely been proportionate to American influence.) As historian Richard Bushman said at the end of his biography of Smith:

> His was a religion for and by the people. . . . In his theology, unexceptional people could aspire to the highest imaginable glory. In belated recognition of this populist side, Joseph Smith's Mormonism came to be understood in the twentieth century as an American religion.[32]

THE LEGACY OF JOSEPH SMITH

As might be expected from such a quintessentially American religion, Smith's ideas could not stand immutable. True to their pioneer spirit, Smith's followers have successively added to his collection of authoritative writings. For example, Smith's successor Brigham Young taught that before he became God, the Lord lived on Kolob, a star Smith had associated with God's throne room. Building on Smith's idea that there is little difference between God and man, Young taught that Jesus had not been born by the Holy Spirit, but through God

31. In his inaugural Tanner Lecture for the Mormon History Association, Gordon Wood noted, "Mormonism was born at a peculiar moment in the history of the United States, and it bears the marks of that birth. Only the culture of early-nineteenth century evangelical America could have produced it" [Reid Larkin Neilson, Terryl Givens, Joseph Smith, Jr., *Reappraisals After Two Centuries* (Oxford: Oxford University Press, 2009), 37]. Similarly, Fawn M. Brodie has suggested that *The Book of Mormon* "can best be explained, not by Joseph's ignorance nor by his delusions, but by his responsiveness to the provincial opinions of his time." Fawn M. Brodie, *No Man Knows My History: The Life of Joseph Smith*, (New York: Vintage, 1971), 69.

32. Bushman and Woodworth, *Joseph Smith*, 559.

the Father's sexual relations with Mary.[33] Other Mormon teachers, being recognized as prophets by the LDS leadership, taught that Jesus and Satan had been spirit brothers, while the rest of us were born as their siblings before coming to earth. But Smith's successors have not merely claimed the authority to add to his revelations. Believing they are continuing the legacy of an ongoing prophetic tradition, they have authoritatively altered the original documents. Indeed, the current *Book of Mormon* contains more than four thousand variants from the original 1830 edition, including some significant doctrinal shifts.

The commitment to continuing revelation has left the LDS with a legacy of extreme subjectivism. A highly pragmatic and individualistic people, Americans have always had the tendency to use personal experience as the barometer of truth. This was evident in the Second Great Awakening, when revivalists tried to evoke a variety of emotional experiences as proof of authentic conversion. This subjective criterion remains evident in the approach taken by contemporary Mormon missionaries. "When you pray and ask the Lord if the *Book of Mormon* is from Him, His answer will come in the form of an experience," young Mormons are taught before they become missionaries. Sometimes this experience may be miraculous, but more often than not it is a quiet sense that these things are true. You will simply *feel* that Joseph Smith is a prophet. As you read the *Book of Mormon* with an open mind, you will experience a "burning in your bosom" or some other experiential authentication. This is God's way of answering your prayer and showing you that it is true.

Armed thus with the unanswerable argument of personal experience, Mormon missionaries can close their minds to counter-arguments and feel all the more pious for doing so. By making personal experience the final arbiter of truth, Smith's followers continue his legacy by doing homage to one of America's chief idols.

The most amazing aspect of Smith's legacy has to be the number of followers. Today there are over thirteen million worldwide

33. Brigham Young, *Journal Of Discourses By Brigham Young V8, His Two Counsellors, The Twelve Apostles, And Others* (Whitefish: Kessinger Publishing, LLC, 2006), 115; Young, *Journal of Discourses*, 50. For further information on Mormon teaching about the godhead, and a comparison with the Biblical doctrine of the Trinity, see Robin Phillips, "The Trinity: Mormonism vs. Christianity," Alfred the Great Society, http://atgsociety.com/?p=1857 (accessed April 17, 2012).

who have staked their hope on the finished work of Smith.[34] While the Latter Day Saints represent only 1.7 percent of America's adult population, they have the largest retention rate of any religious tradition in America. In his book *Souls in Transition*, Christian Smith showed research establishing that the retention rate for Mormons in the eighteen to twenty-three age group is 72 percent, as opposed to conservative Protestants of the same age where the retention rate is only 64 percent.[35]

LESSONS FROM THE LIFE OF JOSEPH SMITH

The first lesson we learn from the life of Smith is that false prophets always speak what the people around them want to hear. Though false prophets usually like to think of themselves as modern-day Jeremiahs, going against the grain of popular opinion in order to proclaim God's truth, their messages are usually carefully constructed to mesh with the biases already popular within the wider community. Smith's approach was no exception. Like the false prophets described in 2 Timothy 4:2, he offered to the people exactly what their itching ears longed to hear. Consider the following two ways he did this.

First, in Smith's theological system, the pioneer mentality of the self-made man reached its apex. Taking Finney's do-it-yourself pragmatism one stage, further he taught Americans not simply that they

---

34. "Joseph Smith holds the keys of this last dispensation, and is now engaged behind the veil in the great work of the last days . . . no man or woman in this dispensation will ever enter into the celestial kingdom of God without the consent of Joseph Smith. From the day that the Priesthood was taken from the earth to the winding-up scene of all things, every man and woman must have the certificate of Joseph Smith, junior, as a passport to their entrance into the mansion where God and Christ are—I with you and you with me. I cannot go there without his consent. He holds the keys of that kingdom for the last dispensation—the keys to rule in the spirit-world; and he rules there triumphantly, for he gained full power and a glorious victory over the power of Satan while he was yet in the flesh, and was a martyr to his religion and to the name of Christ, which gives him a most perfect victory in the spirit-world. He reigns there as supreme a being in his sphere, capacity, and calling, as God does in heaven" (Brigham Young, *Journal of Discourses*, 289).

35. Christian Smith and Patricia Snell, *Souls in Transition: The Religious and Spiritual Lives of Emerging Adults* (Oxford: Oxford University Press, 2009).

could achieve salvation through their own efforts,[36] but that they could also attain divinity. Not content to merely colonize the western frontier, Mormons have followed Smith in the hope of one day colonizing an entire planet with their celestial offspring. Good Mormon children can aspire, not simply to become President one day, but to be a god.

Secondly, Smith constructed a utopian worldview that sanctified the revolutionary, schematic, and elitist leanings of nineteenth-century American Christians. The entire history of Christendom between the Apostles and Smith came crashing down under the hammer of his "restoration." To achieve this revolution, Smith masterfully drew on the anti-institutional impulses of nineteenth-century evangelicalism, using them to strip away all structures but his own. Although he began his career with a stinging denouncement of the denominational system, it was only by invoking the popular spirit of sect and schism that Smith was able to launch the largest indigenous denomination in American history.

Were it not for the energy with which Smith's followers have continued his tradition, his name would now be lost among a host of other nineteenth-century fanatics. The way the Latter Day Saints have achieved self-perpetuation has not primarily been through conversion but through organic growth from within. The encouragement to have large families plays a key part in this process. But even more significant is the fact that Mormon children are raised not

36. Mormonism from Joseph Smith to the present day has been very clear that both salvation and future deification are earned through works. Salvation is not a free gift of grace. As the Mormon Francis Lyman summarized the matter in a Conference Report in 1898: "All the requirements of the Lord must be accomplished if we would attain to all that is to be obtained in the celestial kingdom of our Father. And every Latter-day Saint has started out for that—the obtaining of eternal life, and the greatest degree of glory that can be obtained in the celestial kingdom. Then to obtain this I say that the full and perfect law of the Father must be observed. We are to be rewarded for our works. We must earn what we obtain." *The Year of Jubilee: A Full Report of the Proceedings of the Fiftieth Annual Conference of the Church of Jesus Christ of Latter-day Saints, Held in the Large Tabernacle, Salt Lake City, Utah, April 6th, 7th and 8th, A. D. 1880; Also a Report of the Exercises in the Salt Lake Assembly Hall, on the Sunday and Monday Just Preceding the Conference*, vol. 1 (Salt Lake City: Deseret News Printing and Publishing Establishment, 1897), 47.

simply to accept their parents' religion, but to *love* it. In Solzhenitsyn's Nobel lecture he noted, "In vain does one repeat what the heart does not find sweet."[37] Mormons repeat what they are taught because they have been trained to find it sweet. One major reason for this is the sense of community shared by those within the movement—a strange antidote to the individualism in which the movement was birthed. The Latter Day Saints look after each other, put a high premium on loyalty to the extended family, practice hospitality in one another's homes, and intentionally structure their parishes in a way to facilitate a sense of community among their members. Children growing up in this environment simply do not want to leave it.

The rest of us stand to learn a valuable lesson here. The task of Christian parents is not merely to pass on the truth to their children, but also to show the next generation that the truth is lovely. Many Christian young people have willingly walked away from a faith they once believed to be true because they were enticed by the illusory attractiveness of idols. But few will abandon a faith they believe to be both true *and* beautiful. The deceptiveness of Mormonism is that it is packaged in such a way so that the youth find it beautiful.

QUESTIONS FOR DISCUSSION

1. If a Mormon missionary urges you to read the *Book of Mormon* and pray that the Lord will show you whether it is true, should you do it? How are Paul's comments in Galatians 1:8 relevant here?

2. Had Smith begun his career claiming the types of things he later did in the King Follett discourse, is it likely that as many people would have followed him?

3. Are all men created equal?

4. In matters of theology when, if ever, is it helpful to have a pioneer mentality?

---

37. Aleksandr Isaevich Solzhenitsyn, *The Solzhenitsyn Reader: New and Essential Writings, 1947–2005,* ed. Edward E. Ericson and Daniel J. Mahoney (Wilmington: ISI Books, 2006), 514.

5. Should every Christian interpret the Bible for himself, no matter where this leads?

6. Is it ever appropriate for an evangelist to use psychological manipulation to reach his audience?

7. How does the philosophy of Edmund Burke help us to understand what was wrong with Joseph Smith?

8. Does Irenaeus's teaching about public truth (chapter 2) help to undermine any of Joseph Smith's claims?

9. Why do you think those movements which aimed to strip Christianity of all traditions and creeds often wound up bringing their people into bondage to new sets of traditions?

10. When fourteen-year-old Joseph decided to pray and ask the Lord which church was the correct one, did this reveal a basic misunderstanding of the nature of the church in the first place?

11. Many of Smith's predictions clearly never came true. Does this automatically mean that he was a false prophet by the standard of Deuteronomy 18:22? If so, how does this differ from a prophet like Jonah, who prophesied that Nineveh would be destroyed even though it wasn't? Does Deuteronomy 13:1–5 assist us with this question?

12. Does God still give people prophecies today?

13. What might be some reasons that Christians have such poor success in passing on their faith to the next generation?

14. Is denominational division inevitable within Protestantism? Should this be looked upon as a good thing, a bad thing, or a bad by-product of a good thing? Is there any possible solution?

15. What are some key ways that parents can show their children that the Christian faith is beautiful as well as true?

PERSONAL CHALLENGE

What aspects of Mormonism might you be tempted to find appealing?

CHAPTER 14

CLOTHING TRUTH WITH BEAUTY

The Mythic Vision of George MacDonald (1824–1905)

In 1916, C. S. Lewis was eighteen and preparing to enter the university at Oxford. On a Friday afternoon after a day in town, he stood on a railway platform waiting for the train that would take him back to his lodgings. As Lewis'ss mind was fixed on "the glorious week end of reading"[1] that awaited him, his attention turned naturally to the station's bookstall. On it sat a curious looking volume, an Everyman edition of George MacDonald's novel *Phantastes: A Faerie Romance for Men and Women.*

Having journeyed through this station every week, Lewis had seen this book before but had never decided to buy it. This afternoon as he waited for the train, he picked up the book and took a closer look. At this stage in Lewis's life he was, to use his own term, "waist-deep in Romanticism,"[2] and this book seemed similar to other romantic literature he enjoyed. So he decided to buy it.

---

1. C.S. Lewis, *Surprised by Joy: The Shape of My Early Life* (New York: Harvest Books, 1955), 172.

2. C.S. Lewis, *George Macdonald: An Anthology: 365 Readings* (New York: Touchstone Books, 1996), xxxvii.

That evening, when Lewis opened *Phantastes* and entered into MacDonald's imaginary landscape, he was haunted by the dream-like narrative in which ordinary life becomes transformed into the world of faerie. The story, he later reflected, "had about it a sort of cool, morning innocence, and also, quite unmistakably, a certain quality of Death, *good* Death."[3]

The thick, moving, emotionally-satisfying prose of *Phantastes* conveyed all the qualities that had charmed Lewis in other writers such as Malory, Spenser, and William Morris. Yet MacDonald's story also contained something more that he couldn't quite put his finger on. "It is as if I were carried sleeping across the frontier, or as if I had died in the old country and could never remember how I came alive in the new."

Lewis was later able to convey something of this feeling in his story *The Lion, the Witch and the Wardrobe* when he described the Pevensie children first hearing the name of Aslan:

> None of the children knew who Aslan was . . . but the moment the Beaver had spoken these words everyone felt quite differ-ent. Perhaps it has sometimes happened to you in a dream that someone says something which you don't understand but in the dream it feels as if it had some enormous meaning . . . so beautiful that you remember it all your life.[4]

Though the young Lewis felt that *Phantastes* had some enormous meaning, there was one problem: at the time he was an atheist and MacDonald was a Christian. Initially, MacDonald's theism was merely an annoyance to the young Lewis, who felt "it was a pity he had that bee in his bonnet about Christianity. He was good *in spite of it.*"[5] As he grew and read more of MacDonald's writings, however, Lewis eventually came to understand that the peculiar quality he encountered in *Phantastes* was not separate from MacDonald's faith, but a *result* of it. "I did not yet know (and I was long in learning) the

---

3. Ibid., xxxviii.

4. C.S. Lewis, *The Lion, the Witch and the Wardrobe* (London: HarperCollins Children's Books, 2011), 76–77.

5. Lewis, *Surprised by Joy, 206.*

name of the new quality, the bright shadow, that rested on the travels of Anodos. I do now. It was Holiness."[6]

In his autobiography *Surprised by Joy*, Lewis said that his discovery of MacDonald baptized his imagination. It would be many years before his intellect would follow. Nevertheless, that afternoon at the station represented the beginning of the slow and twisted spiritual journey that would eventually culminate in Lewis's conversion to Christ. When Lewis did convert, he looked upon MacDonald as his spiritual master, saying, "I know hardly any other writer who seems to be closer, or more continually close, to the Spirit of Christ Himself.... I have never concealed the fact that I regarded him as my master."[7]

FATHERHOOD AT THE CORE

George MacDonald was born in Huntly Scotland on December 10, 1824, the second son of his parents' nine children. His boyhood was a happy one, filled with rural fun and boyish adventures.

His father, a hard-working farmer and miller, was the most lasting influence on George's life. A strict disciplinarian when filial obedience was in question, he nevertheless turned a blind eye to his sons' frequent mischief and escapades. Though life on the family farm was difficult and at times stressful, the senior MacDonald was a man of exuberant joy, deep personal faith, and an abiding concern for the spiritual welfare of his nine children. George learned much about the Lord, not so much from what his father said (though his enthusiastic retellings of Bible stories left a lasting impact on the lad), but from the fruit of the Spirit emanating from his life. C. S. Lewis was hardly exaggerating when he noted that, "An almost perfect relationship with his father was the earthly root of all his wisdom. From his own father, he said, he first learned that Fatherhood must be at the core of the universe."[8]

Through his father and others, George was exposed to the tradition of Celtic folklore and fairy tales. This inspired his imagination in a

---

6. Ibid., 173.
7. Lewis, *George Macdonald: An Anthology*, xxxv–xxxvii.
8. Ibid., xxiii.

way that would later manifest itself in his own fairy tales, together with a strong tendency towards Gaelic mysticism.

George and his brothers spent much of their childhood outdoors, making up imaginary lands and enjoying a close bond with their natural surroundings. One might almost be tempted to describe George's childhood, like his relationship with his father, as being idyllic, were it not for the fact that his mother died when he was eight. Though this left a deep and lasting impression on the sensitive child, the trauma was mitigated by the close bond he enjoyed with his father. It also helped when his father married again to a woman that proved to be the kindest of stepmothers.

Besides his father, the other great influence in George's life was his paternal grandmother, Isabella Robertson MacDonald. After his mother died, Isabella took on a prominent role in the lives of the Mac-Donald children. Isabella was a woman of great piety whom George always respected, yet she was terribly severe. As a young woman she had been responsible for the family joining the dissenting church, which embodied a particularly narrow type of religion which John Piper described as "a certain brand of gloomy, lifeless Calvinism."[9] The prevailing outlook saw God as fundamentally a God of wrath. Although salvation was technically by grace, you could only know if you were among the elect through a strenuous program of good works. MacDonald scholar Kerry Dearborn tells how this "produced a great sobriety in religion that distrusted the imagination, frowned on the arts (especially theatre and music) and enforced a strict Sabbatarianism."[10] Grandmother MacDonald even burnt the violin belonging to George's uncle, lest it lead young men "beyond reach of the Divine Grace."[11] When he later described a character based on his grandmother in his novel *Robert Falconer*, MacDonald wrote that "frivolity . . . was in her eyes a vice; loud laughter almost a crime;

9. John Piper, *The Pleasures of God* (Colorado Springs: Multnomah Books, 2000), 168.

10. Kerry Dearborn, *Baptized Imagination: The Theology of George MacDonald* (Burlington: Ashgate Publishing, 2006), 11.

11. Michael R. Phillips, *George MacDonald, Scotland's Beloved Storyteller* (Minneapolis: Bethany House, 1987), 95.

cards, and *novelles,* as she called them, were such in her estimation, as to be beyond my powers of characterization."[12]

The village schoolmaster also embodied this same outlook. An embittered man of almost legendary cruelty, the schoolmaster's whip was said to have been responsible for the death of George's younger brother.

If his grandmother and schoolmaster had been the only influences in his life, George might have turned out quite differently. But while he learned to fear God from his grandmother and schoolmaster, it was from his father that he learned to love Him. From an early age he instinctively felt that his Heavenly Father could not be less loving and good than his earthly father, and he struggled to reconcile what he was taught about God with what he knew of his father.

FROM STUDENT TO TUTOR

MacDonald's love of nature led to an interest in science. When he was sixteen he won a scholarship to study natural science at King's College, Aberdeen. During his university days, MacDonald was known to exhibit the same qualities that would forever characterize his life. His fellow student Robert Troup wrote that "he was studious, quiet, sensitive, imaginative, frank, open, speaking freely what he thought. His love of truth was intense, only equaled by his scorn of meanness, his purity and his moral courage."[13]

During his college days MacDonald discovered books by poets such as Chaucer as well as the type of German romances that would later exercise such a formative role on his own fantasy works. His childhood exposure to the tradition of Gaelic folklore had helped to birth in him a Celtic mysticism that found much common ground with German Romantic authors such as Novalis and Hoffmann. As a result of these books, MacDonald's interest began to shift from science to the imagination, although he always retained a keen interest in the workings of the natural world. Even so, he continued with his

---

12. George MacDonald, *Robert Falconer,* Christian Classics Ethereal Library, http://www.ccel.org/ccel/macdonald/rfalconer.html (accessed January 9, 2012).

13. Greville Macdonald, *George Macdonald and His Wife* (London: G. Allen & Unwin, 1924), 76.

scientific studies and graduated in April 1845 with a master's degree in chemistry and natural philosophy (physics).

Originally MacDonald intended to go on and study medicine. However, because he lacked funds to study under the best doctors, he chose to take on work as a tutor while he decided what to do next. With the help of a family friend, he secured a position in London.

MacDonald's student years had also given rise to a gradually deepening crisis of faith. His reading of poetry and the German romances had stirred his imagination with images of loveliness, while his close affinity with the natural world constantly fed a deep attraction for things of beauty. This, however, seemed at odds with the religion of his upbringing, which he associated not with beauty but with ugliness. He no doubt spoke of his own childhood impressions when he later wrote that the fictional Robert Falconer felt that church was "weariness to every inch of flesh upon his bone."[14] In his novel *David Elginbrod,* he would go so far as to suggest sarcastically that the Scottish reformers had purposely attempted to create ugly models of worship:

> One grand aim of the reformers of the Scottish ecclesiastical modes appears to have been to keep the worship pure and the worshippers sincere, by embodying the whole in the ugliest forms that could be associated with the name of Christianity.[15]

This created a dichotomy in MacDonald's mind between beauty and faith, religion and loveliness. MacDonald was helped to bridge this gulf by reading the Bible, as well as Christian poets such as George Herbert and Henry Vaughan. The more he read, the more he saw that his religious and poetic sides were not in competition with each other but were actually complementary. Writing to his father in April 1847, he confessed, "One of my greatest difficulties in consenting to think of religion was that I thought I should have to give up my

14. MacDonald, *Robert Falconer.*
15. George MacDonald, *David Elginbrod,* Christian Classics Ethereal Library, http://www.ccel.org/ccel/macdonald/elginbrod.toc.html (accessed January 9, 2012).

beautiful thoughts and love for the things God has made."[16] He went on to say how reading the Bible was changing his perspective:

> I love my Bible more, I am always finding out something new in it. I seem to have had everything to learn over from the beginning. Imust get it all from the Bible again...if [the gospel of Jesus] be true, everything in the universe is glorious, except sin...Religion must pervade everything—absorb everything into itself. To the perfectly holy mind, everything is religion. It seems to glorify everything...I find that the happiness spring-ing from all things not in themselves sinful is much increased by religion. God is the God of the beautiful, Religion the love of the Beautiful, and Heaven the House of the Beautiful—na-ture is tenfold brighter in the sun of Righteousness, and my love of nature is more intense since I became a Christian—if indeed I am one.[17]

MacDonald came to understand that his imagination and love of beauty were not separate from his relationship with Christ but integrally connected to it. In her book *Baptized Imagination: The Theology of George MacDonald,* Kerry Dearborn describes how

> [r]ather than viewing the imagination and the arts as satanic snares, MacDonald began to consider them as intimately con-nected with God's good creation. . . . he not only saw the imagi-nation's potential to harmonize with God's creative ways, but also to convey something of God's nature.[18]

MacDonald would later express this understanding in his book *England's Antiphon,* in which he put forward what Dearborn has called "the basic interconnectedness of theology and poetry."[19] As this harmony began to unfold in his thinking, he increasingly began

---

16. Macdonald, *George Macdonald and His Wife,* 108.

17. George MacDonald, *An Expression of Character: The Letters of George Mac-donald* (Grand Rapids: Eerdmans Publishing Company, 1994), 17–18.

18. Dearborn, *Baptized Imagination,* 18–19.

19. Ibid., 27.

to consider a career, not in science, but in the pulpit where he could point others to God.

During his years as a tutor in London, MacDonald made the acquaintance of Louisa Powell, the daughter of a prosperous leather merchant. As the pair shared poetry together and corresponded about the Lord, they developed a deep love for one another. They were engaged to be married in 1848, the same year MacDonald entered a Congregationalist seminary in the city to prepare for the ministry.

FROM PASTOR TO NOVELIST

With a background in science, some writers have puzzled as to why MacDonald decided to enter the ministry. The reason seems to be that he felt a genuine call to preach the message of God's Fatherhood in opposition to what he believed were monstrous ideas about God that were circulating at the time. One such idea was a particularly extreme theory of substitutionary atonement, which MacDonald believed turned God into a vindictive abuser not unlike his boyhood schoolmaster.

In reacting against the crude atonement theology of Scottish Presbyterianism, MacDonald often lapsed into **semipelagian** views of salvation[20] as well as **universalism**. Though he passionately believed that all things would eventually be reconciled to God through Christ, he distanced himself from **syncretistic** views of universalism that were gaining ground at the time among Unitarians. Such views bypassed the work of Christ and diminished the reality of God's wrath. MacDonald not only believed in God's wrath, but in his *Unspoken Sermons,* he wrote about hell in terrifying terms. Yet he believed that even God's wrath was an expression of His love—a love that would not rest content until He had put everything to rights. Following church fathers like Origen (c. 185–254) and Gregory of Nyssa (c. 335–390s), he taught that hell is a temporary purifying process culminating in the reconciliation of all to God in Christ.

20. See Robin Phillips, "George Macdonald and the Anthropology of Love *North Wind: A Journal of George MacDonald Studies* 30 (2011).

When his seminary training was finished in 1850, he accepted a pulpit at Arundel, a small village in the South Downs of West Sussex. That same year he and Louisa were married.

In his biography *George MacDonald and His Wife*, MacDonald's oldest son Greville wrote, "Those were happy days indeed, with plenty to do among a people, simple, eager to learn, and very grateful."[21] Unfortunately, these happy days were not to last. MacDonald's ministry as a pastor was cut abruptly short in 1853 after some of the church's more wealthy patrons decided that his theology was not sufficiently orthodox. It is uncertain exactly what the issues were, but Greville mentions that his father's position on Sabbath-keeping together with his views that animals would share in the afterlife, caused particular consternation. To make matters worse, MacDonald had translated into English some poems by the German Romanticist Novalis and in those days anything coming from Germany was considered (not without some warrant) to be unorthodox. However, the most likely explanation is that the wealthy deacons were deeply uncomfortable with the young minister's denunciation of mammon-worship, cruelty, and self-seeking.

At first the church's patrons tried to induce MacDonald to leave by radically cutting his salary. This was a great hardship to him and Louisa, who now had an infant daughter to support. However, the peasants of the village rose to the occasion, making up for their cut in income by bringing the family fresh fruit, cauliflowers, potatoes, home-brewed beer, and other simple gifts.

Eventually, the dissension grew too great and MacDonald was forced to resign to preserve the peace of the congregation. The family moved to Manchester and then London, where MacDonald took whatever work he could find, mostly teaching and lecturing. (Because of his asthma, he was never able to permanently return to the cold, damp climate of his beloved Scotland, though he always remained a Scotsman at heart.) Despite MacDonald's abilities, he had trouble finding permanent work. It was often challenging to determine where the next meal would come from.

In an attempt to generate some much-needed income, MacDonald decided to begin writing. His first publication was an epic poem

21. Macdonald, *George Macdonald and His Wife*, 154.

he had composed some years earlier titled *Within and Without*. Although the work did not generate enough income to feed the family, it did bring him to the attention of Lady Byron, the widow of Lord Byron. In the winter of 1856, as the family was facing poverty, Lady Byron decided to become MacDonald's patron. This helped the family to survive until the writing began to support them. Lady Byron also made it possible for the family to spend time in Algiers, Italy where the change of climate greatly restored MacDonald's health.

His next book was *Phantastes: A Faerie Romance for Men and Women*. Though this book suggested that his talents lay in the genre of fantasy, his publisher urged him to try his hand at novels. "If you would but write novels," he said, "you would find all the publishers saving up to buy them of you! Nothing but fiction pays."[22] MacDonald took the advice and five years after the publication of *Phantastes* he published *David Elginbrod*, a novel inspired by the life of his father. For the rest of his career MacDonald wrote approximately one novel a year.

His reasons for writing novels were not entirely economic. His son Greville noted that the world was sorely in need of his message and that his father hoped the novels would provide more scope for getting this message across.

Though his novels were received with increasing enthusiasm by the public, he still had to take a variety of other jobs to support his family. These jobs included lecturing in science and English literature, editing a magazine for children, and even work as a professional dramatist with other members of his family. He also spent time substitute preaching but never accepted any money for it. It was not until his career was at its height in the 1870s that the family was finally free of their financial hardships. (In part this was due to the existence of so many pirated versions of his books. He did not receive royalties from many of the American editions, even though they were best sellers.)

But why were MacDonald's novels so popular? As works of literature, they can hardly be considered great and often suffer from being heavy and didactic. So what was it about them that struck such a chord for Christians in the latter half of the nineteenth century?

22. Ibid., 318.

MAKING GOODNESS ATTRACTIVE

MacDonald thought of his novels as an extension of his failed pulpit ministry. As such, they convey to us that righteousness is attractive. MacDonald retained the strong emphasis on good works that was a prominent feature of the Scottish non-conformists, but unlike the dour moralism of his grandmother, he showed that obedience to Christ is lovely. John Piper, while questioning certain aspects of MacDonald's theology in his book *The Pleasures of God*, nevertheless spoke for many when he noted that MacDonald's stories inspire us by a "new zeal to be pure," holding out to us models of "radical commitment" to Christ.[23] The protagonists in his novels demonstrate what it means to breathe grace in the midst of conflict, to give charitably in the midst of poverty, to model Christ's love in the midst of suspicion and mistrust, to bring hope in the midst of suffering, and to live according to Christ's commands in the midst of hypocrisy, compromise, and self-centeredness.

While MacDonald's characters constantly remind us that nothing is as important as doing our duty in the next five minutes, his characters also show us that there is nothing quite so exciting. In this he paved the way for apologists like G. K. Chesterton and Dorothy Sayers, who were likewise concerned to defend Christianity as much from the charge of tedium as from the charge of falsehood.

The ability to make goodness attractive is also a dominant feature of MacDonald's fantastical works. While his fairy tales take us into dream-worlds full of strange creatures and fantastic occurrences, they are not escapist, for they help us to view the real world, and our role in it, with greater clarity, insight, and wonder. "Not only can fairy tales be enjoyed because they are moral," G. K. Chesterton once noted, "but morality can be enjoyed because it puts us in fairyland, in a world at once of wonder and war."[24] This is exactly what MacDonald's stories do for us. After accompanying Mr. Vane through the mysterious landscape of *Lilith,* following Diamond's travels with Lady North Wind in *At the Back of the North Wind,* or journeying with Curdie to Gwyntystorm in *The Princess and Curdie,* we begin to see the mystery and enchantment with which the "real

---

23. Piper, *The Pleasures of God,* 167.
24. G. K. Chesterton, *All Things Considered* (London: Methuen, 1908), 258.

world" has been infused. We begin to feel that the world of Faerie, as MacDonald liked to spell it, has invaded the world of men or as Chesterton put it when writing about MacDonald, that "the fairy-tale was the inside of the ordinary story and not the outside."[25] His mythic vision, encapsulated in his fantastic works, invites us to see the world not primarily as facts but as a wonderful story in which we are participants.

This is what C. S. Lewis discovered in MacDonald and why it helped to nudge him away from the materialism of his atheistic worldview. "The quality which had enchanted me in his imaginative works," Lewis wrote in his anthology of MacDonald's works, "turned out to be the quality of the real universe, the divine, magical, terrifying and ecstatic reality in which we all live."[26] MacDonald himself articulated something like this in the essay "A Sketch of Individual Development" in his book *A Dish of Orts*. Here he suggests that our world is every bit as magical, every bit as wonderful, and every bit as enchanted as the world of Fairyland. In the same work he goes on to write movingly about what happens when "the world begins to come alive around [a person]:"[27]

> He begins to feel that the stars are strange, that the moon is sad, that the sunrise is mighty. He begins to see in them all the something men call beauty. He will lie on the sunny bank and gaze into the blue heaven till his soul seems to float abroad and mingle with the infinite made visible, with the boundless condensed into colour and shape. The rush of the water through the still twilight, under the faint gleam of the exhausted west, makes in his ears a melody he is almost aware he cannot understand.[28]

Here MacDonald was on common ground with nineteenth-century romantics like Wordsworth and Tennyson, who also saw the world

25. G. K. Chesterton, *In Defense of Sanity: The Best Essays of G.K. Chesterton* (San Franscisco: Ignatius Press, 2011), 303.

26. Lewis, *George Macdonald: An Anthology*, xxxviii.

27. George MacDonald, *A Dish of Orts: Chiefly Papers on the Imagination, and on Shakespeare* (London: Sampson, Low, Marston, 1893), 49.

28. Ibid.

as pervaded with spirituality. Yet MacDonald goes one step further. He showed that it is *goodness* which infuses our world with meaning and makes it beautiful. In contrast both to the prosaic moralism of his grandmother, which sucked all beauty out of goodness, as well as the subjective sentimentalism of the Romantic movement, which untethered beauty from its foundations in objective goodness, MacDonald showed that beauty and objective goodness cannot be separated. It is precisely this that makes his works so appealing. "I should have been shocked in my 'teens," wrote C. S. Lewis, "if anyone had told me that what I learned to love in *Phantastes* was goodness. But now that I know, I see there was no deception. The deception is all the other way round—in that prosaic moralism which confines goodness to the region of Law and Duty, which never lets us feel in our face the sweet air blowing from 'the land of righteousness,' never reveals that elusive Form which if once seen must inevitably be desired with all but sensuous desire."[29]

THE MACDONALD FAMILY

Though MacDonald could be serious at times, haunted with melancholy moods, he maintained a jovial and humorous atmosphere for his family. The MacDonald home was always lively, full of love, games (charades was one of his favorites), drama, music, and—when they could afford it—generous hospitality to other families. Despite his busy writing schedule, MacDonald was never too busy to delight in the unique personality of each of his children, to assist Louisa with the homeschooling, and to play with his children (he especially enjoyed imagining fairy lands with them). The family also enjoyed many hours of acting together and even began to professionally perform some of Shakespeare's plays, *Pilgrim's Progress,* and some fairy tales.

Despite their poverty, George and Louisa did what they could to give their children a rich upbringing, filled with the same joy, love, and freshness that permeated MacDonald's writings. Through their parents, the children came to know many of the leading literary figures of Victorian England, including Charles Kingsley, Frederick

29. George MacDonald, *Lilith: A Romance* (Grand Rapids: Wm. B. Eerdmans Publishing, 1981), xii.

Maurice, John Ruskin, and Charles Dodgson. (Dodgson, whose pen name was "Lewis Carroll," first tested his *Alice in Wonderland* on the MacDonald children when trying to decide whether it was good enough to publish.)

Even more importantly, the children received the same type of love and discipline from their father that he had received from his. They, in turn, were able to pass onto their own children this same simple, childlike trust in God's Fatherhood. One of the ways MacDonald passed this vision on to his children was, of course, through his teachings, but even more important was the example of his own life. "There has probably never been a writer whose work was a better expression of his personal character," wrote his son Ronald in *From a Northern Window*.[30]

When their children were grown, George and Louisa remained close to each of them. The letters they exchanged show that MacDonald maintained a deep concern for each of their spiritual lives. Even after they had moved away from home, the children would often write to their father to ask him questions about God, love, and life. In one letter, answering questions that his daughter "Elfie" (the nickname for his daughter Mary) had asked him about love, he ended by replying, "Ask me anything you like, and I will try to answer you—if I know the answer. For this is one of the most important things I have to do in the world." Elsewhere in the same letter he encouraged Elfie by reminding her that

> God is so beautiful, and so patient, and so loving, and so generous that he is the heart & soul & rock of every love & every kindness & every gladness in the world. All the beauty in the world & in the hearts of men, all the painting all the poetry all the music, all the architecture comes out of his heart first. He is so loveable that no heart can know how loveable he is—can only know in part. When the best loves God best, he does not love him nearly as he deserves, or as he will love him in time.[31]

30. Ronald MacDonald, *From a Northern Window: A Personal Reminiscence of George MacDonald by His Son* (Eureka: Sunrise Books, 1989), 24.

31. MacDonald, *An Expression of Character*, 170.

Perhaps the greatest testimony to MacDonald's life is the fact that his children picked up and carried on the same vision of God that he had labored to articulate throughout his writings.[32]

By 1872 MacDonald had developed such a reputation that he was able to cash in on the American lecture circuit. Taking with him Louisa and Greville, he remained in America for nine months, travelling as far west as Chicago and as far north as Canada. MacDonald was an instant hit, lecturing on the Romantic poets (the Americans derived particular satisfaction on hearing him discourse on Robert Burns), Dante, Shakespeare, Chaucer, and Milton. Sometimes his audiences would reach into the thousands. Famous American writers paid him homage, including Ralph Waldo Emerson, Henry Wadsworth Longfellow, John Greenleaf Whittier, Oliver Wendell Holmes, and Mark Twain. So admired was MacDonald by the Americans that they tried to keep him in the country by offering him a pastorate for a Fifth Avenue church in New York for $20,000 a year—an unheard-of sum in those days. Throughout the trip, however, the MacDonalds' greatest joy was meeting the ordinary people who had been inspired to deeper faith and obedience through George's novels.

FINAL DAYS

One of MacDonald's final books, *Lilith*, drew on the fruits of his mature imagination. Filled with what Greville called "symbolic allusiveness," the narrative is haunting and obscure, dealing with ultimate themes of death and redemption. While this is probably MacDonald's most respected work, his own wife Louisa was troubled by the book's dark imagery. MacDonald began to doubt his literary abilities and it was only after Greville read some drafts and gave a

---

32. The following quotation from Greville MacDonald shows the extent that MacDonald's poetic understanding etched itself deep into his children's consciousness: "So the immanence of God is the secret of all Beauty, and God is knowable to us only through Beauty. Human fatherhood invites the imagining of the Divine Fatherhood; man's power over the world and its forces implies a personal power, immeasurably mighty, in the Creator; Man's love, faithful to the death, makes possible the belief in that Spirit Who so loved the world that, through vicarious suffering, He is saving it" (Macdonald, *George Macdonald and His Wife*, 551).

positive verdict that husband and wife were both happy for the book to proceed.

In 1900, five years after the publication of *Lilith,* MacDonald suffered a stroke and permanently lost the ability to speak. He spent the last five years of his life in virtual silence, peacefully waiting to pass from this life and meet his Master. To the very end, his family tenderly cared for him, especially after Louisa passed away in 1902. The death of Louisa came as a great blow to MacDonald, and though he couldn't speak a word, he wept bitterly when the news was communicated to him.

The following words, written in 1880, shortly after the deaths of two of his children, describe the feeling of expectation that must have also given him peace in his silent vigil as he waited to meet his Maker and be reunited with his wife:

> Yet hints come to me from the realm unknown;
> Airs drift across the twilight border-land,
> Odoured with life; and, as from some far strand
> Sea-murmured, whispers to my heart are blown
> That fill me with a joy I cannot speak.[33]

THE LEGACY OF GEORGE MACDONALD

At a time when the Industrial Revolution was reducing people to machines and driving people into depression, when the world seemed bleak and wonderless, MacDonald bequeathed to us an opposite vision. His was a universe filled with enchantment, saturated in wonder, and infused with grace. It was a sacramental vision that drew heavily on the Middle Ages, especially the medieval notion that the external things surrounding us are outward signs of inward spiritual graces. As MacDonald expressed it in *The Miracles of Our Lord,* "With his divine alchemy, [God] turns not only water into wine, but common things into radiant mysteries, yea, every meal into a Eucharist, and the jaws of death into an outgoing gate."[34]

---

33. George MacDonald, *The Diary of an Old Soul* (Minneapolis: Augsburg Publishing House, 1975), 57.

34. George MacDonald, "The Miracles of Our Lord," Project Gutenberg, http://www.gutenberg.org/ebooks/9103 (accessed February 16, 2012).

His novels conveyed this sacramental vision. Although they may technically fall under the category of "realistic fiction," there was always something fantastic about them. The literary critic Marion Lochhead has compared them to Hans Andersen's fairy tales in possessing "the gift of turning homeliness into beauty."[35]

In his book *Saint Francis of Assisi,* G. K. Chesterton noted that Francis "was a poet whose whole life was a poem. He was not so much a minstrel merely singing his own songs as a dramatist capable of acting the whole of his own play."[36] Chesterton might just as well have been talking about George MacDonald, and it was not without warrant that when he came to write the introduction to *George MacDonald and His Wife,* Chesterton referred to MacDonald as the "St. Francis of Aberdeen." MacDonald, like Saint Francis, was gifted with the ability to see "the same sort of halo round every flower and bird."[37] This sacramental vision represented what Scottish religion would have been if it had continued within the template of Scottish medieval poetry—a religion which, to quote Chesterton again, "competed with the beauty and vividness of the passions, which did not let the devil have all the bright colours, which fought glory with glory and flame with flame."[38]

C. S. Lewis and G. K. Chesterton were not the only authors who drank deeply from the wells of MacDonald's sacramental vision. Frances Hodgson Burnett, Lewis Carroll, E. Nesbit, J. R. R. Tolkien, and Madeleine L'Engle are among those touched by him. But his influence stretches beyond specific individuals, for he pioneered what Marion Lochhead has called "a renaissance of wonder in books for children." He also brought respectability to the genre of the adult fantasy, laying groundwork for what would later reach fruition in Tolkien's masterpiece, *The Lord of the Rings.*

MacDonald left behind over fifty books, representing the extraordinary breadth of his interests. His corpus includes poetry, literary criticism, novels, fantasies, essays, plays, and theology. Until the end of the nineteenth century, he was a household name in the United

35. Marion Lochhead, *The Renaissance of Wonder in Children's Literature* (Edinburgh: Canongate, 1977), 2.

36. G. K. Chesterton, *Saint Francis of Assisi* (New York: Image Books, 1957), 89.

37. MacDonald, *George Macdonald and His Wife,* 14.

38. Ibid., 13–14.

Kingdom and even in America he enjoyed a popularity that was perhaps only rivaled by Dickens and Scott. Although *Phantastes, Lilith, At the Back of the North Wind,* and the Curdie books have remained enduring classics, most of his other writings fell into neglect until the first half of the twentieth century. In the early 1980s, his novels again became bestsellers after this author's own father, Michael Phillips, edited eighteen of them for Bethany House Publishers.

C. S. Lewis's words about MacDonald's *Unspoken Sermons* remain the testimony of countless others: "My own debt to this book is almost as great as one man can owe to another: and nearly all serious inquirers to whom I have introduced it acknowledge that it has given them great help—sometimes indispensable help toward the very acceptance of the Christian faith."[39]

LESSONS FROM THE LIFE OF GEORGE MACDONALD

One important lesson we learn from MacDonald is that beauty was never meant to be an end in itself, but something that points us beyond the universe to God and His goodness. In failing to discern God's goodness behind beauty, many of the English Romantic poets never went far enough. John Keats' poem "Ode on a Grecian Urn" exemplifies this:

> Beauty is truth, truth beauty,—that is all
> Ye know on earth, and all ye need to know.[40]

By contrast, MacDonald taught that there was something more we needed to know, namely that there is an ultimate Source from which all beauty springs. Though he didn't conflate truth and beauty as Keats did, he agreed that they were connected and spoke of hoping "for endless forms of beauty informed of truth."[41] The connection between truth and beauty arose by virtue of each having their home in God. As MacDonald wrote in his poem "A Book of Dreams," "God's

---

39. Lewis, *George Macdonald: An Anthology,* xxxiv.
40. Sir Arthur Quiller-Couch, ed., *The Oxford Book of English Verse 1250–1918, New Edition.* (Oxford: Oxford University Press, 1939), 730.
41. MacDonald, *Orts,* 25.

heart is the fount of beauty."[42] He took up this same theme later in some of the essays in *A Dish of Orts*. In an essay on Wordsworth's poetry he wrote,

> Let us go further; and, looking at beauty, believe that God is the first of artists; that he has put beauty into nature, knowing how it will affect us, and intending that it should so affect us that he has embodied his own grand thoughts thus that we might see them and be glad.[43]

A lesson related to this is the interconnectedness of goodness, truth, and beauty. The Calvinism of MacDonald's upbringing had been mediated through a dry rationalism that fixated on the legal categories but had little room for beauty and imagination. But truth without beauty was regretful to MacDonald, who once wrote that, "beauty is the only stuff in which Truth can be clothed."[44] Yet Mac-Donald also rejected the sentimentalism of the English Romantics who landed in the opposite ditch by emphasizing beauty without any ultimate truth behind it. In one of his sonnets he spoke of the unfortunate disconnect between beauty and truth among those that cared little for the latter:

> From the beginning good and fair are one,
> But men the beauty from the truth will part,
> And, though the truth is ever beauty's heart,
> After the beauty will, short-breathed, run,
> And the indwelling truth deny and shun.[45]

42. George MacDonald, *A Hidden Life and Other Poems* (Rockville: Prime Classics Library, 2004), 82.

43. MacDonald, *Orts*, 246–247.

44. Ibid., 315.

45. George MacDonald, *The Poetical Works of George Macdonald* (London: Chatto & Windus, 1893), 259. While MacDonald saw goodness, truth, and beauty as intimately related, he also recognized that in a fallen world beauty can sometimes distract people from imbibing what is true and good. Thus, in the rest of the sonnet just cited, he goes on to describe how God's words came to man "in common speech, not art" and that "for Truth's sake even [beauty's] forms thou didst disown:/ Ere, through the love of beauty, truth shall fail." As important as

MacDonald understood that in Christ, truth and beauty were as integrally connected as goodness and beauty. The interconnectedness between the trinity of goodness, truth, and beauty meant that to separate any of these three was to do violence to the others. In this he anticipated the thought of the twentieth century Roman Catholic theologian Hans Urs von Balthasar, who wrote,

> We no longer dare to believe in beauty and we make of it a mere appearance in order the more easily to dispose of it. Our situation today shows that beauty demands for itself at least as much courage and decision as do truth and goodness, and she will not allow herself to be separated and banned from her two sisters without taking them along with herself in an act of mysterious vengeance.[46]

Such mysterious vengeance occurred when, around the end of MacDonald's life, the Romantic movement trailed off into obscuration and perversity. With prophetic insight he had inadvertently predicted this in his essay, "A Sketch of Individual Development," when he observed that "the soul departs from the face of beauty, when the eye begins to doubt if there be any soul behind it."

In some of MacDonald's fairy tales he explores what happens when beauty becomes disconnected from goodness and truth. The characters of Lilith in his book *Lilith* or the Alder tree in *Phantastes* give a stark portrayal of beauty disengaged from goodness and truth. This was also a theme that MacDonald explored in one of his sonnets:

> Men may pursue the Beautiful, while they
> Love not the Good, the life of all the Fair;
> Keen-eyed for beauty, they will find it where
> The darkness of their eyes hath power to slay
> The vision of the good in beauty's ray,
> Though fruits the same life-giving branches bear.[47]

---

beauty was to MacDonald, he was ever ready to discard it if it got in the way of people following the truth in Jesus.

46. Hans Urs von Balthasar, *The Glory of the Lord: A Theological Aesthetics* (San Francisco: Ignatius Press, 1989), 18.

47. George MacDonald, *Poems* (London: Longman, Brown, Green, Longmans, & Roberts, 1857), 301.

Thirdly, MacDonald helps us to understand the role that beauty plays in education. Echoing Plato, who once observed that the object of education is to make us love what is beautiful, MacDonald understood that if the good and the true are not clothed in beauty, they will have little formative influence on the human person. More recently, Stratford Caldecott took up the same theme in his book *Beauty for Truth's Sake,* noting that "beauty is the radiance of the true and the good, and it is what attracts us to both."[48]

Fourthly, MacDonald helps us to understand that suffering can be redemptive. His was not an easy life. Providing for eleven children was always a great weight on his mind, even after his books began to sell. Witnessing the death of four of his children was even harder. MacDonald also experienced physical suffering, struggling all his life with eczema, asthma, and bronchitis. Moreover, he often experienced periods of intense doubt, depression, and dryness. However, throughout all these trials, he retained a childlike trust in God, believing that his heavenly Father was using everything that happened to him—including the challenging circumstances—to make him more like Jesus. This perspective helped him to see his periods of spiritual dryness as gifts sent for the perfecting of his faith. "That man is perfect in faith," he once wrote, "who can come to God in the utter dearth of his feelings and desires, without a glow or an aspiration, with the weight of low thoughts, failures, neglects, and wandering forgetfulness, and say to Him, 'Thou art my refuge.'"[49]

QUESTIONS FOR DISCUSSION

1. "Truth and beauty are distinguishable but not divisible." Discuss.

2. If we say that all of life is in some way "sacramental," does this diminish the important of the specific biblical sacraments of baptism and the Eucharist?

48. Stratford Caldecott, *Beauty for Truth's Sake: On the Re-enchantment of Education,* 1st ed. (Grand Rapids: Brazos Press, 2009), 31.
49. Lewis, *George Macdonald: An Anthology,* 1.

3. Hans von Balthasar wrote that "beauty demands for itself at least as much courage and decision as do truth and goodness."[50] What might he have meant by it and how might this be applied in our own lives?

4. In his novel *David Elginbrod,* MacDonald describes the experience he has as a child of feeling that he didn't want God to love him unless God loved all people. Does God love everyone? If God loves every person, then would it follow that every person would have to be saved?

5. Some historians have argued that the Romantic movement was doomed to failure from its outset. How does MacDonald's philosophy of beauty help us to see why such an assessment may be correct?

6. Is the genre of fantastic literature as important for adults as it is for children? Why or why not?

7. If someone disagrees that Christianity is true, you can try to persuade the person by having a debate. But if someone does not perceive the Christian faith as being lovely, what can be done to show the person otherwise?

8. MacDonald's writings often drift towards theological liberalism. Because of this, some Christians think we should stay away from his writings. Is this an appropriate position to adopt? How much error can be permitted before we consider a writer to be a false teacher?

9. Is the following a true statement: "The worldview we adopt with our mind tends to follow those images of the good life that have first captivated our hearts"? If so, then what are the implications for Christian nurture and discipleship?

10. What are some examples of truth without beauty? What are some examples of goodness without truth? What are some examples of beauty without goodness? What are some examples of goodness without beauty?

---

50. Urs von Balthasar, *The Glory of the Lord,* 18.

11. MacDonald complained that the church services he was used to were ugly. How important is it that our worship of God be beautiful?

PERSONAL CHALLENGE

Has the Lord ever used periods of spiritual dryness to strengthen your own faith?

CHAPTER 15

LIVING A LIFE OF COSTLY GRACE

The Gratefulness of Dietrich Bonhoeffer (1906–1945)

On February 4, 1906, Dietrich Bonhoeffer was born in Breslau, Germany (now part of Poland). Dietrich and his twin sister, Sabine, were two of eight children born to Karl and Paula Bonhoeffer. At the age of fourteen, Dietrich surprised his parents by announcing his intention to become a theologian. Eight years later, at twenty-one, he received his doctorate in theology from the University of Berlin. Too young to be ordained in Germany, Bonhoeffer accepted a post as curate for a German community in Barcelona, Spain. Though he was invited to stay for a second year, he chose to resume his studies at the University of Berlin. The following year he went to New York as an exchange student at Union Theological Seminary.

The experience in America had a profound effect on the young minister, especially after being introduced by a fellow student to the Abyssinian Baptist Church—a passionate African-American church in Harlem, New York. With their emphasis on social engagement, the African-American community helped Bonhoeffer appreciate the need for Christians to work for justice in the world. While this was not a radical idea, it stood in contrast to the church in Europe, which largely accepted the Enlightenment notion that the message of Christ applied only to one's private life, independent of the public world.

Returning to Berlin in 1931, Bonhoeffer was ordained and took up the post of student chaplain. He also worked closely with the poor and impoverished in one of Berlin's worst areas.

THE NAZIFICATION OF THE GERMAN CHURCH

As Bonhoeffer ministered in Berlin, he was shocked to see what was happening around him. Not only was the Nazi movement gathering support from Germany's leading intellectuals, but most of the German church saw Hitler's rise as a good thing.

Hitler won support from traditionalist members of German society by emphasizing family values, encouraging women to stay at home and raise large families, defending German folk traditions against modern influences, being tough on crime, bringing social stability, and by opposing recent innovations like Bolshevism. Moreover, Hitler intentionally appealed to categories Christians were comfortable with in order to make them feel that he was on their side. "The Church's interests," Hitler once said,

> cannot fail to coincide with ours alike in our fight against the symptoms of degeneracy in the world of to-day, in our fight against the Bolshevist culture, against an atheistic movement, against criminality, and in our struggle for the consciousness of a community in our national life, for the conquest of hatred and disunion between the classes, for the conquest of civil war and unrest, of strife and discord. These are not anti-Christian, these are Christian principles.[1]

Though there were many voices of dissent, most of the Christians in Germany not only went along with Hitler's plans but believed that he was indeed championing Christian principles. Thus it was that most of the churches in Germany willingly folded into the Nazi-sponsored German National Church (*Reichskirche*). In his article "Radical Resistance," Dr. Richard V. Pierard explained that

---

1. Adolf Hitler, *The Speeches of Adolf Hitler, April 1922–August 1939* (New York: H. Fertig, 1969), 386–387.

some churchmen even referred to the "turning point in history" where "through God's providence our beloved fatherland has experienced a mighty exaltation." Pastor Siegfried Leffler declared that "in the pitch-black night of church history, Hitler became, as it were, the wonderful transparency for our time, the window of our age, through which light fell on the history of Christianity. Through him we were able to see the Savior in the history of the Germans." Pastor Julius Leutheuser added that "Christ has come to us through Adolf Hitler.[2]

Pastor Julius Leutheuser added that "Christ has come to us through Adolf Hitler.[3] Hermann Grüner, spokesman for the Reichskirche, was even more emphatic:

> The time is fulfilled for the German people in Hitler. It is because of Hitler that Christ, God the helper and redeemer, has become effective among us. Therefore National Socialism is positive Christianity in action. . . . Hitler is the way of the Spirit and the will of God for the German people to enter the Church of Christ.[4]

Bonhoeffer, on the other hand, saw Hitler for what he was from the very beginning and labored tirelessly to restrain the German church from its headlong rush to destruction.

BONHOEFFER AGAINST THE NAZIS

From the fall of 1933 to the spring of 1935, Bonhoeffer removed himself from the growing storm by serving as a pastor of two German-speaking Lutheran congregations in London. Still concerned about his homeland, Bonhoeffer used his radio broadcasts to oppose the anti-Semitism and blasphemy of Nazi ideology. In 1933 a lecture of his

2. Dr. Richard V. Pierard, "Radical Resistance," *Christian History* 32 (1991).
3. Ibid.
4. Ruth A. Tucker, *Parade of Faith: A Biographical History of the Christian Church* (Grand Rapids: Zondervan, 2011), 464.

was broadcast over Berlin radio as Germany was celebrating Hitler's appointment to the position of Chancellor. In it, Bonhoeffer said:

> [S]hould the leader allow himself to succumb to the wishes of those he leads, who will always seek to turn him into an idol, then the image of the leader will become the image of the mis-leader. This is the leader who makes an idol of himself and of his office, and who thus mocks God.[5]

The broadcast was cut off before Bonhoeffer had a chance to finish.

In 1934, while still living in England, Bonhoeffer joined with Karl Barth to organize German pastors who were opposed to the Nazi control of the Lutheran church. (Earlier in his life, Barth's writings had been instrumental in alerting Bonhoeffer to the primacy of God's Word and some of the dangers of Lutheran liberal theology.) This group of pastors became known as the Confessing Church. The Confessing Church was not a resistance movement: its goal was to preserve Christianity in Germany, not to topple Hitler. Of special concern to the group was the mounting racism and the need to offer support to those who were the victims of the state.

At this point in his life, Bonhoeffer was still wrestling through the appropriate Christian response to the growing evil. A friend of his from Union Theological Seminary had persuasively argued that Christ's Sermon on the Mount excluded all forms of fighting. Intrigued by the pacifist solutions to civil injustice, Bonhoeffer prepared to travel to India to study non-violent resistance with Gandhi.

THE SECRET SEMINARY

Bonhoeffer canceled his trip to India when the opportunity arose to form an underground seminary in Germany for the Confessing Church. The seminary was designed to give aspiring ministers a theological education at a time when all the other seminaries had been taken over by the *Reichskirche*. But the school did more than

---

5. Charles Colson and Ellen Santilli Vaughn, *God and Government: An Insider's View on the Boundaries Between Faith and Politics* (Grand Rapids: Zondervan, 2007), 144.

merely train minds: it was an opportunity to put into practice what Bonhoeffer believed to be an essential aspect of the gospel—Christian community.

His views on Christian community again collided with the Enlightenment paradigm that religion is the province of the solitary individual. The church, he believed, is not just a collection of individuals who happen to be Christians, but a new community. "Christ is really present only in the community," he had argued in his doctoral dissertation. "The church is the presence of Christ just as Christ is the presence of God." His thesis had gone on to suggest that in order to be fully human, we must be in relationship with our fellow brothers and sisters in Christ. Bonhoeffer was grieved to see this unity undermined by denominational, economic, and ethnic division within the body of Christ.[6]

The secret seminary at Finkenwalde was a chance for Bonhoeffer to put into practice his ideas about community. Structured around prayer, love, meditation, Bible readings, fraternal service, and deep theological reflection, the small group practiced everything that the Nazis stood against.

The Nazis also claimed to be interested in forming a new community and in finding true humanity through relationships; however, for them salvation lay in one's relationship to the state, and the only community that mattered to them was that of the German people.

CHEAP GRACE

In September 1937, two years after Bonhoeffer had formed the seminary, Hitler's secret police discovered its existence and shut it down. This did not stop Bonhoeffer from continuing to train students, which he did in secret for the next two years in "collective pastorals." However, when Hitler's armies marched on Bohemia and Moravia in 1939, it became clear that Bonhoeffer was no longer safe. Friends made arrangements for him to flee to the United States where he could wait out the rest of the war in safety.

6. Dietrich Bonhoeffer, *A Testament to Freedom: The Essential Writings of Dietrich Bonhoeffer* (New York: HarperOne, 1990) 56–57.

After a brief stay with his friends in New York, Bonhoeffer decided to return to Germany. He believed that if he was to be an effective minister after the war, it would be necessary to stay and suffer with his fellow Germans during their time of trial. The decision would prove costly.

Significantly, in 1939 Bonhoeffer published a book titled *The Cost of Discipleship*, which he had written during his time at Finkenwalde. Based on the Sermon on the Mount, the book sets out the necessary Christian response to a world engulfed in spiritual warfare. "The older the world grows," Bonhoeffer wrote, "the more heated becomes the conflict between Christ and Antichrist, and the more thorough the efforts of the world to get rid of the Christians."[7]

The Cost of Discipleship called Christians to respond to the conflict by abandoning the half-hearted, watered-down versions of the gospel, which he called "cheap grace." "Cheap grace," he wrote, is

> the preaching of forgiveness without requiring repentance, baptism without church discipline, Communion without confession, absolution without personal confession. Cheap grace is grace without discipleship, grace without the cross, grace without Jesus Christ, living and incarnate.[8]

Bonhoeffer sharply contrasted cheap grace with the costly grace presented in the Gospels. Real grace, he wrote,

> is costly because it calls us to follow, and it is grace because it calls us to follow Jesus Christ. It is costly because it costs a man his life, and it is grace because it gives a man the only true life. It is costly because it condemns sin, and grace because it justifies the sinner. Above all, it is costly because it cost God the life of his Son: "ye were bought at a price," and what has cost God much cannot be cheap for us. Above all, it is grace because God did not reckon his Son too great a price to pay

7. Dietrich Bonhoeffer, *The Cost of Discipleship* (New York: Scribner Book Company 1959), 266.
   8. Ibid., 44–45.

for our life, but delivered him up for us. Costly grace is the Incarnation of God.[9]

DOUBLE AGENT

In 1940, Bonhoeffer was recruited into the resistance by his brother-in-law, Hans von Dohnanyi. As an advisor to high government officials, von Dohnanyi had access to the Justice Ministry's most secret documents and knew many of the leading Nazis. As a result of his privileged position, he learned of the heinous crimes being committed by the Nazis against the Jews—atrocities of which many in the military were still ignorant.

Through von Dohnanyi, Bonhoeffer got an opportunity to join the resistance as a "confidential agent" in the *Abwehr* (German military intelligence). Bonhoeffer quickly became a key member of the inner circle of the resistance within the high echelons of the German military. To many in the outside world, however, it appeared that Bonhoeffer had had a change of heart and was now working for the Nazis.

As Bonhoeffer traveled throughout Europe to perform "pastoral visits" and visit his ecumenical contacts, the Nazis believed that he was scouting intelligence information for them. In reality, he was working as a courier and secret diplomat to the British government on behalf of the German resistance.

As a minister, Bonhoeffer also played a key role in helping other members of the resistance to overcome their scruples in breaking the oaths of loyalty they swore before entering the military.

When not traveling on behalf of the resistance, Bonhoeffer stayed in a Benedictine monastery at Ettal and worked on his *Ethics*. In this work, published after his death, Bonhoeffer articulated the theological basis for resistance, based on the fact that the lordship of Christ applies to every sphere of the world, including government.

THE "JULY 20 PLOT" OF 1944

For years the resistance had been conspiring to assassinate the Führer and overthrow the Third Reich. "If we claim to be Christians,"

9. Ibid., 45.

wrote Bonhoeffer, "there is no room for expediency. Hitler is anti-Christ. Therefore we must go on with our work and eliminate him whether he is successful or not."[10]

The resistance made careful plans not only to kill Hitler, but to set up an emergency government that would follow in his wake. To achieve the latter, they needed to first negotiate the future terms of surrender with the Allies as well as seek any assistance they might have to offer. That is where Bonhoeffer came into play. In 1942 he traveled to Sweden to meet with his friend Bishop Bell of England, a member of the British Parliament. Bonhoeffer gave Bell the details of the conspiracy, asking him to inform the British and ask for help.

After some deliberation, the British decided against helping the German resistance. They were suspicious of dealing, in advance, with a new German regime that would come about only through a military coup. Moreover, the Allies called for an unconditional surrender from Germany and had no interest in negotiating in advance the terms of surrender should the plot succeed.

Although the failure to win outside support came as a great blow to the fragile resistance movement, it did not deter its members from pressing forward with their scheme.

Known as the "July 20 Plot," and dramatized in the 2008 film *Valkyrie,* the conspiracy to assassinate Hitler was the culmination of years of careful planning on the part of the German underground. The plan called for Colonel Claus von Stauffenberg, a German war hero and collaborator with the resistance movement, to place a briefcase containing a bomb beneath a table in the conference room where Hitler would meet with his staff inside the Wolfsschanze, the German military headquarters for the Eastern Front.

From our vantage point it seems normal and straightforward that a German Christian would want to help topple one of the worst regimes in history. However, at the time it was unprecedented for a Protestant theologian to engage in treasonous activities to overthrow the government. Many of Bonhoeffer's closest friends were confused by his double life and his ability to so easily tell lies in order to cover his seditious activities.

---

10. Richard L. Rubenstein and John K. Roth, *Approaches to Auschwitz: The Holocaust and Its Legacy* (Louisville: Westminster John Knox Press, 2003), 262.

Bonhoeffer and his associates did not have the encouragement of knowing that history would judge them positively, and none of them felt like heroes as they betrayed the oaths of loyalty they had taken.

IMPRISONMENT

A year before the assassination plans were put into action, money used to help Jews escape to Switzerland was traced to Bonhoeffer. He was immediately arrested and sent to jail. At this point, Bonhoeffer was merely accused of embezzling money for personal gain.

When it became clear that Bonhoeffer had been working for the resistance, the authorities interrogated and threatened him with torture. Yet he did not disclose a single name. Using his linguistic skills, he misled his interrogators, even writing papers aimed at deceiving them.

Outside the prison walls, the assassination plot was being put into action. Events transpired exactly as planned until the very last moment. In Wolfsschanze, Hitler and his generals gathered to discuss plans. Stauffenberg entered the room carrying the loaded briefcase and requested a seat next to Hitler, explaining that his hearing was impaired. He was placed two seats away. Stauffenberg leaned the briefcase against the nearest table leg before receiving a planned phone call as an excuse to leave the room.

The plan would have worked perfectly, but shortly before the bomb was set to detonate, the briefcase apparently bumped against the foot of an officer, who moved it to the other side of the heavy table leg, and thus further away from where Hitler sat. When the explosion occurred, three officers died, but Hitler received only minor injuries.

The German high command immediately began to track down members of the resistance that had been involved in the plot. It would be a while, however, before the investigation led them to the imprisoned Bonhoeffer.

Meanwhile, Bonhoeffer was not idle in jail. He used his time to write some of his best work. His *Letters and Papers from Prison*, which were smuggled out and later published, demonstrate that even in the midst of hardship he never became cynical, never lost his sense of hope, and retained both his love for humanity and his sense of humor. His confinement impressed upon Bonhoeffer a sense of the fragility of life, which made him eager to get the most out of every day, whatever difficulties it might hold.

Bonhoeffer befriended the prison guards and used these friendships as a means for secretly communicating with the outside world. At one point he was offered a chance to flee with one of the guards. However, as he was preparing to escape, news reached him that his brother Klaus had been arrested. Fearing the repercussions against his brother and family were he to escape, Bonhoeffer chose to remain in prison.

EXECUTION

It was only a matter of time before Bonhoeffer's complicity in the plot was discovered. When Hitler learned of it, he personally ordered Bonhoeffer's execution from his bunker in Berlin.

On the morning of April 8, 1945, Bonhoeffer was conducting a worship service for some of the other prisoners. One of these prisoners, an English officer, later wrote,

> Pastor Bonhoeffer . . . spoke to us in a way that went to the heart of all of us. He found just the right words to express the spirit of our imprisonment, the thoughts and the resolutions it had brought us. He had hardly ended his last prayer when the door opened and two civilians entered. They said, "Prisoner Bonhoeffer, come with us." That had only one meaning for all prisoners—the gallows. We said good-by to him. He took me aside: "This is the end, but for me it is the beginning of life."[11]

The next morning, Bonhoeffer was led naked into the execution yard while prison guards jeered and ridiculed him. At the foot of the scaffold, Bonhoeffer paused to kneel and pray, and then climbed the steps to the gallows to be hung.

Bonhoeffer was thirty-nine when he died. Eleven days later, American soldiers liberated the prison.

---

11. Dietrich Bonhoeffer, *Life Together: The Classic Exploration of Christian Community* (New York: HarperCollins, 1978), 13.

The Lord seemed to have been preparing Bonhoeffer for the hour of his death for many years. "When Christ calls a man," Bonhoeffer had written in *The Cost of Discipleship*, "he bids him come and die. It may be a death like that of the first disciples who had to leave home and work to follow him, or it may be a death like Luther's, who had to leave the monastery and go out in to the world. But it is the same death every time—death in Jesus Christ, the death of the old man at his call."[12]

THE LEGACY OF DIETRICH BONHOEFFER

Although Dietrich Bonhoeffer's legacy may seem to be one of failure, it was largely because of his death that his writings reverberated throughout the world to achieve the impact that they have. His teachings on obedience, grace, community, and the way of the cross remain a powerful inspiration for Christians. The testimony of his amazing life continues to draw both scholars and lay people to plumb the depths of his thought. Such a task is not always easy, as Bonhoeffer was a highly complex thinker.

It is partly for this reason that Bonhoeffer's legacy remains one of intense debate. When I told an evangelical friend that I was including a chapter on Bonhoeffer in this book, he asked whether he would be one of my heroes or villains. This is because Bonhoeffer remained a product of German liberal theology despite being influenced by American evangelicalism during his time in New York. Consequently, he occasionally made remarks that sound far from orthodox. This has led some evangelicals to denounce him, even as it has led other conservatives to claim him for their own camp. However, trying to put Bonhoeffer in a box remains as difficult today as it was during his own life. Moreover, even if his speculative theology can be ambiguous or even heterodox at times, it would be foolish if this prevented us from seeing the value of his legacy and the wisdom that he has to offer us.

12. Bonhoeffer, *The Cost of Discipleship*, 89.

LESSONS FROM THE LIFE OF DIETRICH BONHOEFFER

Although the life of Bonhoeffer furnishes us with dozens of lessons about the Christian walk, from the importance of courage to the need for Christian unity, I will focus on just one: gratefulness.

"I think we honor God more if we gratefully accept the life that he gives us with all its blessings, loving it and drinking it to the full," Bonhoeffer once wrote.[13] Even in the midst of the agonizing circumstances of a Nazi prison, Bonhoeffer never ceased to overflow with gratitude to God. Facing the daily possibility of death, he regarded each day as a precious gift from the Lord, to be received with thankfulness and joy.

One English officer imprisoned with him later commented: "Bonhoeffer always seemed to me to spread an atmosphere of happiness and joy over the least incident and profound gratitude for the mere fact that he was alive."[14]

Thankfulness did not come easy to Bonhoeffer. He had much to be troubled over. His worst torment was the separation from his beloved fiancée, Maria, and the uncertainty of not knowing whether she was safe.

During these sufferings, Bonhoeffer's approach was not merely to refrain from complaining. Nor was it to be joyful in spite of the hardship. Rather, he teaches us that we can be grateful not just *in* suffering but *for* the suffering itself. Bonhoeffer believed that difficult circumstances, no less than pleasant ones, come from the hand of God.[15] Writing to his brother-in-law from prison on April 5, 1943, he reflected:

13. Dietrich Bonhoeffer, *Letters and Papers from Prison, Updated* (New York: Touchstone, 1997), 192.

14. Bonhoeffer, *Life Together*, 13.

15. This echoed the teaching of Alfred Plummer who, in his commentary on James 1, wrote, "This doctrine of joy in suffering, which at first sight seems to be almost superhuman, is shown by experience to be less hard than the apparently more human doctrine of resignation and fortitude. The effort to be resigned, and to suffer without complaining, is not a very inspiriting effort. Its tendency is towards depression. It does not lift us out of ourselves or above our tribulations. On the contrary, it leads rather to self-contemplation and a brooding over miseries. . . . It is in the long run easier to rejoice in tribulation, and be thankful for it, than to be merely resigned and submit patiently. And therefore this 'hard saying' is really a merciful one, for it teaches us to endure trials in the spirit that will make

For you must know that there is not even an atom of reproach or bitterness in me about what has befallen the two of us. Such things come from God and from him alone, and I know that I am one with you and Christel in believing that before him there can only be subjection, perseverance, patience—and gratitude. So every question "Why?" falls silent, because it has found its answer. Until recently, until father's seventy-fifth birthday, we have been able to enjoy so many good things together that it would be almost presumptuous were we not also ready to accept hardship quietly bravely—and also really gratefully from prison.[16]

The following poem, written by Bonhoeffer in the concentration camp shortly before his death, reveals the depth of his constant gratitude:

By gracious powers so wonderfully sheltered,
And confidently waiting come what may,
We know that God is with us night and morning,
And never fails to greet us each new day.

Yet is this heart by its old foe tormented,
Still evil days bring burdens hard to bear;
Oh, give our frightened souls the sure salvation
For which, O Lord, You taught us to prepare.

And when this cup You give is filled to brimming
With bitter suffering, hard to understand,
We take it thankfully and without trembling,
Out of so good and so beloved a hand.

Yet when again in this same world You give us
The joy we had, the brightness of Your Sun,
We shall remember all the days we lived through,
And our whole life shall then be Yours alone.[17]

us feel them least" (Alfred Plummer, *The General Epistles of St. James and St. Jude* [London: Hodder & Stoughton, 1891], 65).

16. Bonhoeffer, *Letters and Papers from Prison*, 32.

17. John Richard Watson, *An Annotated Anthology of Hymns* (Oxford: Oxford University Press, 2002), 402.

QUESTIONS FOR DISCUSSION

1. Was it right for Bonhoeffer to lie to his enemies? Why or why not?

2. Bonhoeffer believed that in order to be an effective minister after the war, it was necessary to stay and suffer with his fellow Germans. Do you think he made the right decision?

3. When, if ever, is it appropriate for a Christian to violently overthrow a reigning government?

4. Bonhoeffer said, "Christ is really present only in the community." Is there biblical support for this? What are some practical ramifications of this idea?

5. Some people think that faith is a personal and private matter only. What are some ways that this notion has affected you or people you know?

6. According to a misunderstanding of Luther's two kingdoms theology which was prevalent in pre-war Germany, God has ordained two kingdoms: that of the church and that of the state. The church is responsible only for the inward, "spiritual" sphere, while the state is concerned for the public and political order. Could this two kingdoms theology have anything to do with why the German clergy were so quick to embrace national socialism?

7. Bonhoeffer believed it was possible to be grateful not just *in* suffering but *for* suffering. Should this be our approach during times of trial?

8. In Hitler's day, many German Christians adopted a synthesis of *Volkstum* (German national identity) and Christianity, thus blending the worship of God with the worship of the state. Do Christians in America also have a tendency to see God as "the God of America"?

9. If the assassination plot against Hitler had succeeded, would Bonhoeffer and his associates have been guilty of murder in God's eyes?

10. What would Bonhoeffer have thought of those Christians that believe violence is justified to protect the unborn? In what ways is the fight against abortion both similar to and different from Bonhoeffer's fight against Nazism?

11. By an apparent fluke, the July 20 plot failed to succeed in killing Hitler. Does it therefore follow that God wanted Hitler to continue perpetuating evil? How does God's control over all things apply to situations like this?

12. In Romans 13 the Apostle Paul says that all governing authorities are appointed by God. Does this mean that Hitler was appointed by God? If so, by attempting to kill Hitler, was the German resistance working against God?

PERSONAL CHALLENGE

Does Bonhoeffer's teaching on gratitude challenge attitudes in your personal life?

CHAPTER 16

THE QUIET REVOLUTION

Antonio Gramsci (1891–1937) and the Frankfurt Movement

On June 12, 1987, President Ronald Reagan stood at the Brandenburg Gate in West Berlin, where the Berlin Wall separated the free world from the communist empire.

In one of the most memorable speeches in living memory, Reagan offered a direct challenge to Mikhail Gorbachev, general-secretary of the Soviet Union's Communist Party. Gorbachev had claimed that he wanted to reform the Communist Party on the principles of *perestroika* (restructuring) and *glasnost* (openness). But Reagan believed that there was one thing left for Gorbachev to do to prove his earnestness.

"General Secretary Gorbachev," Reagan entreated, "if you seek peace, if you seek prosperity for the Soviet Union and Eastern Europe, if you seek liberalization: Come here to this gate. Mr. Gorbachev, open this gate. Mr. Gorbachev—Mr. Gorbachev, tear down this wall!"[1]

Two years later, on November 9, 1989, East Germans began dismantling the wall. As if in silent answer to Reagan's words, Gorbachev did nothing to stop them. Earlier in the same year, Gorbachev

---

1. Ronald Reagan, *Ronald Reagan* (Washington: Government Printing Office, 1982), 22.

had allowed the first open elections since 1917 to be held in the Soviet Union. Also in 1989 the USSR lost control of its satellite nations in Eastern Europe. For the next two years, the free world rejoiced as it witnessed the systematic downfall of communism in Eastern Europe. Communism had failed. Reagan and the free world had won.

Or had they?

The communism of the Soviet Union had been based on the economic theories of Karl Marx and Friedrich Engels, who had taught that the basic substructure of civilization was economic. All of history, they argued in *The Communist Manifesto,* had been characterized by the struggle between competing economic groups. In particular, this struggle found focus in the tension between the bourgeoisie (the wealthy and ruling classes) and the proletariat (the working classes). This struggle could resolve itself only by means of a working class revolution. Such a revolution would abolish private property and give the workers control over the means of production.

Communism, as such, never worked. Even during the heyday of the Soviet Union, the outcomes that Marx predicted never materialized. Yet even as the visible symbols of Marxism came crashing down at the close of the twentieth century, there was another, more subtle, version of Marxism coming to fruition. The apparent downfall of communism merely masked the imminent victory of a new variant, one that was less visible yet more subversive, less observable yet more insidious. It was a type of Marxism that owed its genesis to the Italian revolutionary, Antonio Gramsci (1891–1937).

THE YOUNG GRAMSCI

Antonio was born in 1891, the fourth of seven children, in the Italian city of Ales on the island of Sardinia. His childhood was far from happy. Antonio's father was imprisoned for five years on a charge of embezzlement in 1898, reducing the family to poverty. They were forced to move to Ghilarza, where Antonio suffered an accident that left him hunch-backed and permanently stunted.

At eleven Antonio had to leave school and get a job to support the struggling family. He was later able to complete his schooling, distinguishing himself as an exceptional student. He earned a scholarship to study philosophy at the University at Turin, where he gained a reputation as a writer of remarkable ability.

Like many of the youth in the Italian universities of the early twentieth century, Gramsci was attracted to the new revolutionary ideas. He wrote frequently about the views of Karl Marx, whose *Communist Manifesto* had been energizing workers throughout Europe ever since its appearance in 1848.

In 1914, three years after Gramsci moved to Turin, World War I broke out, triggering a series of events that would result in most of Marx's socialist theories becoming a reality in Russia.

GRAMSCI AND THE BOLSHEVIK REVOLUTION

Revolutionaries in Russia were able to mobilize the working classes by exploiting the climate of discontent. Faced with the unprecedented casualties Russia was experiencing in the war, together with soaring inflation and fuel shortages, the exhausted Russians were amenable to the utopian promises of the revolutionaries.

When the Tsar was forced to abdicate in February 1917, it looked initially as though Russia might adopt a political system similar to that of America. A provisional government was set up, headed by moderate Constitutional Democrats drawn primarily from the middle-class and aristocracy. They emphasized free speech and freedom of religion and advocated assemblies designed to maintain these and other liberties. However, the exiled Marxist revolutionary Vladimir Lenin (1870–1924) had other plans. He realized that the time was ripe to complete his agenda of a communist Russia, modeled on Marx's idea of the classless society.

Lenin arrived on the scene from Switzerland in April 1917. He immediately set to work mobilizing small revolutionary councils peppered throughout the country, known as "soviets." Lenin promised to redistribute land to the peasants, to transfer factories and industries from private owners into the hands of the workers, and to give the people "Peace, Land, Bread." Increasing numbers rallied to his side.

By the end of October 1917, Lenin's "Bolshevik" party had taken control of the various soviet councils in the capital, St. Petersburg, and in Moscow. During the night of November 6, they seized power in St. Petersburg. However, gaining control over all of Russia was another matter. It would take more than three years and a protracted civil war before Lenin and the communists ("Red Russians") would achieve victory against the anti-communists ("White Russians").

While Russia's civil war—known as the Bolshevik Revolution—was raging in Russia, Gramsci was trying to foment revolution in Italy. Together with his friend Palmiro Togliatti, he formed the Italian Socialist Party, in addition to starting the periodical *The New Order,* through which he disseminated the ideas of the revolution. A year after the Bolsheviks won control of Russia and turned it into the Union of Soviet Socialist Republics (USSR), Gramsci traveled to the nation as a delegate for the Italian Socialist Party.

Gramsci spent eighteen months in the Soviet Union, learning from the communists. Though he identified himself with the aims of the Bolsheviks and hoped that their goals could spread throughout the entire world, he held reservations about their brutal methods. Moreover, he could not detect the "class consciousness" that Marx had theorized about. He was dismayed that when the Great War had broken out in 1914, the proletariat throughout Europe—including those previously aligned with Marxism—had flocked to the causes of their own nations. He reasoned that if the working classes possessed the sort of class consciousness Marx had postulated, they ought to have understood that participating in the conflict was not in their best interests.

LIQUIDATING WESTERN CIVILIZATION

These were the questions that occupied Gramsci before and after his visit to the Soviet Union. He came to realize that the problems standing in the way of communism becoming an international reality were more basic than mere class struggle. Most workers had deep loyalties that went far deeper than economic considerations—loyalties such as family and religion. "Mediating institutions," like the church and family, served to insulate workers from the power of the state, blocking government's attempts to bring the communist utopia. Even in the Soviet Union, where Marxism appeared to work, Gramsci saw that it could only be sustained through the continual threat of terror.

At first Gramsci sought a solution that was consistent with traditional Marxist doctrine. However, he eventually came to see that communists like Marx and Lenin had things the wrong way around. Whereas Marx had argued that the substructure of civilization was economic, Gramsci came to see it as cultural.

What this meant in practice was that power did not rest only with those who controlled the means of production; rather, it depended on those that controlled the institutions and disciplines of culture, including philosophy, politics, art, literature, media, religion, and most importantly, the educational systems from elementary school to university. Only by concentrating on these domains could the hearts and minds of the proletariat be reached and a classless society achieved.[2] The real way to accomplish the Marxist revolution, therefore, was not first through economic adjustments, but cultural and institutional change.

What was needed in particular was to undermine the institutional hegemonies rooted in years of civic and ecclesial ideologies. This involved an attack on the very root of Western civilization: Christianity itself. This wasn't just because Christianity was inexplicably connected with the principles of the free market, though that was part of the picture. More crucially, Christianity attached importance to transcendent truths and values, in direct opposition to Marxism's insistence that everything valuable in life can be attained by tinkering with man's external environment.

The cultural legacy wrought by Christianity thus made the proletariat immune to the liberating influences of Marxism. Even among those individuals who had abandoned the Christian faith, their basic instincts were still deeply rooted in the residual **mores** of Christian society. As Malachi Martin describes it in *The Keys of This Blood:*

There would be no Marxist inspired violent overthrow of the ruling "superstructure" by the working "underclasses."

2. Ideas and culture had been important to classical Marxists, but only as a superstructure built on top of a substructure of economics. At least, that is how Marx was generally interpreted up until 1932, when some of his earlier manuscripts were published. In these manuscripts he argued that capitalism's real dangers were spiritual. This suggests that Gramsci may have had more in common with Marx than he realized.

Because no matter how oppressed they might be, the "structure" of the working classes was defined not by their misery or
their oppression but by their Christian faith and their Christian culture.[3]

It followed, Gramsci realized, that the proletariat revolution could
never succeed until the integrity of the culture that was blocking it
had been compromised. Before the political hegemony of communism could emerge, the ideological hegemony of Christianity would
first have to be dismantled. Workers must begin to see themselves as
being separated from the ruling classes not through economics but
through ideology. Marxist categories must first be internalized by
the masses before they could be externalized by the socialist political
parties. This could happen only to the degree that such categories
came to permeate every level of society, becoming part of the very
air people breathed. Once the new values formed the unchallenged
assumptions—the collective "common sense"—of society, the aims
of the revolution could be brought to bear. When that happened, a
revolution would not be necessary, for the people would willingly
embrace the communist solution. To quote again from Martin,

> What was essential, insisted Gramsci, was to Marxize the inner
> man. Only when that was done could you successfully dangle
> the utopia of the "Workers' Paradise" before his eyes, to be ac-
> cepted in a peaceful and humanly agreeable manner, without
> revolution or violence or bloodshed.[4]

Gramsci's strategy for "Marxizing" the inner man has come to be
known as "cultural Marxism" to distinguish it from classical economic
Marxism. In 1921, the same year that Gramsci founded the Italian Socialist Party, he wrote about this method of cultural subversion:

---

3. Malachi Martin, *The Keys of This Blood: Pope John Paul II Versus Russia
and the West for Control of the New World Order* (New York: Simon and Schuster,
1991), 245.
    4. Ibid., 248.

Nothing in this field is foreseeable except for this general hypothesis: there will be a proletarian culture (a civilization) totally different from the bourgeois one and in this field too class distinctions will be shattered. Bourgeois careerism will be shattered and there will be a poetry, a novel, a theatre, a moral code, a language, a painting and a music peculiar to proletarian civilization, the flowering and ornament of proletarian social organization. What remains to be done? Nothing other than to destroy the present form of civilization. In this field, "to destroy" does not mean the same as in the economic field. It does not mean to deprive humanity of the material products that it needs to subsist and develop. It means to destroy spiritual hierarchies, prejudices, idols and ossified traditions.[5]

FROM PARLIAMENT TO PRISON

Gramsci was in the Soviet Union in 1924 when Lenin died and Stalin seized the reigns of power. He decided to return to Italy, partly to protect himself against Stalin's party purges. Because Gramsci had opposed the methods of classical Leninism, he knew it would only be a matter of time before Stalin's police arrested him. But Gramsci also wanted to return to his homeland to join the struggle against the fascist Mussolini, whose party had held power since 1922.

The same year Mussolini's party came to power Hitler had commented that the communists and fascists were brothers together in the revolution for the liberation of the world. Fascism was not too distinct from communism. They were, in fact, rival brands of socialism. Both were left-wing political movements which had their origins in the legacy of the French Revolution. Both communism and fascism opposed the free market, both claimed to represent the way of progressive reform, both attempted to achieve their goals through an overthrow of the established order. Moreover, both were totalitarian, believing that government alone held the answer to all of life's problems. (When Mussolini first coined the term "totalitarianism," it was not a pejorative slur, nor was it something connoting tyranny.

5. Vassiliki Kolocotroni, *Modernism: An Anthology of Sources and Documents* (Chicago: University of Chicago Press, 1998), 215.

Rather, he used the word to refer to a humane society in which every-one was taken care of and looked after by a state which encompassed all of life within its grasp.)

Where fascism and communism differed was in the single-factor explanation for ushering in the socialist utopia. For communism, the explanation lay in the glorification of the working class; for fascism, it was the glorification of the nation-state and the races with which the nation was associated. (In Italian fascism, the racist element arose comparatively late as a result of German influence.)[6] Fascism told all citizens that they were the victims of other *nations and races;* communism told the workers that they were victims of other classes. In calling on the workers of the world to unite as one, the *Communist Manifesto* had implicitly downplayed the importance of nationhood. By contrast, the means by which fascism sought to bring a **planned economy** was through calling the people of the *nation* to unite and whipping the masses up into a nationalistic frenzy.

Gramsci's nemesis, Mussolini, had begun his career within the communist camp. But he had been influenced by the political thinker Georges Sorel (1847–1922), who argued that Marx's contribution was not in describing what had to come about (he disagreed with Marx's **historical determinism**) but, rather, a prescription for what *could* happen if the working classes were sufficiently inspired by Marx's "energizing myth." What was important was not whether a particular "energizing myth" was actually true, but whether it had the power to mobilize the masses. After observing the way workers flocked to defend their nations in 1914, Mussolini and other Italian Marx-ists became convinced that the nation-state would serve as a more compelling energizer than class consciousness for ushering in the socialist utopia. Mussolini thus abandoned Marxism for fascism.

In 1926, Mussolini's party began a purge of all its political oppo-nents. Gramsci was condemned as a communist and sentenced to twenty years behind bars. By sentencing Gramsci to prison, however,

---

6. In 1932 Mussolini wrote an entry on fascism for the Italian encyclopedia, noting, "The foundation of Fascism is the conception of the State, its character, its duty, and its aim. Fascism conceives of the State as an absolute, in comparison with which all individuals or groups are relative, only to be conceived of in their relation to the State" (Jackson J. Spielvogel, *Western Civilization: Volume II: Since 1500,* 8th ed. [Belmont: Wadsworth Publishing, 2011], 825).

Mussolini was unwittingly perpetuated his legacy, for it was during his confinement that Gramsci wrote his most lasting and influential works. When he died in 1937, he left behind nine volumes of his writings.

A DIFFERENT TYPE OF MARXIST

His time in prison had given Gramsci opportunity to reflect further on the problem of bringing the revolution to a culture so saturated in the principles of Christianity and the free market. In his *Prison Notebooks* he argued that effective control of the political and economic mechanisms of the state could only occur after what has been called the long march through the culture. The Judeo-Christian culture of Europe would have to be made to implode slowly, anonymously, and gradually, so that people would be unaware of what was happening around them. Moreover, it would have to be done in the name of man's dignity, liberty, and human rights. Only through years of steady chipping away at the foundation of Western society could the proletariat be oriented to look favorably on the communist solution. This process of undermining the social foundation would work through, in, and with the democratic mechanisms and political parties entrenched in the various nations, a position considered to be heretical by classical Leninists.

Gramsci realized and appropriated a truth that Solzhenitsyn would later articulate so profoundly: "Evil makes its home in the individual human heart before it enters a political system."[7] In getting to the heart of the matter, Gramsci's masterplan resembles Aldous Huxley's *Brave New World* more closely than George Orwell's *1984*. No force would be required to make the population subservient because they would be rendered cooperative by degrees. Gramsci considered it deeply offensive that leaders like Stalin could only maintain the workers' "paradise" through a regime of terror. Under the blueprint Gramsci offered, government did not need to wrest culture into line like Stalin was doing, because culture itself would eventually provide the revolutionary government with its constituency. After a long

7. Solzhenitsyn, *The Solzhenitsyn Reader*, 581.

process of cultural warfare the very infrastructure of Western culture could be exploited and funneled towards the goal of subversion.

Throughout the twentieth century, various individuals and institutions attempted to apply Gramsci's strategy. The most successful of these attempts was the influential Frankfurt School.

FRANKFURT AND THE GRAMSCIAN STRATEGY

The devastation and sheer futility of World War I, together with the Spanish Influenza that followed on its heels,[8] produced a generation of exhausted and cynical intellectuals ready to embrace either the false optimism of fascism, or the scathing pessimism of cultural Marxism. Many who adopted the latter course grouped together in the Institute for Social Research at the University of Frankfurt in Germany (formerly called Institute for the Study of Marxism). Their movement was characterized by a unique intellectual vision that came to be known as "the Frankfurt school." That vision was essentially Gramscian, funneling the principles of cultural Marxism towards the liquidation of Western civilization.[9]

The Frankfurt think-tank would come to include sociologists, art critics, psychologists, philosophers, sexologists, political scientists, and a host of other "experts" united in the aim of converting Marxism from a strictly economic theory into a cultural reality.

Among the intellectuals associated with the movement were Theodor Adorno, Max Horkheimer, Herbet Marcuse, Erich Fromm, Walter Benjamin, Leo Lowenthal, Wilhelm Reich, and Georg Lukács. What these men shared was a disillusion with the traditional Marxist doctrine of economic determinism. The failed revolution by German workers in 1919 seemed to indicate that a working class takeover was far from being the inevitability predicted by Marx. Echoing Gramsci, the thinkers of the Frankfurt school believed that the groundwork for this takeover would be laid by eviscerating the values on which

8. A fact not widely appreciated is that the flu pandemic of 1918 killed more people than World War I, wiping out 2.5 to 5 percent of the human population.

9. In relating the Frankfurt school to Gramsci's theories, I am not claiming that any of the thinkers associated with the movement were self-consciously appropriating the theories of Gramsci, or that the latter caused the former. But I am claiming that there is an important correlation.

Western culture was built. Georg Lukács, who helped to found the school, said that its purpose was to answer this question: "Who shall save us from Western Civilization?"[10]

When Hitler became chancellor in 1933, the school was forced to disband, relocating to Geneva. When most of its intellectuals later fled to the United States, the institute was transplanted to Columbia University, where its ideas were disseminated throughout American academic life.

The Gramscian tactics of the Frankfurt school were remarkably cunning. On the surface of things, post-war America seemed like the last place that would give their anti-Western philosophy a hearing. After all, this was a time when the entire Western world, and especially America, was acutely conscious of the way fascism had nearly wiped out their civilization. By taking as his paradigm the pre-Christian primitivism of the "noble savage," Hitler had represented the antithesis of Western values. Moreover, the Nazis rode to power on a wave of a fashionable neo-paganism and primordial tribalism that had presented itself as a secular alternative to the culture of the modern West. In a number of ways, therefore, the defeat of Hitler represented the victory of Western values. In America this victory was accompanied with the renewed cultural optimism characteristic of the late 1940s and 1950s. Such optimism manifested itself in the birth of the baby boomers, the production of happy films like "Singing in the Rain," and the popular music of crooners such as Bing Crosby and Frank Sinatra.

The genius of the Frankfurt School was its ability to convert this newfound confidence in American society into a force for sabotaging American society. The strategy involved a clever redefining of Fascism as an extreme right-wing heresy. According to this narrative, Nazism had been the outgrowth of a society entrenched in capitalism. ("Whoever is not prepared to talk about capitalism should also remain silent about fascism," commented Frankfurt sociologist Max Horkheimer.[11]) Cultures that attached strong importance to family,

---

10. György Lukács, Judith Marcus, and Zoltán Tar, *Georg Lukács: Selected Correspondence, 1902–1920: Dialogues with Weber, Simmel, Buber, Mannheim, and Others* (New York: Columbia University Press, 1986), 18.

11. Goldberg, *Liberal Fascism*, 287.

religion, patriotism, and private ownership, they argued, were virtual seedbeds of fascism.

On purely historical grounds, this explanation of fascism is questionable. However, by mixing complex social theories with Freudian psychoanalysis and pseudo-scientific cultural analysis, then stirring in a heavy dose of historical revisionism, the Frankfurters produced a cocktail of ideas that effectively associated social conservatism with the Nazis. This association has stuck long after the psychobabble and pseudo-science that produced it has lain dormant in the garbage heap of discredited academia. The net result is that it became intellectually respectable for Americans to embrace many of Hitler's goals, but to do so under the flag of an anti-fascist agenda.

The historical revisionism reached its height in the writings of Herbert Marcuse, the most well-known member of the movement.[12] For him—and the academics who followed in his wake—the only answer to the problem of fascism was communism. "The Communist Parties are, and will remain, the sole anti-fascist power," he declared. "[T]he denunciation of neo-fascism and Social Democracy must outweigh denunciation of Communist policy. The bourgeois freedom of democracy is better than totalitarian regimentation, but it had literally been bought at the price of decades of prolonged exploitation and by the obstruction of socialist freedom."[13]

THE "F-SCALE"

The apex of the pseudo-scientific sociology of the Frankfurt School was Theodor Adorno's book *The Authoritarian Personality,* written in 1950, after his move from Columbia to Berkeley. The book reported and evaluated a study of American society in which various individuals were polled using a questionnaire. Their answers indicated how well they scored on "the F-Scale." F, of course, stood for fascism.

The purpose of the study was to identify and analyze the profile of the "potential fascist character." However, as Daniel Flynn

12. For more information on Marcuse, see my article "The Illusionist: Herbert Marcuse Is the Godfather of Political Correctness," *Salvo* 20, Spring 2012.

13. Rolf Wiggershaus, *The Frankfurt School: Its History, Theories, and Political Significance* (Cambridge: MIT Press, 1995), 391.

pointed out in his discussion of the survey in *Intellectual Morons,* "what the authors took to be signs of fascism were merely indications of conservatism."[14] Sometimes the participants were simply asked whether they agreed or disagreed with certain statements. One statement was, "Now that a new world organization is set up, America must be sure that she loses none of her independence and complete power as a separate nation."[15] Those who answered that they agreed with this scored a point on the F-scale.

The study purportedly identified fascism as a specific psychological personality type, one that was deeply embedded in the authority structures of the patriarchal family and sustained by the conditions of the free market. Interestingly, the survey did not make any attempt to study actual fascist characters.

What Adorno "discovered" was that America was virtually on the brink of lapsing into fascism. Strongly-Christian families were among the telltale signs of a society on the verge of succumbing to the fascist impulse. According to the Frankfurt narrative, daughters obey their fathers only because their unresolved hatred of them has been converted into an attraction. This primes the culture for later falling under the spell of leaders like Mussolini and Hitler. The dynamic at work was articulated by the Frankfurt psychoanalyst Wilhelm Reich, who suggested that "familial imperialism is ideologically reproduced in national imperialism."[16] Max Horkheimer suggested similarly: "When the child respects in his father's strength a moral relationship and thus learns to love what his reason recognizes to be a fact, he is experiencing his first training for the bourgeois authority relationship."[17]

The opposite of the fascist personality was what Erich Fromm called the "openness" of the healthy personality. "Open" individuals were those who noted "that man is the center and purpose of his life; that the growth and realization of man's individuality is an end

14. Daniel J. Flynn, *Intellectual Morons: How Ideology Makes Smart People Fall for Stupid Ideas,* 1st ed. (New York: Crown Forum, 2004), 18.

15. Ibid.

16. Wilhelm Reich, *The Mass Psychology of Fascism,* 3rd ed. (New York: Farrar, Straus and Giroux, 1980), 59.

17. Max Horkheimer, *Critical Theory: Selected Essays* (New York: Continuum International Publishing Group, 1972), 101.

that can never be subordinated to purposes which are supposed to have greater dignity."[18]

"CRITICAL THEORY"

The Frankfurt thinkers established that those who held conservative views were not just wrong, but neurotic. By converting ideas into pathologies, the Frankfurt school set in motion the trend of silencing ideas through diagnosis rather than dialogue. "Psychologizing" their political opponents became a substitute for critical engagement.

It wasn't just their political opponents that fell under the hammer of this type of psychoanalysis. By pioneering a discipline known as "Critical Theory," the Frankfurt School was able to deconstruct all of Western civilization. Instead of showing that the values of the West were false, they diagnosed the culture as being inherently patriarchal, institutional, patriotic, capitalist, and "logo-centric." No aspect of Western society, from cleanliness to Shakespeare, was immune to this penetrating critique. Even the act of whistling fell under the deconstruction of Adorno, who thought that whistling indicated "control over music" and was symptomatic of the insidious pleasure Westerners take "in possessing the melody."

Reason itself was not without the taint of the authoritarian, fascist personality. Echoing what would later become a truism of **postmodern** social theory, Adorno and Horkheimer argued that fascism, like capitalism, was birthed in the Western cult of reason. They would be echoed by Marcuse in 1964, when he suggested that logic was a tool of domination and oppression.

In place of rationality, they followed Nietzsche in asserting the primacy of the mythic, primordial, and spontaneous urges of pre-Christian society, which exactly paralleled the preoccupations of their fascist nemeses. For Marcuse, the reunion to a more primitive state also involved a rejection of personal hygiene and the freedom to embrace a "body unsoiled by plastic cleanliness."[19]

18. Erich Fromm, *Escape from Freedom* (Austin: Holt, Rinehart and Winston, 1961), 265.

19. Herbert Marcuse, *An Essay on Liberation* (Boston: Beacon Press, 1969), 36.

"A WORLDWIDE OVERTURNING OF VALUES"

"Terror and civilization are inseparable" wrote Adorno and Horkheimer in *The Dialectic of Enlightenment.*[20] The solution to terror was therefore simple: dismantle civilization. Marcuse expressed their goal like this: "One can rightfully speak of a cultural revolution, since the protest is directed toward the whole cultural establishment, including morality of existing society."[21] Georg Lukács argued similarly: "I saw the revolutionary destruction of society as the one and only solution to the cultural contradictions of the epoch."[22] And later,"Such a worldwide overturning of values cannot take place without the annihilation of the old values and the creation of new ones by the revolutionaries."[23]

Lukács used the Hungarian schools as a front for reaping this redemptive cultural **nihilism**. Through a curriculum of radical sex education, he hoped to weaken the traditional family nucleus. History PhD William Borst recounts how

> Hungarian children learned the subtle nuances of free love, sexual intercourse, and the archaic nature of middle-class family codes, the obsolete nature of monogamy, and the irrelevance of organized religion, which deprived man of pleasure. Children were urged to deride and ignore the authority of parental authority, and precepts of traditional morality.[24]

Unlike the other members of the Frankfurt School, Lukács took refuge in the Soviet Union after Hitler came to power. Meanwhile, those that had immigrated to the United States continued to develop ever more sophisticated methods for liquidating Western values.

20. Max Horkheimer, Theodor W. Adorno, and Gunzelin Schmid Noerr, *Dialectic of Enlightenment: Philosophical Fragments* (Stanford: Stanford University Press, 2002), 180.

21. Andrew Breitbart, *Righteous Indignation: Excuse Me While I Save the World!* (New York: Grand Central Publishing, 2011), 114.

22. Michael Löwy, *Georg Lukács—From Romanticism to Bolshevism* (London: NLB, 1979), 93.

23. Ibid., 130.

24. William A Borst, "A Nation of Frogs," Catholic Culture, http://tinyurl.com/7lfvhcl (accessed February 20, 2012).

One of these—again echoing the genius of Gramsci—was to make oppressed groups feel that the world owed them something. What Marx did for groups defined by their economic status, the Frankfurt school did for groups defined by race, ethnicity, gender, and minority status (Marcuse added homosexuals to the list).

The Frankfurt School sought to build a base among academics who were willing to write about these oppressed peoples. By encouraging these groups to think of themselves as victims of Western oppression, the Frankfurt School sought to harness their energy in the fight against Christian values. The itinerary was being set for Western culture to splinter into numerous competing factions whereby America's diversity (previously one of its strengths) would become a fatal weakness. Under the shadow of Frankfurt, multiculturalism would shift from being *descriptive* to *prescriptive*—from describing a fact of American life to dictating policy. The former gave cohesion to American society, the latter would bring disintegration by fueling antagonism between different groups competing for legal privileges and exemptions.

During the 1960s Herbert Marcuse popularized these ideas and disseminated them to college radicals. By mobilizing the anti-war movement, the quiet revolution of Gramsci began to increase in volume. The counter-culture adopted Marcuse as their intellectual guru, and he in turn provided the youth with a steady stream of propaganda to sanctify their movement. (It was Marcuse who invented the catchphrase "Make Love, Not War.")

Instead of seeking to give the working classes control over the means of production, Marcuse sought to give groups aligned with the Left control over the intellectual infrastructures of the West. One of the ways he approached the goal was through redefining the notion of tolerance. Marcuse considered that the traditional way of conceiving tolerance—permitting another person's viewpoint regardless of how one personally felt—to be "repressive tolerance." What was needed instead was what he termed "liberating tolerance." Significantly, liberating tolerance involved "intolerance against movements from the Right and toleration of movements from the Left."[25]

---

25. Herbert Marcuse, *The Essential Marcuse: Selected Writings of Philosopher and Social Critic Herbert Marcuse* (Boston: Beacon Press, 2007), 50.

Movements from the Left included various groups that Marcuse encouraged to self-identify as oppressed, including homosexuals, women, blacks, and immigrants. Only groups such as these could be considered legitimate objects of tolerance.

What emerged under the shadow of this new tolerance was a type of intellectual redistribution. Instead of redistributing capital from the middle class to the working class, as traditional Marxism had urged, the new tolerance followed Gramsci in seeking to redistribute cultural capital. Marcuse made no secret that these were his ultimate goals, reflecting once, "I suggested...the practice of discriminating tolerance in an inverse direction, as a means of shifting the balance between Right and Left by restraining the liberty of the Right."[26] Marcuse also made no secret of the fact that he was willing to stamp out academic freedom in order to shift this balance of power. Significantly, he acknowledged that this new model of tolerance involved "the withdrawal of toleration of speech and assembly from groups and movements which promote aggressive policies," while "the restoration of freedom of thought may necessitate new and rigid restrictions on teachings and practices in the educational institutions which, by their very methods and concepts, serve to enclose the mind within the established universe of discourse and behavior."[27]

By the 1960s the ideologies forged at Frankfurt had become the dominant position for most college radicals. Many of them then entered academia, media, or politics with the deliberate purpose of changing the world. The change they would bring would be along the lines that Aldous Huxley articulated in his foreword to *Brave New World*: "A really efficient totalitarian state would be one in which the all-powerful executive of political bosses and their army of managers control a population of slaves who do not have to be coerced, because they love their servitude."[28]

26. Ibid., 56–57.
27. Ibid., 45.
28. Aldous Huxley, *Brave New World* (New York: HarperCollins, 1932), xiv.

THE LEGACY OF CULTURAL MARXISM

A. N. Whitehead once described all of Western philosophy as simply
a series of footnotes to Plato. It might be similarly urged that all of
contemporary liberalism is merely a footnote to Gramsci. Indeed, his
theories, mediated through the **deconstructionism** of the Frankfurt
school, form the bedrock for the type of neo-Marxism fashionable
today (though the term "Marxism" is no longer in vogue). As Gene
Veith observed in *Postmodern Times:*

> Today's left wing shows little concern for the labor movement
> and economic theory, unlike the Marxists of the last genera-
> tion. Instead, the Left emphasizes *cultural change.* Changing
> America's values is seen as the best means for ushering in the
> socialist utopia. This is why the Left today champions any
> cause that undermines traditional moral and cultural values
> and why leftists gravitate to culture-shaping institutions—
> education, the arts, and the media.[29]

There are many practical areas in which the legacy of cultural
Marxism has found fruition today. One of these is in the network of
tendencies that are popularly referred to as "political correctness."

In his book *The Retreat of Reason,* journalist Anthony Browne
gives concisely defines political correctness as "an ideology that clas-
sifies certain groups of people as victims in need of protection from
criticism, and which makes believers feel that no dissent should be
tolerated."[30] Browne rightly identifies political correctness as a species of cultural Marxism. Instead of merely transferring wealth from
the bourgeois to the working class, it has become politically correct
for government to transfer power from the powerful to the powerless,
or to groups perceived to be victims.

Browne's analysis was echoed by Jonah Goldberg in his landmark
study, *Liberal Fascism.* Goldberg showed that in the latter half of the

---

29. Gene Edward Veith, *Postmodern Times: A Christian Guide to Contemporary
Thought and Culture* (Wheaton: Crossway Books, 1994), 161.

30. David Conway and Anthony Browne, *Retreat of Reason: Political Correctness & the Corruption of Public Debate in Modern Britain,* 2nd ed. (London: Civitas, 2006), 4.

twentieth century, civil rights shifted from describing a legal system that is color blind to race or religion, to describing a system that must show preferential treatment to those groups which are assumed to have "victim status." The result has been "identity politics" and a new tribalism, whereby people define themselves by their group and then compete with those in other communities.[31]

The legacy of Frankfurt is also felt in a pervasive bent towards what C. S. Lewis called "bulverism" in *God in the Dock,* whereby an idea is attacked by identifying its source rather than refuting its grounds. Also known as the "genetic fallacy," this tendency is manifested whenever an argument is silenced through diagnosis rather than discussion. One does not have to penetrate very deeply into our public discourse to see this trick at work. Following in the footsteps of Adorno and the Frankfurters, one does not need to show how a truth claim is false provided one can label it as being "sexist," "homophobic," "patriarchal," "racist," "logo-centric," or even "Islamophobic." Such terms can be bandied about to short-circuit rational debate and render large swaths of public assumptions immune to analysis.

The power of these labels, even when they may be legitimately descriptive, normally functions to bypass critical engagement, stir up prejudice, and harness the "new and rigid restrictions on teachings and practices in the educational institutions."[32] The result is frequently to induce a state of affairs described by George Orwell when he remarked that "at any given moment, there is a sort of all-pervading orthodoxy—a general tacit agreement not to discuss some large and uncomfortable fact."[33]

But above all, the arm of Frankfurt is seen in the antipathy to Christian values which permeates much of our current public discourse.

LESSONS FROM GRAMSCI AND THE FRANKFURT SCHOOL

Gramsci and the Frankfurt School understood that culture is not spiritually neutral but is religion externalized. There is a crucial lesson we can learn from this. Our art, language, architecture,

31. Goldberg, *Liberal Fascism.*
32. Marcuse, *The Essential Marcuse,* 45.
33. Martin, *The Keys of This Blood,* 266.

technologies, economics, music, clothing, schools, and every other aspect of culture all point to a certain worldview, whether it is explicitly acknowledged or not.

Another lesson we learn from Gramsci and the Frankfurt School is that a self-deceived man will always see in other people his own faults. One of the traits that the Frankfurt School took to be characteristic of the fascist character type was a rigid commitment to dominant values. Yet it seems undeniable that the ideology which emanated from their think-tank involved an exceedingly rigid commitment to the values of deconstructionism. To the extent that they used reason to attack reason, and used the freedoms of the West as a safe haven from which to attack those very freedoms, the architects of Frankfurt became the prototypes for the postmodern embrace of **contrarieties**.

If Gramsci had lived to see the Soviet Union's downfall, I don't think he would have been surprised. The Soviets attempted to impose a communist regime on Europeans who still thought and functioned as capitalist Christians. Gramsci understood that in order to change the system of a society, you must first change the hearts of the people. That must be done through a process of persistent enculturation, beginning when children are very young.

President Ronald Reagan also understood this principle. He understood that the root of the struggle between the communists and the free world was more than simple economics: it was a spiritual struggle rooted in the conflict of ideas. As Reagan put it in 1982,

> The ultimate determinate in the struggle now going on for the world will not be bombs and rockets but a test of wills and ideas—a trial of spiritual resolve; the values we hold, the beliefs we cherish and the ideas to which we are dedicated.[34]

34. Robert C. Rowland and John M. Jones, *Reagan at Westminster: Foreshadowing the End of the Cold War* (College Station: Texas A&M University Press, 2010), 72.

QUESTIONS FOR DISCUSSION

1. Compare and contrast classical Marxism with cultural Marxism.

2. Gramsci was concerned that traditional Marxism could never achieve its goals. Was he correct in this? What are some reasons why traditional Marxism doesn't work?

3. How does the Trinitarian balance between the one and the many help to counter the particular type of multiculturalism introduced by the Frankfurt thinkers?

4. What are some ways that structures such as the church and the family help to insulate a person against the power of the state?

5. What temptations of sinful man did Marxism appeal to? What temptations of sinful man did fascism appeal to? What temptations of sinful man did the Frankfurt movement appeal to?

6. Was Gramsci correct that control of society rests with those who control the institutions and disciplines within culture?

7. What does the Bible teach about tolerance, particularly tolerance towards those who hold different worldviews?

8. What are some ways that the phenomena of "political correctness" functions to short-circuit rational debate of specific issues and to make certain issues functionally immune to critique?

9. "A self-deceived man will always see in other people his own faults." Discuss.

10. What are some ways that the goals of Gramsci and the Frankfurt School have been successfully realized in today's culture?

11. Were the Russian revolutionaries right to overthrow the Tsar?

12. What are some collective "common sense" assumptions of our society that are not biblical?

PERSONAL CHALLENGE

Revolutionaries in Russia were able to mobilize the working classes by taking advantage of their discontent. What are some ways that the devil tempts you to sin by exploiting your areas of discontent?

CHAPTER 17

THE ALIVENESS OF ALL THINGS

The Passionate Intellect of Dorothy Sayers (1893–1957)

"A FESTIVAL NOT A MACHINE"

When medieval man looked up into the sky and contemplated the heavens, he was greeted not with a deep vacuity, but with a delightful dance; not a mechanical unwinding like clockwork, but a magnificent, unfolding play. It was a cosmos that C. S. Lewis described as "tingling with anthropomorphic life, dancing, ceremonial, a festival not a machine."[1]

The writings of thirteenth-century poet Dante Alighieri were animated by this same vision. Dante's universe was alive, pulsating with the energy of God and His angels, bathed in radiance and glory:

The glory of Him who moves all things soe'er
Impenetrates the universe, and bright
The splendor burns, more here, and lesser there.[2]

---

1. C.S. Lewis, *English Literature in the Sixteenth Century, Excluding Drama* (Oxford: Clarendon Press, 1954), 4.
2. Dante Alighieri, *The Divine Comedy Part 3: Paradise,* trans. Dorothy L. Sayers (Baltimore: Penguin Classics, 1962), 53.

According to C.S. Lewis, all Christendom shared this same vision until roughly the seventeenth century. Under the impetus of advances in science, man began to complete a process Lewis describes as "emptying" the universe. Man, with his new powers of observation and scientific analysis, "became rich like Midas but all that he touched had gone dead and cold."[3]

It was not that thinkers at the advent of the modern age stopped believing that the universe was created by God. Rather, they began to view the machinery of the universe as *separate* from spiritual categories. The universe that emerged under the telescope of modern science was "dead and cold" precisely because it was an autonomous mathematical machine, no longer radiating with *aliveness*.

The cosmos was further disenchanted when philosophers in the eighteenth century used the discoveries of Newton to bolster a cosmology of materialism. By reducing God to an irrelevant "First Cause," this materialistic philosophy (often called Modernism) rendered asunder the realms of spirit and matter. The realm of the spiritual, they argued, is invisible, private, and subjective; the material world is visible, public, and objective.

This dualistic approach was boosted in 1859, when Charles Darwin published *On the Origin of Species*. Darwin gave scientific legitimacy to Modernism, showing how biological systems could evolve over time independent of any divine reference point. Consequently, by the early 1900s the disconnection of the material world from the spiritual realm became the unquestioned orthodoxy of the scientific community.

By the twentieth century, this separation of matter and spirit not only permeated universities like Oxford and Cambridge but had affected the outlook of much of the British church. In the Church of England, it began to be seen as a badge of intellectual sophistication for clergy to water down, and sometimes even reject completely, the supernatural aspects of the Christian faith. The Anglican laity were hardly any better, having imbibed a sentimentalized, moralistic faith that had become unhinged from any spiritual reference point. Even those Englishmen committed to espousing a biblical faith often colluded with the modernist separation of the physical from

---

3. Lewis, *English Literature in the Sixteenth Century*, 4.

the spiritual. This false separation resulted in the British church imbibing a Gnostic-like spirituality which failed to see how the world of ordinary things—work, matter, creativity, culture, to say nothing of the universe itself—was spiritually infused and dynamic.

It may be a mark of God's sense of humor that one of the most penetrating critiques of this modernist worldview came from a most unlikely quarter: a woman who first gained an audience by writing popular murder mysteries.

EARLY LIFE

Dorothy Sayers was born in 1893, the only daughter of Henry and Helen Sayers. Almost immediately it was evident that Dorothy was an exceptional girl. She was acutely sensitive to the splendor of the world, the beauty of abstract patterns, logical forms, and what one biographer has called "the glow of the order of things."[4] By the age of four, Dorothy could read English, and her father started her on Latin at six. By her teens she was fluent in French and German.

From an early age Dorothy had a bristling imagination which reveled in the fantastic, the dramatic, and the poetic. She exhibited what her literary colleague Barbara Reynolds has aptly termed "a Chestertonian gusto for life."

Unfortunately, Sayers' very enthusiasm and exuberance contributed to a sense of alienation from the "stuffy" Christianity of her parents. Although her father was a clergyman, she received no theological instruction from him. Reflecting on the time when her parents insisted on having her confirmed into the church as a teenager, she wrote that it "gave me a resentment against religion which lasted a long time . . . the cultivation of religious emotion without philosophic basis is thoroughly pernicious."[5]

Dorothy may have completely rebelled against Christianity had not the writings of G. K. Chesterton come to her rescue. "It was stimulating to be told," she later reflected, "that Christianity was

---

4. David Coomes, *Dorothy L. Sayers: A Careless Rage for Life* (Oxford: Lion Publishers, 1992), 36.

5. Barbara Reynolds, *Dorothy L. Sayers: Her Life and Soul* (New York: Macmillan, 1997), 38.

not a dull thing but a gay thing; not a stick-in-the-mud thing but an adventurous thing; not an unintelligent thing but a wise thing, indeed a shrewd thing."[6]

In 1912, Dorothy won a scholarship to attend Somerville College, Oxford, from which she graduated with a first-class honors degree in modern languages and a master's degree in medieval French. After graduating she was employed first as an editor by the publisher, Blackwell, and then as a copywriter for the advertising agency, Benson's, where her wild imagination and quirky sense of humor were harnessed in the advertising of products.

LOVE AND MARRIAGE

At twenty-nine, Dorothy fell deeply in love with the novelist John Cournos. She wanted to marry him and have children, but he refused, claiming that he did not believe in marriage. When the relationship unraveled, Sayers was utterly heartbroken. On the rebound she formed a physical relationship with an unemployed motor car salesman, Bill White. When he learned that he had made her pregnant, he abandoned her.

The child, a baby boy named John Anthony, was born in 1924 when Sayers was thirty. Wishing to shield her aging parents from the news of her indiscretion, Sayers arranged for the boy to live with her cousin, Ivy. She hoped that a day would come when he could live with her. The opportunity seemed to present itself two years later when she met and married Oswald Fleming, a divorced man twelve years her elder. However, Fleming made it clear that John would not be welcome in their home. This, together with the fact that Sayers and her husband drifted apart as the years went by, seems to have taken an emotional toll on her.

Soon after joining Benson's, she published her first Lord Peter Wimsey novel, *Whose Body?* The public took an immediate liking to Wimsey—a quixotic gentleman that solved mysteries as a hobby. By 1931 the novels were providing enough income for Sayers to quit her job and write full-time.

6. D. J. Conlon, *G.K. Chesterton: A Half Century of Views* (Oxford: Oxford University Press, 1987), 123.

FROM CRIME NOVELIST TO CHRISTIAN DRAMATIST

Possessing what she termed "a careless rage for life," Sayers tended to throw herself with abandon into whatever she was doing. As a girl, she was known to march down the High Street singing at the top of her voice, "Fling wide the gates, for the Savior waits." Yet as the years went by, Sayers hardened in response to being hurt so many times. In 1992 David Coomes published many of Sayers' intimate letters in his biography, *A Careless Rage for Life*. What we find is that behind her bombastic and overbearing exterior was a vulnerable and often lonely woman.

Sayers' sufferings may have played a part in keeping her faith at bay for so many years. Coomes notes that "battered by poverty, lost love, the weakness of the flesh and an unhappy marriage, she was to grow weary of the faith and allow it to lie dormant for nearly twenty years."[7] When Sayers did finally emerge on the scene as a prominent spokeswoman for Christianity it was, perhaps, as much of a surprise to herself as to anyone else.

It all began when she was asked to write a play for the Canterbury Festival in 1937. The production, *The Zeal of Thy House*, tells the story of a French architect and gave Sayers the opportunity to explore themes of creativity, work, pride, and the Incarnation. The production was an instant success, although it puzzled her that many people responded to the Christian theology in the play as if it were a novelty of her own invention.

Captivated by the stage, Sayers dropped her focus on detective novels and threw her energies into the theatre.

THE DOGMA IS THE DRAMA

As all Sayers' plays had theological undertones, the editor of the *Sunday Times* invited her to contribute an article for Passion Sunday 1938. Her article, "The Greatest Drama Ever Staged is the Official Creed of Christendom," reflected on the responses she had received from her Canterbury play. "The action of the play," she observed, "involves a dramatic presentation of a few fundamental Christian

---

7. Coomes, *Dorothy L. Sayers*, 68.

dogmas" and yet "all these things were looked upon as astonishing and revolutionary novelties, imported into the faith by the feverish imagination of a playwright."[8] Sayers recalled how she "protested in vain against this flattering tribute" to her "powers of invention" and instead referred her inquirers "to the creeds, to the Gospels, and to the offices of the Church."[9] The article went on to articulate what would be a recurring theme throughout her life: that the creedal Christianity of the church is based on the most dramatic story the world has ever encountered.

> I insisted that if my play was dramatic it was so, not in spite of the dogma but because of it—that, in short, the dogma was the drama. The explanation was, however, not well received; it was felt that if there was anything attractive in Christian philosophy I must have put it there myself.[10]

> The Christian faith is the most exciting drama that ever staggered the imagination of man—and the dogma is the drama. That drama is summarized quite clearly in the creeds of the Church.[11]

> This is the dogma we find so dull—this terrifying drama of which God is the victim and hero.

> If this is dull, then what, in Heaven's name, is worthy to be called exciting? The people who hanged Christ never, to do them justice, accused him of being a bore—on the contrary, they thought him too dynamic to be safe. It has been left for later generations to muffle up that shattering personality and surround him with an atmosphere of tedium.[12]

---

8. Dorothy Leigh Sayers, *Letters to a Diminished Church: Passionate Arguments for the Relevance of Christian Doctrine* (Nashville: Thomas Nelson, 2004), 15.
9. Ibid.
10. Ibid., 15.
11. Ibid., 1.
12. Ibid., 4.

In 1940 the BBC commissioned Sayers to write a play on the life of Christ for Children's Hour. She used this opportunity to prove again how dynamic traditional Christian dogma could be. Her play, *The Man Born to Be King*, employed several devices aimed at bringing the Christian message to common men and women who, like Sayers in her youth, felt alienated from the church. One way she achieved this was by having Jesus and His disciples speak with working-class accents. This did not sit well with some of the conservative evangelical societies of the day, one of whom accused Sayers of "irreverence bordering on the blasphemous." Even before the play was broadcast, the Protestant Truth Society and the Lord's Day Observance Society launched an expensive campaign to ban the work. They even delivered a petition to Prime Minister Winston Churchill and the Archbishop of Canterbury, William Temple, demanding they ban the broadcast. But the Archbishop was a devoted Wimsey fan and an even more devoted advocate of Sayers, especially when she began to evangelize to people that the church had failed to reach.

The play aired as planned and was an immediate success. Sayers, now middle-aged, built on her notoriety by writing works which brought Christian theology alive in a way no one had done since G. K. Chesterton. In *Begin Here, The Mind of the Maker,* and *Creed or Chaos?* she defended the historic creeds of Christendom, not so much from the charge of falsehood, but from the far more pernicious accusation of dullness. She showed that the confessional theology of the church is just as exciting as a good murder mystery. Like her friend and fan, C. S. Lewis, she breathed new life into Anglican theology, not by abandoning its doctrines for innovations, but by showing how exciting the church's traditional teachings actually were.

DISCOVERING DANTE

In 1944 Sayers sat huddled with others taking refuge in a bomb shelter while German V1 rockets screamed over the city. Oblivious to the explosions, she was engrossed in her grandmother's copy of the *Inferno*. At fifty-one years of age, this was her first encounter with Dante. For the rest of her life she would be consumed with a passion for *The Divine Comedy*.

Sayers' obsession with Dante is not surprising. With penetrating clarity he had presented the same vision of a living cosmos that she had also articulated. It was a vision of a universe alive with hierarchy, order, and purpose:

> And, as the soul that dwells within your dust
> Diffuses through the limbs, that variously
> To various powers shape themselves and adjust,
> So through the stars in great diversity
> The Intelligence its goodness multiplies
> Revolving still on its own unity.[13]

It was not only Dante's worldview that left Dorothy spellbound. She also adored him because he was a riveting storyteller. She spent the final years of her life laboring to translate the three books of Dante's *Divine Comedy*. The first appeared as a Penguin Classic in 1949, the second in 1955. At the time of her death on December 17, 1957, the third translation was unfinished. It was completed in 1962 by Barbara Reynolds.

UNITING WHAT MAN HAS RENT ASUNDER

Sayers left a rich body of writing in which she continually opposed the modernist assertion that the universe could be understood independent from any spiritual reference point. She turned to the older, pre-modern worldview and its contention that the universe is animated with God's life and pulsating with His creative energy. As Sayers put it in a 1940 lecture, "the whole material universe is an expression and incarnation of the creative energy of God, as a book or a picture is the material expression of the creative soul of the artist."[14]

Maintaining what she called a "sacramental" view of matter, Sayers found the modernist separation of spirit and matter particularly insidious. In a letter to the *Church Times* on May 16, 1941, Sayers criticized what she called the "perverse" and "unsacramental" theology

---

13. Dante, *Paradise*, canto II. 133–136.
14. Sayers, *Diminished Church*, 64.

that denied "the intimate unison between spirit and matter which is in fact a denial of the Incarnation."

The bringing together of the spiritual and the physical had implications, not just for how Sayers understood the universe, but in how she approached the world, its institutions, and life itself. "[T]here is a fundamental error," she wrote,

> about the Church's attitude to the Active Life—a persistent assumption that Catholic Christianity, like any Oriental Gnosticism, despises the flesh and enjoins a complete detachment from all secular activities. Such a view is altogether heretical. No religion that centres about a Divine Incarnation can take up such an attitude as that. What the Church enjoins is quite different: namely, that all the good things of this world are to be loved because God loves them, as God loves them, for the love of God, and for no other reason.[15]

The false separation of the physical and the spiritual had led to an unofficial theology which stressed that the fundamental Christian hope is immortality rather than physical resurrection. This notion was reinforced by the Platonic bent of post-Victorian evangelicalism, in which the word "resurrection" began to be used simply as an approximation for the soul's immortality. It even became fashionable for Anglican bishops to spiritualize away Christ's own resurrection. "When I was a girl," Sayers reflected, "G. K. Chesterton professed belief in the Resurrection, and was called whimsical. When I was at college, thoughtful people expressed belief in the Resurrection 'in a spiritual sense,' and were called advanced."[16] The down-to-earth Sayers had little time for this type of crypto-Gnosticism. Christ rose in the flesh, she taught, not only to redeem man's invisible soul, but to bring salvation to the *whole* person, including our bodies. Any "excessive spirituality" that left the physical body out of the picture

15. Dorothy Leigh Sayers, *Introductory Papers on Dante* (New York: Barnes & Noble, 1969), 113.

16. Dorothy Leigh Sayers, *The Poetry of Search and the Poetry of Statement: And Other Posthumous Essays on Literature, Religion, and Language* (London: Gollancz, 1963), 69.

was not Christianity, but Gnosticism. As Sayers put it in *Further Papers on Dante:*

> [T]he doctrine of the immortality of the soul, though Christians do in fact believe it, is not particularly characteristic of Christianity, nor even vital to it. No Christian creed so much as mentions it, and theoretically, it would be quite compatible with Christian belief if soul as well as body had to undergo the experience of death. The characteristic belief of Christendom is in the Resurrection of the Body and the life everlasting of the completely body-soul complex. Excessive spirituality is the mark, not of the Christian, but of the Gnostic.[17]

In Sayers' 1940 BBC broadcast, "The Sacrament of Matter," she had argued similarly, urging that the goodness of matter is foundational to the doctrines of the Church, since it is central to a correct understanding of the Incarnation.

"THE LOST TOOLS OF LEARNING"

Education was always close to Sayers' heart. She understood that the primary goal in education is for the student to love learning and, as a consequence, to better know and enjoy God, this in turn leading to wisdom and virtue.

Sayers' 1947 Oxford address, "The Lost Tools of Learning," has been enormously influential in the field of education. While acknowledging that the literacy rate in Western Europe was never higher, she noted that the influence of mindless advertising (something of which she had firsthand experience) and mass propaganda had also reached unprecedented levels. Although schools were churning out students with a large amount of knowledge, this coexisted with a deficit in understanding. Schools were not training their students how to think, to hone their imaginations, or to make connections between the different "subjects." As Sayers herself put it,

17. Dorothy Leigh Sayers, *Further Papers on Dante* (London: Taylor & Francis, 1957), 93.

Is not the great defect of our education today, that although we often succeed in teaching our pupils "subjects," we fail lamentably on the whole in teaching them how to think: they learn everything, except the art of learning.[18]

As a solution, Sayers drew inspiration from what she believed to have been medieval educational pedagogy, and she speculated about what that would look like if applied in a contemporary setting. According to her insight, a student would be equipped with the tools of learning long before he is expected to apply them to any subject, just as a student of carpentry is taught how to hold and wield a hammer and chisel before being given a block of wood on which to work. In this early period, known as the Grammar Stage, the child learns the "grammar" embedded in any subject. For example, the grammar of history comprises facts and dates; the grammar of math calls for memorizing sums, number groups, and geometrical shapes; the grammar of science requires the identification and naming of natural phenomena, and so on. All this occurs at a time in the child's life when he naturally gravitates to learning by rote (what Sayers called the "Poll-Parrot stage").

When the child is a little more advanced (perhaps around seventh or eighth grade, though Sayers didn't specify), he becomes naturally argumentative. This is the perfect time for the teacher to step in and teach the student how to construct logical arguments, detect fallacies, and apply these skills in all fields. This second phase is the Logic Stage and involves learning how to reason on facts already acquired.

The third and final stage, known as the Rhetoric or Poetic stage, is when the student is taught how to express himself in language. Here he is taught the skills for honing his imagination. The things learned in the previous two stages now synthesize into a coherent whole.

18. Dorothy Leigh Sayers, *The Lost Tools of Learning: Paper Read at a Vacation Course in Education, Oxford, 1947* (London: Methuen, 1948), 7.

LEGACY

"I have never met anybody who compared with her in energy and expanse of mind or breadth of vision," said Sayers' friend and fellow-translator Barbara Reynolds.[19]

A true polymath, Sayers is remembered today as a novelist, scholar, essayist, poet, advertiser, theologian, literary critic, journalist, scholar, playwright, translator, and Christian apologist. Her play *The Man Born to Be King* has been translated into numerous languages, while many consider her Wimsey stories to be among the best detective fiction ever written. Yet Sayers' greatest legacy remains spiritual. Her commitment to "the aliveness of all things" breathed new life into the sleepy Anglican church of the mid-twentieth century. She showed that the Church's message is radical, not in spite of her creeds, traditions, and institutions, but *because* of them.

One important aspect of Sayers' spiritual legacy has been her impact on education. Many schools now exist which structure a "Great Books" or "classical" education around Sayers' educational schema. Though her descriptions of medieval education have been criticized (her proposals are actually an improvement on medieval pedagogy rather than an accurate reflection of what actually occurred in the medieval classroom), there is something to be said for working with, rather than against, the God-given stages of cognitive development. In our era, young children are continually being pressured to engage in self-expression before they are shown how to think coherently, and they are pressured to engage in reasoning before they are given the facts with which to reason. The result is not intellectual freedom but enslavement, for someone that is never taught how to think is by default trained to be a bondservant to the latest fad or fashion.

LESSONS FROM THE LIFE OF DOROTHY SAYERS

Valuable lessons can be derived, not simply from Dorothy Sayers' thought, but from the example of her life. She was a woman deeply touched by beauty, glory, and splendor. Yet for all her "careless rage

---

19. Barbara Reynolds, "Dorothy Sayers: 'The dogma is the drama,' An interview with Barbara Reynolds by Chris Armstrong," *Christian History* 88 (2005).

for life," she felt little in the way of what we might call "religious emotion." She once confessed:

> I am quite without the thing known as "inner light" or "spiritual experience." I have never undergone conversion. . . . But since I cannot come at God through intuition, or through my emotions, or through my "inner light" . . . there is only the intellect left.[20]

But Sayers was far from being just a brain: she lived out her Christianity. This did not come easy for Sayers, bereft as she was from all spiritual emotion. "If I ever do a disagreeable duty," she noted, "it is in the spirit of the young man in the parable who said 'I go not,' but afterwards (probably in a detestable temper) went grumbling off and did the job."[21]

There were many disagreeable duties to which Sayers faithfully applied herself throughout her life. As her husband aged, he became increasingly irritable and showed little interest in the things that were important to her. Yet she cared for him faithfully until his death in 1950, and there is no record of her complaining about him, save for some coded references to their unhappy marriage in her novels.

Sayers' dedication to the work God had given her was rooted in her theology of vocation. All of life, she taught, has been sanctification through Christ, and this includes work, even work which may not seem particularly glorious at the time. As she put it in an address delivered at St. Martin-in-the-Fields on February 6, 1942: "Christianity demands that *all* work should be done in a Christian way—Christianity proclaims that *all* work, all that is well done, does reveal God and may be offered to God in worship."[22] However, as she pointed out in *Creed or Chaos?*,

> the Church's approach to an intelligent carpenter is usually confined to exhorting him not to be drunk and disorderly in

---

20. Dorothy Leigh Sayers and P. D. James, *The Letters of Dorothy L. Sayers: 1951–1957 : In the Midst of Life* (London: Hodder & Stoughton, 2000), 136–137.

21. Ibid., 137.

22. Laura K. Simmons, *Creed Without Chaos: Exploring Theology in the Writings of Dorothy L. Sayers* (Grand Rapids: Baker Academic, 2005), 118.

his leisure hours, and to come to church on Sundays. What the Church should be telling him is this: that the very first demand that his religion makes upon him is that he should make good tables.[23]

Another lesson we learn from Sayers is the importance of an integrated worldview. She was particularly gifted at showing how things that people viewed as separate and distinct were in fact two sides of the same coin. The false antithesis between faith and fact, work and glory, spirit and matter, religion and reason, dogma and drama, the sacred and the secular, the head and the heart, and many other false dualisms came crashing down under the hammer of her incisive logic. By emphasizing that redemption involves the *whole* personality, she showed that there is no part of creation untouched by the magic of the Incarnation. There is no aspect of life separate from the demands of Christ's lordship.

QUESTIONS FOR DISCUSSION

1. Modern science has achieved a comparatively sophisticated level of scientific precision concerning the material universe. Has this knowledge led to a greater understanding of the cosmos?

2. List some ways in which Christians have imbibed the modern idea of a universe that is "dead and cold" rather than pulsating with aliveness.

3. Describe some ways that Christians still separate the spiritual from the material without being aware of it. What are some Scriptural passages which show that such separation is not appropriate?

4. Those who have special enthusiasm and exuberance for life sometimes feel alienated from the church. Why? What could be done to prevent this?

5. Should we try to avoid the hardening process that often follows being hurt? If so, how?

23. Dorothy Leigh Sayers, *Creed or Chaos?* (Manchester: Sophia Institute Press, 1995), 106.

6. List some ways in which we may be guilty of muffling the shattering personality of Christ and surrounding Him with an atmosphere of tedium.

7. There have been many creeds throughout the history of the church. How should we decide which are foundational to our faith? If we decide based on our individual interpretation of Scripture, then does that negate the need for the creeds in the first place?

8. How did Sayers show that creedal Christianity could be exciting? What can we learn from her example for our own day and age? How might this understanding affect the work of missions?

9. How much freedom, if any, should an artist be allowed in representing Christ on the stage?

10. Many churches today have concluded that in order to be relevant to ordinary people, they must avoid talking about Christian doctrine. How do you think Sayers would respond to this?

11. Sayers contrasted "Catholic [universal] Christianity" with "Oriental Gnosticism." What was the purpose of this contrast, and how does it help us to better understand the Christian teaching?

12. Many Christians talk about going to heaven when you die as the ultimate Christian hope. Is this a biblical view?

PERSONAL CHALLENGE

Dorothy Sayers believed that many things that Christians separated were actually two sides of the same coin. In what ways might you be guilty of dividing that which the Lord has brought together? How does Sayers' example inspire you?

CHAPTER 18

DYING TO GAIN
WHAT HE COULD NOT LOSE

The Evangelism of Jim Elliot (1927–1956)

Philip James ("Jim") Elliot was born in 1927 in Oregon, the third child of Fred and Clara Elliot. Above everything else, the Elliots desired that their children would grow to love Jesus and walk in His ways.

The Elliot home was marked by joy, kindness, and humor, as well as strict standards of obedience and personal honesty. In her book *Shadow of the Almighty*, Elisabeth Elliot describes the atmosphere of the Elliot household during Jim's formative years:

> Fred Elliot read the Scriptures daily to his children, seeking to show them the glory of Christ above all else, striving always to avoid legalisms or a list of "don'ts." "I prayed with them as well as for them," [Fred] says. And each of the children at an early age heard the call of Jesus and set his face to follow.[1]

Jim and his brothers were encouraged to take initiative and given frequent opportunity to enjoy outdoor work, recreation, and adventure.

---

1. Elisabeth Elliot, *Shadow of the Almighty: The Life and Testament of Jim Elliot* (New York: HarperCollins, 1989), 25.

All of this helped to instill in Jim a rugged piety, a willingness to take risks, and a desire to try impossible things.

Ever hospitable, the Elliots often had missionaries lodging in their home. The stories Jim heard about the spread of the gospel around the world left a profound impression on the young lad.

HIGH SCHOOL AND COLLEGE

In high school Jim was popular, known for his talent in athletics, acting, and oratory. But above all, he was seen as a man of uncompromising convictions. He was conscientious but not timid, confident but not arrogant, and meticulously responsible without being uptight or legalistic.

Always eager for any opportunity to share his faith, in the fall of 1945 Jim entered Wheaton College with the aim of preparing for the mission field. During the summer following his second year of college he traveled to Mexico on mission work. At the end of his third year, after a meeting with a missionary from Brazil, the Lord placed a burden on Jim's heart for South America.

As he worked towards completing his degree at Wheaton, Jim continued to think about South America and readied himself for the mission field. Believing that a missionary needed to be physically as well as spiritually fit, he joined a wrestling team. In his third year he began a study of Greek to make it easier for him to later translate the Scriptures into new languages.

Jim was an all-or-nothing person full of immense enthusiasm. If he felt called to be a missionary, he put pressure on his friends to follow him; if he believed that God wanted him to avoid the distractions of romance, he advocated the path of celibacy for everyone. And it was with equal vigor that he threw himself into having a good time. His fellow students still recall that no one on campus was as mischievous and hilarious as Jim.

In spite of his desire to avoid distractions, Jim inadvertently found himself developing feelings for a classmate named Elisabeth Howard. They admitted that they were attracted to each other, but decided not to pursue a serious relationship until they were convinced of God's leading.

After graduating from Wheaton in 1949, Jim returned to his family's home in Portland. The following summer he attended Camp Wycliffe, where he had the opportunity to work with a former missionary to indigenous South Americans who told Him about a tribe of people called the Waodani. Also known as the Auca, this Ecuadorian tribe had never had friendly contact with the outside world. The missionary informed Jim about an abandoned mission station which was available for use. Jim would never forget this encounter.

While preparing to travel to Ecuador as a missionary himself, Jim became involved with a number of local ministries. This included helping to run a radio program, preaching in prisons, holding evangelistic rallies and teaching Sunday School. It was not until February 1952 that the necessary preparations were completed for Jim to travel to South America.

Having recruited another bachelor, Pete Fleming, the two travelled to Ecuador, where they spent six months studying Spanish with a missionary family. In April of the same year Elisabeth arrived in Ecuador to study Spanish and tropical diseases, and to train for medical work. Although they were living in different parts of the country, Elisabeth and Jim kept up frequent contact. Their relationship grew, and the two were married in February of the following year.

During their first year of marriage, Jim worked with the Quechua people, helped by Elisabeth's translation of the New Testament into their native dialect. It was during this period that Jim and Pete met up with the missionary pilot Nate Saint, who was also living in Ecuador with his family.

OPERATION AUCA

Jim had never forgotten what the missionary at Camp Wycliffe had told him about the Waodani or Auca tribe, the murderous group which had never had friendly contact with the West. A plan began to form in Jim's mind about how to reach this people, a plan that would come to be known as "Operation Auca."

The first phase was what Jim believed to be the most important: prayer. "That saint who advances on his knees never retreats," he once remarked.

Jim and Elisabeth were soon joined in their daring undertaking by others: Pete Fleming and his new wife Olive, Nate and Marjorie Saint, Ed and Marilou McCully, and Roger and Barbara Youderian.

A CYCLE OF VIOLENCE

If ever a people were in need of the gospel, it was the Waodani. Scattered across a territory approximately one hundred by one hundred twenty miles wide, the Waodani formed what anthropologists considered to be one of the most brutal cultures on earth.

Waodani society revolved around revenge killings in a cycle of violence that stretched back at least five generations, possibly dozens. More than sixty percent of their deaths resulted from stabbing each other with their deadly eight-foot-long spears. This self-perpetuating feud threatened to drive the tribe into extinction. It was not only against themselves that they directed their violence—they regarded all foreigners as inhuman cannibals.

Jim knew all this. He also knew that the tribe would be extremely difficult to locate. He also knew that even if he could contact them, it would be almost impossible to communicate since their language bore no similarity to any other tongue and had never been learned by an outsider. Yet he was still determined to be God's instrument for bringing the love of Jesus to this people.

AIR CONTACT WITH THE WAODANI

After numerous unsuccessful flights over Waodani territory, Nate Saint finally made visual contact with some of their dwellings. He continued his flights, giving the Waodani a chance to get used to the airplane. Occasionally, Nate and the other missionaries would lower a basket containing gifts, using an ingenious invention Nate had devised which allowed the bucket to remain stationary while the plane circled around it. Sometimes the Waodani would send gifts back in the basket.

In addition to dropping gifts, the missionaries would communicate peaceful phrases they had learned from Dayuma, a young Waodani woman who had become friends with Nate's sister. Dayuma had fled from the jungle as a girl after members of her family had been murdered. She proved a invaluable resource for learning the Waodani language.

There followed a series of flights over the jungle clearings where the tribesmen lived, with gifts exchanged on both sides. Eventually, Jim and his group determined it was time for their operation to progress to the next stage: to leave the safety of the aircraft and make personal contact.

MEETING THE WAODANI

Jim was fully aware of the dangers he and his colleagues might confront. Only five days earlier he had written to his father, "They have never had any contact with white man other than killing. They have no word for God in their language, only for devils and spirits. I know you will pray."[2]

Using a narrow stretch of riverbank as an airstrip, the plane touched down in Waodani territory. The missionaries hoped that the tribespeople would recognize the airplane and come out to see them. Their expectations were realized when two Waodani approached them, curious about the plane and other interesting objects the missionaries possessed. The meeting was cordial enough and one man, whom they called George, even indicated that he wanted to go for a ride in the plane.

ATTACK AT PALM BEACH

Encouraged by their first apparent success, the missionaries landed again on the strip of riverbank they called Palm Beach.

The last words any of the wives ever heard from their husbands was when Nate radioed to say, "Have just sighted a commission of ten. . . . Pray for us. This is the day! Will contact you next at 4:30."[3]

Back at the base the women prayed constantly. One can only imagine what they must have felt when their husbands not only failed to make radio contact that afternoon, but did not return home that evening.

2. Ibid., 243.

3. Russell T. Hitt, *Jungle Pilot, Updated* (Grand Rapids: Discovery House Publishers, 1997), 277.

During the five days that followed, the Ecuadorian Air Force, missionary personnel, and the US Army, Air Force, and Navy swarmed the region, searching for any sign of the missing men. Eventually they discovered what everyone feared: mutilated bodies.

Elisabeth and the other wives received the dreaded news with courage. "The Lord has closed our hearts to grief and hysteria, and filled in with His perfect peace," Barbara Youderian said.[4]

It would be years before the true reason for the attack came to be known. Eager to deflect attention from a potentially deadly marriage dispute, a Waodani man suggested attacking the five missionaries. Always ready to kill foreigners, the others agreed.

THE LEGACY OF JIM ELLIOT

Jim Elliot's legacy did not end with his death. When he was called to minister to the Waodani, little did he realize that it would be through his death, not his life, that this people would ultimately be reached.

Rather than being filled with bitterness, Elisabeth prayed for her husband's murderers. Returning to her work among the Quechua tribe, she remained on the lookout for any opportunity she might have to complete the mission her husband had started.

The opportunity presented itself when two Waodani women, searching for Dayuma, came to live with Rachel Saint. After returning to the jungle, the women later returned with a larger deposition of women asking that Rachel and Elisabeth go with them to the Waodani community. Elisabeth not only joined Rachel in the risky undertaking but took along her three-year old daughter, Valerie. She hoped that by having the child with them, the Waodani would recognize that their intentions were peaceful.

Using Dayuma as a translator, and later learning the complex language themselves, Elisabeth and Rachel taught the tribe the good news of Jesus Christ. Though it was impossible to witness to all of the Waodani living scattered across the Amazonian region of Ecuador, those who did receive the good news had their society transformed from a culture of violence to a culture of love.

---

4. Elisabeth Elliot, *Through Gates of Splendor* (Wheaton: Tyndale House Publishers, 1986), 236.

Elisabeth Elliot left the Waodani in December 1961, after spending two years with them. Rachel Saint continued among them until her death in 1994.

LESSONS FROM THE LIFE OF JIM ELLIOT

The work begun by Jim and finished by Elisabeth and Rachel remains a powerful testimony to the transforming love of Jesus Christ. According to Waodani tradition, the wives, sisters and children of the murdered missionaries should have sought revenge. It was completely unprecedented for Elisabeth to show love and forgiveness to her husband's killers.

As they saw Jim's child Valerie playing side by side with the children of the very men who had killed her father, the Waodani came to realize the power of Christ's love. Nate's children later came and lived in the community, again displaying a different way of being human than the revenge cycle that had previously characterized their society.

Elliot's life also teaches us that when we serve the Lord in faith, our apparent failures can actually become God's greatest successes. As Jim and the other missionaries lay dead on the banks of Palm Beach it looked as though Jim's life had been wasted. It seemed that his burden to reach the Waodani had ended in nothing more than severed flesh and spilled blood. However, the blood of martyrs is never wasted but is the very means by which God builds His Church. Not only did Jim's death make it possible for God to answer his prayer for the Waodani tribe, but his testimony prompted a renewed interest in missions among American youth for years to come.

To this day, the words Jim wrote in his diary on October 28, 1949, continue to inspire thousands of men and women to follow Christ more fully: "He is no fool who gives what he cannot keep to gain that which he cannot lose."

QUESTIONS FOR DISCUSSION

1. Throughout his life Jim paid careful attention to the leading of the Lord. What are some ways that the Lord leads us? How do we know if a decision is God's will?

2. What were some of the qualities that made Jim such a good leader?

3. The conversion of the Waodani people and the subsequent transformation of much of their society illustrates that God is not merely concerned with saving souls, but with the transformation of culture. What are some ways that the gospel is transforming the culture in which you live?

4. The church father Tertullian once remarked that "the blood of the martyrs is the seed of the Church." What do you think Tertullian meant by that, and do you agree with him?

5. After her husband's death, Elisabeth Elliot went to work among the Waodani people. She took her child with her to show her peaceful intentions. Was this a responsible decision for a mother to make? Would you have done the same thing if you were in her position?

6. If Elisabeth and her daughter had been killed by the Waodani and the tribe never converted, would that mean Elizabeth's decision was a mistake?

7. Jim's parents taught him to be pious as well as manly and adventurous. Why is this combination important? What are some ways Christian parents can raise boys to have these qualities?

8. Although Jim and Elisabeth loved each other, they decided not to marry until they were sure it was God's will. Is this a helpful approach?

9. Contemporary missionaries are usually careful not to "Westernize" indigenous peoples. How does a missionary balance the need to respect the culture and customs of a given people, on the one hand, with the need to reform that culture based on the lordship of Jesus Christ, on the other? How does this play out in areas such as clothing, music, courtship, technology, and art?

10. Even though Jim knew about the vicious ways of the Waodani people, he still wanted to minister to them. Do you think he was afraid?

11. Is courage reflected most in a person who is fearless, or in a person who acts bravely in the face of fear? If the latter, then does it follow that in order to be extremely courageous one must first be enormously frightened?

12. Waodani society was characterized by a cycle of revenge. What does the Bible say about revenge? If you feel revenge in your heart, what should you do?

PERSONAL CHALLENGE

Jim Elliot was constantly looking for opportunities to lead people to Christ. Do you also look for opportunities to lead people to Christ? What might be some ways that you could become more of an evangelist?

CHAPTER 19

URGING THE NATIONS TO REPENTANCE

The Impact of Aleksandr Solzhenitsyn (1918–2008)

In 1994, Aleksandr Solzhenitsyn flew from Alaska to Magadan, the former center of the Soviet Union's labor camp system on the Pacific coast. From there he journeyed by a slow train across the expanse of the country, taking his time and talking to ordinary people along the way. Having been an exile from his homeland for twenty years, Solzhenitsyn relished the train journey, which gave him a chance to savor the country and reconnect with the people he loved.

Throughout his travels, Solzhenitsyn was generally well received by the Russian people. But not always. Passing through Siberia, he was met by an angry Russian, who shouted, "It is you and your writing that started it all!"[1] The man was, of course, referring to the collapse of the Soviet Union and the system of communism it had birthed for Russia. As this hostile comment suggests, the people of Russia did not all agree that the collapse of communism had been a good thing for their country. They did, however, generally agree that the writings of Aleksandr Solzhenitsyn had been instrumental in bringing about that collapse.

---

1. David Aikman, *Great Souls: Six Who Changed the Century* (Lanham: Lexington Books, 2003), 129.

FROM CHRISTIAN TO COMMUNIST

Aleksandr Isayevich Solzhenitsyn was born in the city of Kislovodsk in 1918, a year after the Bolshevik Revolution plunged the entire nation into chaos. Aleksandr's father died before he was born, leaving the boy to be raised by his mother and aunt. Under Soviet redistribution policy, the family property was turned into a collective farm in 1930, resulting in poverty for his mother.

Despite the lowly circumstances in which he grew up, the young Aleksandr aspired to receive an education and become a writer. He devoured the great novels of Russian literature, especially Dostoyevsky and Tolstoy (he read Tolstoy's *War and Peace* when he was only ten). His childhood was saturated not only in good literature, but also in Christianity. His aunt Irina was a lady of devout convictions, and when he was not in school, Aleksandr would accompany her to services at the nearby Russian Orthodox Church. The rhythms and rituals of the worship service etched themselves deep in the mind of the young boy.

Another influence in Aleksandr's life, one that threatened to squeeze out Christianity, was communism. When he was ten, a member of the Young Pioneers (the communist version of the Boy Scouts) ripped the cross off Aleksandr's neck to demonstrate their hatred of his faith. Two years later, Aleksandr joined the Pioneers, partly out of peer pressure, but also because the brainwashing he received at school finally convinced him that the communist cause was right.

EDUCATION AND MILITARY SERVICE

Russian communism was the convergence of the slave mentality and the revolutionary mindset. The former instilled in Russians an ancient and deep-rooted sense of needing to blindly submit to those in power, as well as an unquestioning acceptance of violence and cruelty as a normal part of life. The revolutionary mentality, on the other hand, introduced the impulse to advance the goals of the self, or one's group, at the expense of everyone else. It was upon the twin foundations of the slave mentality and the revolutionary impulse that Soviet Communism was erected.

Solzhenitsyn's interest in communism dovetailed with his interest in literature and history, particularly the events that led up to Russia's participation in World War I. But he was unable to attend the university at Moscow and receive the literary training he craved. He settled instead for studying mathematics at the local Rostov University. This was providential, as Solzhenitsyn's mathematical talents would later help to save his life on two occasions.

From 1939 to 1941, Solzhenitsyn had a chance to acquire a literary education by taking a correspondence course from Moscow. The curriculum was heavily weighted with Marxist propaganda, which Solzhenitsyn not only accepted, but embraced with enthusiasm. He supplemented his own studies by devouring all the Marxist and Leninist literature he could get his hands on. It was his genuine enthusiasm for Marxism and Leninism that gave him reservations about the Soviet leader, Stalin, who Solzhenitsyn believed had departed from the basic values of classical communism.

Solzhenitsyn's passion for communism was demonstrated by the fact that he took Marx's *Das Kapital* to read on his honeymoon, following his marriage to Natalia Reshetovskaya on April 7, 1940. The Solzhenitsyns did not have long to enjoy married life together. Shortly after their marriage World War II broke out, and Solzhenitsyn was sent to fight on the front lines with the Soviet Army. He showed great bravery as commander of a sound-ranging artillery battery and was decorated twice.

Solzhenitsyn shared his interest in politics with his high school classmate Vitaly Vitkevich. While serving in East Prussia in 1945 the two men discussed a range of political issues, and this inevitably led to some criticism of Stalin who, the men believed, had departed from the purer form of communism advocated by Lenin. In his correspondence with Vitaly, Solzhenitsyn did not mention Stalin by name, referring to him only as "the whiskered one," a term which in Russian also denoted a gang leader. Even this proved to be a dangerous mistake. Government officials intercepted his letters and charged Solzhenitsyn with anti-Soviet propaganda.

At first he thought the charges against him were a mistake. Being naively confident in the Soviet system, he believed that everything would soon be cleared up. After all, he was a loyal patriot of the Soviet army. However, after being mistreated, deprived of sleep, and interrogated, he was charged with conspiracy to "overthrow, undermine, or weaken the Soviet regime, or to commit individual counter-revolutionary acts." He was sentenced to eight years in a labor prison camp.

PRISON AND EXILE

At the time, the Soviet Union officially denied the existence of their vast network of prison camps. By experiencing the injustices at these camps and hearing the stories of the other prisoners, Solzhenitsyn came to understand the darker side of communism. Even so, his rejection of communist ideology was gradual, spanning years of reflection during his time in captivity.

The first part of his sentence was served in hard labor in a series of correctional facilities. Due to the brutal treatment, the severe cold, and the deprivation of food and sleep, most prisoners died before their sentences were complete. Solzhenitsyn almost certainly would not have survived his eight-year term had it not been for his mathematical training. Recognizing his aptitude, prison officials transferred him to one of the Gulag's secret scientific research facilities in 1946. This was where the better-educated prisoners were sent to help the Soviets with various research projects.

For the next four years Solzhenitsyn enjoyed a relatively comfortable lifestyle. The Soviets realized that prisoners could not think properly if they were struggling to stay alive. Thus, inmates at the research facilities were given sufficient food (even dessert after dinner), nine hours of sleep, and access to books. Even more gratifying was the opportunity to meet some of Russia's finest thinkers. Being already imprisoned, these men felt free to talk about anything they wished, and Solzhenitsyn was able to test many of his emerging convictions in debate with fellow intellectuals.

At first, his criticisms of the Soviets had remained focused against the abuses of Stalinism. However, after enjoying many good debates with some of the Christian intellectuals imprisoned with him, Solzhenitsyn began to rethink the entire atheistic worldview on which communism was founded. He developed a particular friendship with Dimitri Panin, who later became the inspiration for the character of Sologdin in Solzhenitsyn's novel, *The First Circle*. Panin was a devout member of the Russian Orthodox church, as committed to God as he was hostile towards communism. Looking over this period of his life, Solzhenitsyn later reflected on how he began to return to his childhood faith:

> I began to move ever so slowly towards a position that was in the first place idealist, as they call it, that is, of supporting the primacy of the spiritual over the material, and secondly patriotic and religious. In other words, I began to return slowly and gradually to all my former views.[2]

Life at the research institutes was so comfortable that Solzhenitsyn and Panin began to test the waters, subtly refusing to cooperate with their captors. Their resistance came at a heavy cost, and in 1950 Solzhenitsyn was transferred to a newly-established camp for political prisoners in remote Siberia. Here he worked as a miner, a bricklayer, and a foundryman. It was this camp, in a place called Ekibastuz, which provided the material he would describe in his novel *One Day in the Life of Ivan Denisovich*.

Ekibastuz was more inhuman than anything Solzhenitsyn had yet experienced. By keeping the prisoners in a permanent state of malnutrition, the authorities could work them to exhaustion by threatening to reduce their food rations. Hypothermia, malnutrition, and overwork, combined with terrible sanitary conditions, were some of the many factors that killed most inmates. In his chapter on Solzhenitsyn, in *Great Souls*, David Aikman described some of the conditions:

> The daily, brutal labor, the marches to the work sites in rain, or slush, or cold so intense it was like a knife against the skin, the endless searches before you left the camp in the morning, the searches on your return, the waiting in line morning and night for the thin gruel, the absence of books, the conscienceless brutality of the criminal prisoners. All of this for 330 days a year (there were three days of rest each month), killed thousands upon thousands of prisoners, or turned the survivors into cowed, zombielike men.[3]

2. Ibid., 148.
3. Ibid., 151.

While in prison, Solzhenitsyn's interest in being a writer intensified. Although all writing was considered contraband at Ekibastuz, this did not deter him. In his autobiography, *The Oak and the Calf*, Solzhenitsyn describes how he devised a method for memorizing long sections of his own poetry and prose. Using a chain of beads made from chewed bread, he made each bead to represent a passage that he would repeat to himself until he had the entire section memorized. By the end of his prison term, he had memorized twelve thousand lines. Solzhenitsyn would have to take an entire week every month just to silently recite everything he had memorized—a task he performed while undergoing the strenuous routine of camp life.

The intellectual work of composing and memorizing worked as an antidote against what Solzhenitsyn would later describe as "the narrowing of the intellectual and spiritual horizons of a human being, the reduction of the human being to an animal and the process of dying alive."[4] The hope that he might one day be able to write down his works for others to read gave Solzhenitsyn something to live for amid the inhuman conditions of the camp.

It was during his imprisonment at Ekibastuz, in January 1952, that Solzhenitsyn was diagnosed with having a cancerous growth under his right groin. Treatment required an operation. While recovering from the operation in the prison hospital, Solzhenitsyn finished the long process of returning to his faith. He later wrote the following poem to recount his coming back to Christ:

I look back with grateful trembling
At the life I have had to lead.

Neither desire nor reason
Has illumined its twists and turns,
But the glow of a Higher Meaning
Only later to be explained.
And now with the cup returned to me
I scoop up the water of life.
Almighty God! I believe in Thee!
Thou remained when I Thee denied.[5]

4. Solzhenitsyn, *The Solzhenitsyn Reader*, 38.
5. Michael Scammell, *Solzhenitsyn: A Biography* (London: Paladin, 1986), 303.

One month after his eight-year term at Ekibastuz was completed, an administrative decision was made that Solzhenitsyn would not be released but exiled for life to southern Kazakhstan. Once again, he was saved by his knowledge of mathematics. Instead of being made to do hard labor with the rest of the prisoners at Kazakhstan, he was put to work teaching mathematics and physics at a primary school.

At the beginning of his time in Kazakhstan, Solzhenitsyn's cancer returned; he was given three weeks to live. Facing imminent death, his greatest agony was the thought that he might pass silently from the world without ever having had the chance to write down the thousands of lines in his head. Reflecting on this later in *The Oak and the Calf,* he wrote,

> All that I had memorized in the camps ran the risk of extinction together with the head that held it.
>
> This was a dreadful moment in my life: to die on the threshold of freedom, to see all I had written, all that gave meaning to my life thus far, about to perish with me. . . .
>
> In those last few weeks that the doctors had promised me I could not escape from my work in school, but in the evening and at night, kept awake by pain, I hurriedly copied things out in tiny handwriting, rolled them, several pages at a time, into tight cylinders and squeezed these into a champagne bottle. I buried the bottle in my garden—and set off for Tashkent to meet the new year (1954) and to die.[6]

Providentially, instead of dying, Solzhenitsyn actually improved until he regained his entire strength. He put this down to a divine miracle, believing that his life had been returned to him for a purpose. "Since then," he wrote, "all the life that has been given back to me has not been mine in the full sense: it is built around a purpose."[7] That purpose, Solzhenitsyn believed, was to write.

---

6. Aleksandr Solzhenitsyn, *The Oak and the Calf: Sketches of Literary Life in the Soviet Union* (New York: Harper & Row, 1980), 3–4.

7. Ibid., 4.

FREEDOM AND FAME

Solzhenitsyn's exile came to an end in 1956, following the decision by Premier Khrushchev (1953–1964) to release Stalin's political prisoners and empty most of the prisons. The decision was based on policy changes outlined in Khrushchev's secret speech of 1956, in which the Soviet leader expressed a desire to distance himself from the crimes of the Stalinist period.

The Solzhenitsyn that was released was different from the man who had been imprisoned eleven years earlier. In addition to strengthening the Christian faith of his boyhood, his experiences had made him deeply reflective. Moreover, he had formed a strong conviction that the struggle between good and evil cannot be resolved by policies, parties and politics, but is a battle waged within the human heart.

As a free man, Solzhenitsyn continued to teach and to write, but he did not dare to make his works public. He would later reflect on this period, saying,

> During all the years until 1961 not only was I convinced I should never see a single line of mine in print in my lifetime, but, also, I scarcely dared allow any of my close acquaintances to read anything I had written because I feared this would become known.[8]

At the age of forty-two, this secret authorship began to wear him down, mainly because none of his works could be judged by people with literary abilities. In 1961 he felt that conditions might be favorable towards finally getting some of his works published. There was an anti-Stalinist mood even among the high officials of the communist party, and Khrushchev was himself eager to reverse the legacy of the Stalinist era. Thus, he decided to take the risk and offer his novel, *One Day in the Life of Ivan Denisovich,* for publication. The book describes his experiences in prison camp through the experiences of the fictional Ivan.

Surprisingly, *One Day* was well received and was published by the literary magazine *New World,* with the approval of Khrushchev

8. Peter Radetsky, *The Soviet Image: A Hundred Years of Photographs From Inside the TASS Archives* (San Francisco: Chronicle Books, 2007), 156.

himself. The Soviet leader had personally read a copy of the manuscript and it impressed him. "There's a Stalinist in each of you," Khrushchev once remarked, "there's even a Stalinist in me. We must root out this evil."[9] Khrushchev no doubt hoped that the publication of *One Day* would help "root out this evil" and advance his more tolerant policies.

The publication of the novel had huge symbolic value, as this was the first time since the Soviets had come to power that a book critical of the party's ideology was allowed in print. Since everyone in the Soviet Union knew that the book could never have been published without the support of Khrushchev, the communist press felt obliged to praise it. This helped the book to become a bestseller. It was even studied in Soviet Schools. This set the stage for three more of Solzhenitsyn's novels to be approved for publication.

One Day in the Life of Ivan Denisovich also created a sensation outside the Soviet Union, by alerting the world to a side of communism that the Soviet Union had previously kept carefully concealed.

As in the research institute, Solzhenitsyn began to test the waters to see how far he could go. He began speaking at meetings, seminars, and forums, and constantly writing, and his tone of hostility against the Soviets gradually increased. But even as he grew in popularity with the public, he was beginning to be looked upon as a liability by the Soviet government.

BECOMING A NONPERSON

Solzhenitsyn may have had a friend in Khrushchev, but there were many in the government that resented Khrushchev's de-Stalinization policies. This became clear in 1964, when Khrushchev was ousted and replaced by Leonid Brezhnev.

During the years of Brezhnev's leadership (1964–1982), Soviet government morphed from a personal dictatorship into an oligarchy ruled by a privileged minority of hard-line communists. Although the new leadership allowed for increasing Westernization and debate, intellectuals who criticized the State could expect to receive harsh

9. Joseph Pearce, *Solzhenitsyn: A Soul in Exile,* Rev. updated ed. (San Francisco: Ignatius Press, 2011), 164.

treatment. Inevitably, Solzhenitsyn became an immediate target of the strengthened national security agency, the KGB, who banned further publication of his writings, seized the manuscripts he was working on, and declared him a "nonperson." Being declared a "nonperson" meant that he was stripped of his citizenship rights and no longer recognized by the State as even existing. Meanwhile, the full force of the Soviet propaganda machine was unleashed against Solzhenitsyn in an attempt to discredit him in the eyes of the Russian public.

No longer an officially-acclaimed writer, Solzhenitsyn felt released to take an even more critical approach to the government of his country. He continued to smuggle his manuscripts into the West on microfilm, where they were published and widely read. He also wrote a scathing attack of the Soviet censorship system and sent it to other Soviet writers.

The Soviet authorities were incensed when book after book continued to appear in the West with Solzhenitsyn's name on it. Under normal circumstances, a troublesome writer like this would quietly pass out of the public eye, spending the rest of his days heavily drugged in one of the many Soviet mental asylums (non-acceptance of communism was considered to be a symptom of insanity). But the Soviets knew that they had already let Solzhenitsyn go too far. To get rid of him now would be political suicide at a time when they had political incentives for putting on a more friendly face to the rest of the world. Moreover, despite the propaganda against him, Solzhenitsyn only grew as a celebrity within the Soviet Union. A 1967 Soviet poll found that he was overwhelmingly the people's favorite author. The result was that the authorities could not incarcerate him without creating a colossal uproar.

GULAG ARCHIPELAGO

Between 1958 and 1968, Solzhenitsyn had been secretly writing his greatest and most influential work, the monumental *Gulag Archipelago.* This three-volume, non-fiction narrative was a scathing exposé of the Soviet prison camp system, drawing on his own experiences as well as extensive primary research and interviews. Solzhenitsyn not only revealed the camp system in horrifying detail, he also explained the complicity that the Russian people played in allowing the system to develop in the first place. "We didn't love freedom enough," was Solzhenitsyn's simple assessment.

With the help of friends, Solzhenitsyn was able to sneak this manuscript to the West, where it was published in 1973. *Gulag Archipelago* had a greater impact than any of his previous works. The U.S. Kremlinologist George Kennan called the book "the greatest and most powerful single indictment of a political regime . . . in modern times."[10] Many consider the work to have been instrumental in the eventual collapse of the Soviet Union. Prior to its publication, many European liberals had looked favorably on the Marxist experiment. However, after the evils that Solzhenitsyn exposed came to light, the West became increasingly critical of the Soviet system.

When the Soviets discovered that *Archipelago* had been published in the West, they began to give more attention to "the Solzhenitsyn problem." Solzhenitsyn lived in daily fear of his life, sleeping with a pitchfork by the side of his bed for self-defense.

One thing was becoming increasingly obvious to the Soviets: sending him back to prison camp would be political suicide, not least after he had been awarded the Nobel Prize for Literature in 1970. Equally, allowing him to remain in the country would be counter-productive to Soviet aims. As the KGB chief, Yuri Andropov, wrote in a secret memorandum, "If Solzhenitsyn continues to reside in the country after receiving the Nobel Prize, it will strengthen his position, and allow him to propagandize his views more actively."[11]

As a solution, the authorities decided to deport Solzhenitsyn to any country that agreed to have him. West Germany accepted. Solzhenitsyn know nothing about the arrangement when, on February 2, 1974, there was a knock on the door of his apartment. Immediately upon opening the door, he was surrounded by six KGB agents, taken to prison, and then put on an airplane. Having no idea where they were taking him, he was relieved when he finally stepped into the freedom of West Germany. Six weeks after his expulsion, he was joined by his (second) wife, Natalia Svetlova, and their three sons.

10. Aikman, *Great Souls,* 177.

11. Michael Scammell, *The Solzhenitsyn Files: Secret Soviet Documents Reveal One Man's Fight Against the Monolith* (Chicago: Edition Q, 1995), 139.

LIFE IN AMERICA

From Germany the Solzhenitsyn family moved to Switzerland, before finally settling in the United States. They eventually went to live in the small town of Cavendish, Vermont, where Solzhenitsyn kept an incredibly demanding work schedule, writing fourteen to fifteen hours a day, seven days a week, for eighteen years.

During his time in America, Solzhenitsyn resisted becoming a media celebrity and remained isolated, keeping to himself and his family. He hardly ever left his fifty acres and rarely consented to a telephone call. Neighbors protected the family from sightseers by posting a sign saying, "No Directions to the Solzhenitsyns."

It was during his time in Vermont that Solzhenitsyn's Russian Orthodox faith took on an even greater importance in his life. In Joseph Pearce's biography *Solzhenitsyn: A Soul in Exile*, he describes the piety of the Solzhenitsyn home:

> Everyone in the house in Vermont wore a cross, Lent was observed rigorously and Easter was more important than Christmas. The children's saints' days were celebrated as enthusiastically as their birthdays and there was an Orthodox chapel in the library annexe where services were said whenever a priest came to the house.[12]

Despite his reclusive lifestyle, Solzhenitsyn did occasionally consent to speak in public. The most famous of these occasions was the speech he delivered at Harvard. Given his literary achievements, the faculty of Harvard University were thrilled when this guru of human rights agreed to deliver the 1978 commencement address.

In his address, Solzhenitsyn argued that both communism and Western mediocrity are symptoms of forgetting God. Without belief in God and man's religious responsibility, freedom cannot be sustained. As he put it:

> [I]n early democracies, as in American democracy at the time of its birth, all individual human rights were granted on the

12. Pearce, *Solzhenitsyn*, 264.

ground that man is God's creature. That is, freedom was given to the individual conditionally, in the assumption of his constant religious responsibility.[13]

Solzhenitsyn went on to attack the increasing tendency to use the legal structure of rights as a substitute for ethics and personal responsibility. "The defense of individual rights," he said,

has reached such extremes as to make society as a whole defenseless against certain individuals. It is time, in the West, to defend not so much human rights as human obligations. On the other hand, destructive and irresponsible freedom has been granted boundless space. Society has turned out to have scarce defense against the abyss of human decadence, for example against the misuse of liberty for moral violence against young people, such as motion pictures full of pornography, crime, and horror. This is all considered to be part of freedom and to be counterbalanced, in theory, by the young people's right not to look and not to accept. Life organized legalistically has thus shown its inability to defend itself against the corrosion of evil.[14]

Solzhenitsyn's comments about God, his criticisms of Western politics, the American media, and the licentiousness of modern society were not well received by the progressive Harvard audience. The wider American public hardly reacted more favorably. The *New York Times* responded to the speech by saying that his worldview was "dangerous," while the *Washington Post* criticized him for promoting "boundless cold war."[15] To this day, intellectuals throughout the world have joined the chorus of criticizing Solzhenitsyn's Harvard speech with almost the same enthusiasm with which they have condemned communist Russia.

Other intellectuals, such as the human rights guru Jeri Laber, found themselves deeply uncomfortable with the way Solzhenitsyn

---

13. Solzhenitsyn, *The Solzhenitsyn Reader*, 573.
14. Ibid., 566.
15. Aikman, *Great Souls*, 185.

failed to carefully distinguish between Marxism, Stalinism, communism, and socialism. Such distinctions were important to many liberals in the mid- to late-twentieth century, since they looked favorably on Marxism, while at the same time lamenting the direction it had taken in the Soviet Union. For Solzhenitsyn, however, Marxism, communism, socialism, and the abuses of the Soviet system were all part of the same package, rooted in the worldview of atheism. As Alan Wilson put it in his article, "Messianic Statism: A Political Terror," published by *Christianity & Society*:

> For the Russian exile there is no convenient distinction between socialism and the labels "communism" or "Stalinism," which has been the handy method employed by left-wing intellectuals to whitewash their ideology in connection with the inhumane cruelty in the U.S.S.R. (and elsewhere).[16]

RETURN TO RUSSIA

Though Solzhenitsyn's life in America was comfortable, his prayer was to one day return to his homeland. This was made possible in 1990, when Mikhail S. Gorbachev offered to restore his citizenship. However, it was not until the collapse of the Soviet Union in 1994 that he and his family went back.

Solzhenitsyn stayed in Russia until his death on August 3, 2008, at the age of eighty-nine, outliving by nearly seventeen years the Soviet system he had helped to overthrow. To the last he was vocal about politics. He was an outspoken critique of American and British democracy-building projects in the Middle East, in addition to criticizing what he called the "false and dangerous current" in the Western drift towards socialism.[17] He continued to write and even had his own talk show on television for a while.

16. Alan Wilson, "Messianic Statism: A Political Terror," *Christianity & Society* VII.4 (October 1997), 18.
17. Solzhenitsyn, *Solzhenitsyn Reader*, 569.

THE SOLZHENITSYN ENIGMA

If ever there was proof that the pen is more powerful than the sword, Solzhenitsyn was it. In 1976, the British journalist Bernard Levin said that he could not recall any other time in recent history when "a single man with no power—he wasn't a king, a dictator, a general— but with the power of the moral force of his own will and beliefs and character, has compelled the world to listen to him."[18]

Even so, Solzhenitsyn's legacy remains an enigma for the West. Recognized as a great writer and defender of freedom, he alienated himself from many of his former admirers because of his unpopular ideas about the West's misuse of liberty. His reclusiveness, long beard, and hostility to pop culture contributed to the impression that he was something of a freak, a remnant of a bygone era, out of touch with modern life.

Solzhenitsyn even fell out of favor with some of America's presidents. When Gerald Ford was attempting to develop friendly ties with the Soviet Union, he refused to invite Solzhenitsyn to his executive mansion. Ford's secretary of state, Dr. Henry Kissinger, was hardly more receptive, calling Solzhenitsyn's views "an embarrassment even to his fellow dissidents."[19] Similarly, Arthur Schlesinger Jr., erstwhile adviser to President Kennedy, wrote in 1986 that Solzhenitsyn's idea that we should be responsible before God amounted to his advocating "a Christian authoritarianism governed by God-fearing despots."[20]

SOLZHENITSYN'S LEGACY

One neglected aspect of Solzhenitsyn's legacy, which warrants some attention, is his challenge to modernism and postmodernism.

"Modernism" can refer both to a time period in history or to an ideology. As an ideology, it is closely aligned with the worldview of secular humanism, which elevates man and his reason to the center of reality. In contrast to the pre-modern worldview, which stressed that all human knowledge is a subset of God's knowledge, modernism emphasized that unaided autonomous reason could discover

18. Ibid., 129.
19. Aikman, *Great Souls*, 183.
20. Ibid., 185.

absolute truth on its own. Solzhenitsyn challenged these ideas. In his Harvard address he referred to the secular humanist worldview as "the mistake" that was "at the root, at the very foundation of thought in modern times." He continued:

> I refer to the prevailing Western view of the world in modern times. I refer to the prevailing Western view of the world which was born in the Renaissance and has found political expression since the Age of Enlightenment. It became the basis for political and social doctrine and could be called rationalistic humanism or humanistic autonomy: the proclaimed and practiced autonomy of man from any higher force above him. It could also be called anthropocentricity, with man seen as the center of all.[21]

Not only did Solzhenitsyn challenge the worldview of modernism; his message of national repentance also confronted the fashionable relativism of the late twentieth and early twenty-first centuries. Relativism—one subset of postmodernism—is the worldview which asserts that individuals or groups create truth for themselves. While agreeing with modernism that man is at the center, relativism denies that unaided autonomous reason can discover absolute truth for itself, since it rejects the very notion of absolute truth. Within the worldview of the relativist, every person creates meaning for himself. Solzhenitsyn opposed this idea as fervently as he opposed modernism. He argued that eternal values such as truth and justice do not depend on man for their existence but have a concrete existence outside of oneself. As Solzhenitsyn wrote in a **samizdat** letter while he was living in the Soviet Union, "Justice exists, even if there are only a few individuals who recognize it as such. . . . There is nothing relative about justice just as there is nothing relative about conscience."[22]

When Solzhenitsyn was deported from the Soviet Union, he found this message of moral absolutes was just as distasteful to the West as it had been to the Soviets. When *The New York Times* editorial declared that Solzhenitsyn was "dangerous," one of the crimes laid

---

21. Solzhenitsyn, *Solzhenitsyn Reader*, 572.
22. Aikman, *Great Souls*, 167.

at his door was that he believed he was "in possession of The Truth." But these criticisms did not stop Solzhenitsyn from asserting the existence of objective truth against the voices of postmodern relativism.

His rejection of postmodernism had direct ramifications for his view of art. In his Nobel Prize lecture, published in 1972, he contrasted two types of artists. "One artist imagines himself the creator of an autonomous spiritual world" while "another artist recognizes above himself a higher power and joyfully works as a humble apprentice under God's heaven."[23] Solzhenitsyn urged artists to adopt the latter approach. Reality, including spiritual reality, is not something that we create for ourselves, since it exists external to us. He expanded on this in a 1993 speech delivered to the National Arts Club, following his acceptance of the Medal of Honor for Literature:

> For a post-modernist the world does not possess values that have reality. He even has an expression for this: "the world as text," as something secondary, as the text of an author's work, wherein the primary object of interest is the author himself in his relationship to the work, his own introspections. . . . A denial of any and all ideals is considered courageous. And in this voluntary self-delusion, "postmodernism" sees itself as the crowning achievement of all previous culture, the final link in its chain... There is no God, there is no truth, the universe is chaotic, all is relative, "the world is text," a text any post-modernist is willing to compose. How clamorous it all is, but also—how helpless.[24]

LESSONS FROM THE LIFE OF ALEKSANDR SOLZHENITSYN

Among the many important lessons furnished by the life and writings of Aleksandr Solzhenitsyn, the most important may be this: the pathway to healing lies in repentance. Solzhenitsyn urged that repentance was the solution, not only to the sins of Soviet Communism, but also the evils of Western materialism and secularism.

23. Solzhenitsyn, *Solzhenitsyn Reader*, 513.
24. Ibid., 588–590.

"I have grown used to the fact," he said in a 2007 interview, "that, throughout the world, public repentance is the most unacceptable option for the modern politician. . . . We should clearly understand that only the voluntary and conscientious acceptance by a people of its guilt can ensure the healing of a nation."[25]

Given the crucial role that repentance played in his thought, Solzhenitsyn cautioned us not to put too much confidence in political solutions, including the solution of democracy. Democratic institutions, he warned, cannot act as a hedge against the latent corruption of the human heart any more than communism could. This is because democracy is just as capable of being corrupted, and Solzhenitsyn pointed to the triumph of mediocrity "under the guise of democratic restraints" as an example.

It followed that the solution to Russia's problems was not, first and foremost, political, but spiritual. As he argued in his *Letter to Soviet Leaders,* written in 1973 shortly before his deportation, Christianity is "the only living spiritual force capable of undertaking the spiritual healing of Russia."[26] Later, in his 1983 Templeton Lecture of 1983, he reiterated this. Reflecting on the vast amounts of time he spent researching the history of Russia's revolution for an eight-volume history of the event, he concluded by saying,

> But if I were asked today to formulate as concisely as possible the main cause of the ruinous Revolution that swallowed up some sixty million of our people, I could not put it more accurately than to repeat: "Men have forgotten God; that's why all this has happened."[27]

Solzhenitsyn's message—enthusiastically accepted when communism was the target, but rejected when it was turned against Western corruption—remains as relevant today as it was during his lifetime. It is a message that, despite its negativity, also offers hope. Healing

25. Alexander Solzhenitsyn, "I Am Not Afraid of Death: Spiegel Interview with Alexander Solzhenitsyn," http://www.spiegel.de/international/world/0,1518,496003,00.html (accessed January 9, 2012).

26. Solzhenitsyn, cited in Aikman, *Great souls,* 181.

27. Solzhenitsyn, *Solzhenitsyn Reader,* 577.

of a nation is possible, Solzhenitsyn assures us, but only through public repentance.

QUESTIONS FOR DISCUSSION

1. The penal codes in the Old Testament never included a prison system. Is imprisonment an unbiblical form of punishment?

2. Solzhenitsyn opposed relativism—the view which says that we create truth for ourselves. Is there any area of life where relativism could be said to have legitimacy?

3. In what way did the slave mentality of the Russian people have continuity with the revolutionary mentality? What was the result of communism harnessing both these impulses?

4. What are some factors in our own culture that lead to "the narrowing of the intellectual and spiritual horizons of a human being, the reduction of the human being to an animal and the process of dying alive"?

5. Solzhenitsyn believed that the struggle between good and evil cannot be resolved by policies, parties and politics, but is a battle that is waged within the human heart. But do political conditions ever help to influence someone's heart in the right direction?

6. Given what we know of Solzhenitsyn's political views, discuss what he might think of political events today.

7. Compare and contrast Solzhenitsyn's thought with that of Rousseau in as many different areas as possible.

8. What are some examples of modernism in our culture?

9. What are some examples of postmodernism in our culture?

10. What are some key areas where there is continuity between modernism and postmodernism? What are some key areas of discontinuity?

11. Solzhenitsyn once remarked, "It is not because the truth is too difficult to see that we make mistakes. It may even lie on the surface;
but we make mistakes because the easiest and most comfortable
course for us is to seek insight where it accords with our emotions—especially selfish ones."[28] Discuss this quotation in relation
to some of the villains you have encountered in this book.

PERSONAL CHALLENGE

Solzhenitsyn contrasted those who try to create autonomous spiritual worlds for themselves with those who think of themselves as
humble apprentices under God. Which of these polarities does your
own life reflect?

28. Robert Andrews, ed., *The Columbia Dictionary of Quotations* (Columbia
University Press, 1993), 929.

GLOSSARY

antinomianism: The viewpoint emphasizing complete freedom from all laws.

asceticism: The practices or beliefs associated with people that attempt to attain a high spiritual ideal through rigorous self-denial, self-mortification ,and/or withdrawal from social life.

autonomous: Self-governing, independent, or self-directed.

baroque: A period within Western art following the Renaissance. It extends from approximately 1600 to 1750 and is characterized by ornate, florid, and sometimes extravagant detail.

Caesaropapism: The idea that both the church and the state should be under the authority of a secular ruler.

catechumen: A convert to Christianity who is receiving biblical instruction prior to baptism.

contrarieties: Things which are contrary to or opposite in character from one another.

Council of Trent: A council of the Roman Catholic Church which began in December 1545 and lasted until December 1563. It culminated in statements that solidified Roman Catholic doctrine, reformed aspects of Roman Catholic practice, and harshly condemned Protestant ideas.

counterpoint: A style of music composition normally associated with the baroque period and characterized by various melodic lines that are equally important. Instead of having one melody line accompanied by several harmonies, each line carries melody that also harmonizes with the other melodic lines.

deconstructionism: A movement that began among literary critics in the 1960s but quickly spread to other disciplines. It is characterized by a radical scepticism of language's ability to convey objective truth and an attempt to overturn the traditional assumptions underpinning academic disciplines.

deft: Able, skillful, or clever.

deism: Belief in an impersonal God; especially the philosophy that after the initial act of creation, God is uninvolved in the world.

despotism: Rule by a person or government that exercises unlimited, and usually oppressive, power.

Diet of Worms: A meeting that took place in 1521 to assess the teachings of Martin Luther. It was here that Luther delivered his famous "Here I Stand" speech. The diet culminated in the emperor issuing the Edict of Worms, declaring Martin Luther to be an outlaw.

ecumenical: Of or relating to unity among the different Christian churches of the world; interdenominational.

egalitarianism/egalitarian: A belief, condition, or philosophy that embraces universal equality and rejects hierarchy.

enculturation: The process of imbibing cultural values through observation and experience.

Erastianism: The doctrine advocated by Thomas Erastus (1524–1583) that the state had authority over all ecclesiastical matters.

ecclesiastical: Of or relating to the church.

ex nihilo: Latin for "out of nothing."

hegemony: Power exercised by one group over other groups.

hermeneutic: Of or relating to the science of interpretation, especially of literary texts (such as the Bible).

historical determinism: The notion espoused by Karl Marx that the course of history unfolds inevitably on the basis of economic laws and conditions.

holiness movement: A nineteenth-century movement that emerged out of Methodism and was heavily influenced by revivalism and pietism. The movement stressed the possibility of Christian perfection through the work of the Holy Spirit.

invention: In music, a short composition with two-part counterpoint.

Jacobins: The members of the radical society in revolutionary France that promoted the Reign of Terror.

mores: Social norms that embody the views or habits of a group.

nemesis: The opponent or arch-rival of a person or group (plural: **nemeses**).

nihilism: (1) A philosophy which claims there is no ultimate reality; (2) an agenda or orientation focused on the total destruction of what has previously been established; (3) the celebration of nothingness in philosophy, art or literature.

oligarchy: A type of government characterized by the rule of a few privileged individuals or a class.

penance: Discipline imposed by the church in which a sinner proves or earns repentance.

planned economy: A system in which a central authority, typically the government, will regulate all aspects of the nation's commercial and fiscal life.

postmodern: (1) of or relating to a philosophy emphasizing that individuals or groups can create truth for themselves. In contrast to the absolutes of the Modern and pre-modern periods, it emphasizes the subjectivity and relativism inherent in thought and experience. (2) of or relating to the historical period directly following the Modern era, considered to have begun somewhere in the mid-twentieth century. (For a fuller explanation, see my article at http://tinyurl.com/7pt8vks.)

samizdat: A secret system within the Soviet Union for publishing and privately circulating forbidden documents.

semipelagian: The theological view which denies man's dependence on God in the beginning of faith while still acknowledging that salvation is effected by God's grace.

statism: (1) the notion that the state is the answer to all of society's problems, (2) an excessive trust in the government, (3) totalitarianism.

syncretism/syncretistic: The reconciling or blending together of opposing viewpoints or religions.

theocratic: A type of government in which laws are believed to be issued directly by a deity.

totalitarianism: In politics, the notion that the state should regulate all aspects of life. The adjective **totaliarian** describes governments or rulers that dictate every facet of their subjects' lives.

universalism: In theology, the doctrine that there will be a universal reconciliation of all souls to God. It denies the doctrine of eternal punishment, either by disputing the existence of hell altogether (as in Unitarian universalism), or by suggesting a purgatorial concept of hell. In the latter model, post-mortem punishment serves as a mechanism for eventually bringing all persons to repentance and salvation.

utopia/utopian: (1) an ideal place or condition, (2) political or social systems designed to bring perfection.

BIBLIOGRAPHY

and Sources

CHAPTER 1: HEROD THE GREAT

Josephus. *Josephus, the Essential Works: A Condensation of Jewish Antiquities and The Jewish War.* Translated by Paul L. Maier. Grand Rapids: Kregel Academic, 1995.

Orr, James, ed. *The International Standard Bible Encyclopaedia.* Chicago: The Howard-Severance Company, 1915.

Phillips, Robin. "Is Jesus' Kingdom of This World?" http://tinyurl.com/2eydyn2 (accessed April 27, 2012).

Richardson, Peter. *Herod: King of the Jews and Friend of the Romans.* Minneapolis: Continuum International Publishing Group, 1999.

Sandmel, Samuel. *Herod: Profile of a Tyrant.* Philadelphia: Lippincott, 1967.

CHAPTER 2: PERPETUA AND IRENAEUS

Irenaeus of Lyons. "Selections from the Work Against Heresies." Early Christian Fathers. http://www.ccel.org/ccel/richardson/fathers.xi.i.iii.html (accessed February 18, 2012).

Leithart, Peter J. *Against Christianity.* Moscow: Canon Press, 2003.

McIntosh, Mark A. *Divine Teaching: An Introduction to Christian Theology*. Malden: Blackwell Publishing, 2008.

Needham, Nicholas R. *2,000 Years of Christ's Power: Part One: The Age of the Early Church Fathers*. London: Grace Publications Trust, 1997.

Osborn, Eric. *Irenaeus of Lyons*. Cambridge: Cambridge University Press, 2001.

Perks, Stephen C. *Common-law Wives and Concubines: Essays on Covenantal Christianity and Contemporary Western Culture*. Taunton: Kuyper Foundation, 2003.

Phillips, Robin. "Resources for Understanding Gnosticism." http://atgsociety.com/?p=1814 (accessed February 20, 2012).

Richardson, Cyril. *Early Christian Fathers*. New York: Simon & Schuster, 1996.

Roberts, Alexander. *The Ante-Nicene Fathers: The Writings of the Fathers Down to A.D. 325 Volume I: The Apostolic Fathers with Justin Martyr and Irenaeus*. New York: Cosimo, 2007.

Schaff, Philip. *History of the Christian Church Volume 2: Ante-Nicene Christianity*. New York: Charles Scribner's Sons, 1910.

Williams, M.A. *Rethinking "Gnosticism": An Argument for Dismantling a Dubious Category*. Princeton: Princeton University Press, 1996.

Wright, N.T. "Paul's Gospel and Caesar's Empire," N.T. Wright Page. http://www.ntwrightpage.com/Wright_Paul_Caesar_Empire.pdf (accessed January 6, 2012).

CHAPTER 3: SAINT COLUMBANUS

Davis, Charles Till. *Sources of Medieval History*. New York: Appleton-Century-Crofts, 1967.

Hillgarth, J. N. *Christianity and Paganism, 350-750: The Conversion of Western Europe*. Philadelphia: University of Pennsylvania Press, 1986.

Jonas of Bobbio. *Life of St. Columban*. Charleston: BiblioLife, 2009.

Olsen, Ted. *Christianity and the Celts*. Oxford: Lion, 2003.

Scherman, Katherine. *The Flowering of Ireland: Saints, Scholars, and Kings*. New York: Barnes & Noble, 1996.

CHAPTER 4: ALFRED THE GREAT

Abels, Richard Philip. *Alfred the Great: War, Kingship, and Culture in Anglo-Saxon England.* London: Longman, 1998.

Anonymous. *Alfred the Great: Asser's Life of King Alfred & Other Contemporary Sources.* New York: Penguin Classics, 1984.

Attenborough, F. L. *The Laws of the Earliest English Kings.* Clark: The Lawbook Exchange, 2006.

Chambers, Robert, and David Patrick. *Chambers's Cyclopaedia of English Literature: A History Critical and Biographical of Authors in the English Tongue From the Earliest Times Till the Present Day, With Specimens of Their Writing.* London: W. & R. Chambers, 1901.

Chesterton, G. K. *The Ballad of the White Horse.* San Fransisco: Ignatius Press, 2001.

Giles, William John Allen. *William of Malmesbury's Chronicle of the Kings of England.* Charleston: BiblioBazaar, 2008.

Lynch, Joseph H. *Christianizing Kinship: Ritual Sponsorship in Anglo-Saxon England.* New York: Cornell University Press, 1998.

Merkle, Benjamin R. *The White Horse King: The Life of Alfred the Great.* Nashville: Thomas Nelson, 2009.

Smyth, Alfred P. *King Alfred the Great.* Oxford: Oxford University Press, 1995.

Somerville, Angus, and R. Andrew McDonald. *The Viking Age: A Reader.* Toronto: University of Toronto Press, 2010.

Whitelock, Dorothy. *The Anglo-Saxon Chronicle.* London: Eyre and Spottiswoode, 1965.

CHAPTER 5: KING JOHN

Churchill, Winston S. *The Birth of Britain: A History of the English-Speaking Peoples,* vol. 1. London: Cassell, 1956.

Johnson, Paul. *The Offshore Islanders; England's People from Roman Occupation to the Present.* New York: Holt, Rinehart and Winston, 1972.

CHAPTER 6: WILLIAM OF ORANGE

Harrison, Frederic. *William the Silent.* London: Macmillan, 1897.

Motley, John Lothrop. *History of the Netherlands,* vol. 1. Charleston: Forgotten Books, 2008.

Simmons, Dawn Langley. *William, Father of The Netherlands*. Chicago: Rand McNally, 1969.

Wedgwood, Cicely Veronica. *William the Silent: William of Nassau, Prince of Orange 1533-1584*. London: Cassell, 1989.

CHAPTER 7: RICHARD BAXTER

Baxter, Richard. *The Godly Home*. Wheaton: Crossway, 2010).

———. *The Practical Works of Richard Baxter: With a Preface, Giving Some Account of the Author, and of This Edition of his Practical Works; an Essay on his Genius, Works and Times; and a Portrait: in Four Volumes*. London: George Virtue, 1838.

———. *The Saints' Everlasting Rest*. Glasgow: W. Collins, 1831.

Orme, William. *The Life & Times of the Rev. Richard Baxter*. Boston: Crocker & Brewster, 1831.

CHAPTER 8: J. S. BACH

Bertram, Ernst, and Robert Edward Norton. *Nietzsche: Attempt at a Mythology*. Urbana: University of Illinois Press, 2009.

David, Hans T., Arthur Mendel, and Christoph Wolff. *The New Bach Reader: A Life of Johann Sebastian Bach in Letters and Documents*. New York: W. W. Norton & Company, 1999.

Dickinson, Edward. *Music in the History of the Western Church: With an Introduction on Religious Music Among the Primitive and Ancient Peoples*. New York: Charles Scribner's Sons, 1902.

Forkel, Johann Nikolaus. *The Bach Reader: A Life of Johann Sebastian Bach in Letters and Documents*. Edited by Hans T. David and Arthur Mendel. New York: W.W. Norton, 1945.

Gladwell, Malcolm. *Outliers: The Story of Success*. New York: Little, Brown and Co., 2008.

Jeffers Ron, and Gordon Paine. *Translations and Annotations of Choral Repertoire: German Texts*. Corvallis: Earthsongs, 2000.

Kavanaugh, Patrick. *Spiritual Lives of the Great Composers*. Grand Rapids: Zondervan, 1996.

Leaver, Robin A. *J.S. Bach and Scripture: Glosses from the Calov Bible Commentary*. St. Louis: Concordia Publishing House, 1985.

Moreland, J.P., and Kai Nielsen. *Does God Exist?: The Great Debate.* Nashville: Thomas Nelson, 1990.

Wilbur, Gregory, and David Vaughan. *Glory and Honor: The Musical and Artistic Legacy of Johann Sebastian Bach.* Nashville: Cumberland House Publishing, 2005.

Stapert, Calvin. *My Only Comfort: Death, Deliverance, and Discipleship in the Music of Bach.* Grand Rapids: W.B. Eerdmans, 2000.

Terry, Charles Sanford. *Bach: A Biography.* Whitefish: Kessinger Publishing, 2003.

Wilson, A.N. "Can you love god and agree with Darwin?: AN Wilson on his return to faith after a period of atheism." New Statesman. http://www.newstatesman.com/religion/2009/04/returning-to-religion (accessed January 6, 2012).

CHAPTER 9: JEAN-JACQUES ROUSSEAU

Cavanaugh, William T. *Theopolitical Imagination: Christian Practices of Space and Time.* Edinburgh: T & T Clark International, 2003.

Colebatch, Hal G.P. "Britain's Escalating War on Christianity." *The American Spectator* (November 8, 2007), http://spectator.org/archives/2007/11/08/britains-escalating-war-on-chr/1 (accessed April 27, 2012).

Cranston, Maurice William. *The Noble Savage: Jean-Jacques Rousseau, 1754-1762.* Chicago: University of Chicago Press, 1991.

Gentile, Emilio. *Politics As Religion.* Princeton: Princeton University Press, 2006.

Goldberg, Jonah. *Liberal Fascism: The Secret History of the American Left, From Mussolini to the Politics of Meaning.* New York: Doubleday, 2008.

Hampson, Norman. *Enlightenment: An Evaluation of Its Assumptions Attitudes and Values.* Harmondsworth: Penguin, 1968.

Hicks, Stephen R. C. *Explaining Postmodernism: Skepticism and Socialism From Rousseau to Foucault.* Phoenix: Scholargy Publishing, 2004.

Huizinga, Jakob Herman. *Rousseau: The Self-made Saint.* New York: Grossman Publishers, 1976.

———. *The Making of a Saint: The Tragi-Comedy of Jean-Jacques Rousseau.* London: H. Hamilton, 1976.

Johnson, Paul M. *Intellectuals: From Marx and Tolstoy to Sartre and Chomsky*. New York: Harper Perennial, 1990.

Olasky, Marvin N. *Central Ideas in the Development of American Journalism: A Narrative History*. Hillsdale: L. Erlbaum Associates, 1991.

Richards, Ellen Henrietta. *Euthenics, the Science of Controllable Environment: A Plea for Better Living Conditions as a First Step Toward Higher Human Efficiency*. Boston: Whitcomb & Barrows, 1910.

Rousseau, Jean-Jacques. *The Confessions of Jean Jacques Rousseau*. New York: Modern Library, 1945.

———. "Constitutional Project for Corsica." The Constitution Society. http://www.constitution.org/jjr/corsica.htm (accessed January 9, 2012).

———. "A Discourse On a Subject Proposed by the Academy of Dijon: What is the Origin of Inequality Among Men And Is it Authorised by Natural Law?" The Constitution Society. http://www.constitution.org/jjr/ineq.htm (accessed January 9, 2012).

———. *Emile, or On Education*. Sioux Falls: NuVision Publications, 2007.

———. "Jean-Jacques Rousseau, Discourse on the Arts and Sciences, [The First Discourse]." Vancouver Island University. http://records.viu.ca/~johnstoi/rousseau/firstdiscourse.htm (accessed January 6, 2012)

———. *The Social Contract*. London: Penguin Classics, 1968.

Schlossberg, Herbert. *Idols for Destruction*. Wheaton: Crossway Books, 1990.

Veith, Gene Edward. *Modern Fascism: Liquidating the Judeo-Christian Worldview*. St. Louis: Concordia College, 1993.

CHAPTER 10: EDMUND BURKE

Burke, Edmund. *The Best of Burke: Selected Writings and Speeches of Edmund Burke*. Washington: Regnery Publishing, 1963.

———. *Reflections on the Revolution in France*. New York: P.F. Collier & Son, 1937.

———. *The Works of The Right Honourable Edmund Burke*. London: Rivington, 1812.

Prior, Sir James. *A Life of Edmund Burke.* London: G. Bell & Sons, 1891.

Taylor, Irving A. *Life of Madame Roland.* Whitefish: Kessinger Publishing, 2005.

CHAPTER 11: WILLIAM WILBERFORCE

Byrd, Stephanie. *Amazing Dad: Letters from William Wilberforce to His Children.* Longwood: Xulon Press, 2010.

Chesterton, G. K. *What's Wrong with the World.* New York: Dover Publications, 2007.

Dwyer, John. *The War Between the States: America's Uncivil War.* Denton: American Vision Press, 2007.

Hochschild, Adam. *Bury the Chains: Prophets and Rebels in the Fight to Free an Empire's Slaves.* Boston: Mariner Books, 2006.

Metaxas, Eric. *Amazing Grace: William Wilberforce and the Heroic Campaign to End Slavery.* New York: HarperOne, 2007.

Nicoll, Regis. "The Legacy of Wilberforce, Part 3." Break Point. http://www.breakpoint.org/features-columns/breakpoint-columns/entry/2/18743 (accessed March 1, 2012).

Prior, Sir James. *A Life of Edmund Burke.* London: G. Bell & Sons, 1891.

Stock, Eugene. *The History of the Church Missionary Society: Its Environment, Its Men and Its Work.* London: Church Missionary Society, 1899.

Wilberforce, Robert Isaac, and Samuel Wilberforce. *The Life of William Wilberforce.* London: J. Murray, 1939.

Wilberforce, William. "A Practical View of the Prevailing Religious System of Professed Christians, In the Higher and Middle Classes in This Country, Contrasted With Real Christianity." Project Gutenberg. http://www.gutenberg.org/files/25709/25709-h/25709-h.htm (accessed January 9, 2012).

Wilson, N.D. *Dandelion Fire.* New York: Random House, 2009.

CHAPTER 12: THOMAS CHALMERS

Brittain, F.A. *Decadence and Reconstruction.* London: H. Holt, 1923; Quest Reprints, 1991.

Brown, Stewart J. "Chalmers, Thomas (1780-1847)." Oxford Dictionary of National Biography. http://www.oxforddnb.com/view/article/5033 (accessed February 20, 2012).

Chalmers, Thomas. *On the Sufficiency of the Parochial System: Without a Poor Rate, For the Right Management of the Poor.* Glasgow: William Collins, 1841.

Dodds, James. *Thomas Chalmers, A Biographical Study.* Oxford: Oxford University Press, 1870.

Moffat, James. *Chalmers: A Biography.* New York: Culbertson and Brothers, New York, 1854.

CHAPTER 13: JOSEPH SMITH

Brodie, Fawn M. *No Man Knows My History: The Life of Joseph Smith.* New York: Vintage, 1971), 69.

Bushman, Richard Lyman, and Jed Woodworth. *Joseph Smith: Rough Stone Rolling.* New York: Vintage Books, 2007.

Gamble, Richard M. *The War for Righteousness: Progressive Christianity, the Great War, and the Rise of the Messianic Nation.* Wilmington: ISI Books, 2003.

Guinness, Os. *Fit Bodies, Fat Minds: Why Evangelicals Don't Think and What to Do About It.* Grand Rapids: Hourglass Books, 1994.

Hart, D.G. *John Williamson Nevin: High-Church Calvinist.* Phillipsburg: P & R Publishing, 2005.

Mead, Sidney E. *The Lively Experiment: The Shaping of Christianity in America.* Eugene: Wipf & Stock Publishers, 2007.

Nevin, John Williamson. *The Mercersburg Review.* Mercersburg: Alumni Association of Marshall College, 1849.

Nichols, Larry A., George Mather, and Alvin J. Schmidt. *Encyclopedic Dictionary of Cults, Sects, and World Religions: Revised and Updated Edition.* Grand Rapids: Zondervan, 2010.

Noll, Mark A. *A History of Christianity in the United States and Canada.* Grand Rapids: William B. Eerdmans Publishing Company, 1992.

———. *The Old Religion in a New World: A History of North American Christianity.* Grand Rapids: Eerdmans, 2002.

Phillips, Robin. "Evangelicalism and Nationalism." http://tinyurl.com/7nnj6sz (accessed February 20, 2012).

———. "The Trinity: Mormonism vs. Christianity." Alfred the Great Society. http://atgsociety.com/?p=1857 (accessed April 17, 2012).

Rupp, Israel Daniel. *Religious Denominations in the United States, Their Past History, Present Condition, and Doctrines, Accurately Set Forth in Fifty-three . . . Articles Written by Eminent Clerical and Lay Authors . . . Together With Complete and Well-digested Statistics. To Which is Added a Historical Summary of Religious Denominations in England and Scotland.* Philadelphia: C. Desilver, 1861.

Smith, Christian, and Patricia Snell. *Souls in Transition: The Religious and Spiritual Lives of Emerging Adults.* Oxford: Oxford University Press, 2009.

Smith, Joseph Fielding. *Origin of the Reorganized Church and the Question of Succession.* Salt Lake City, The Deseret News, 1909.

Smith, Joseph. *The Doctrines and Covenants 88:87.* The Church of Jesus Christ of Latter-Day Saints. www.lds.org/scriptures/dc-testament/dc/88 (accessed January 9, 2012).

———. "History of Joseph Smith." *The Latter-Day Saints' Millennial Star.* Manchester: P.P. Pratt, 1861.

———. *The Pearl of Great Price: Being a Choice Selection from the Revelations, Translations, and Narrations of Joseph Smith, First Prophet, Seer, and Revelator to the Church of Jesus Christ of Latter-Day Saints.* Salt Lake City: Latter-Day Saints' Printing and Publishing Establishment, 1878.

———. *Teachings of the Prophet Joseph Smith: Taken from his Sermons and Writings as They are Found in the Documentary History and Other Publications of the Church and Written or Published in the Days of the Prophet's Ministry.* Salt Lake City: Deseret Book Company, 1972.

Smith, Joseph, and Heman C. Smith. *History of the Church of Jesus Christ of Latter Day Saints 1836 to 1844, Part Two.* Whitefish: Kessinger Publishing, 2004.

de Tocqueville, Alexis. *Democracy in America.* (Cambridge: J. Allyn, 1862), 43.

The Year of Jubilee: A Full Report of the Proceedings of the Fiftieth Annual Conference of the Church of Jesus Christ of Latter-day Saints, Held in the Large Tabernacle, Salt Lake City, Utah, April 6th, 7th and 8th, A. D. 1880 ; Also a Report of the Exercises in the Salt Lake Assembly Hall, on the Sunday and Monday Just Preceding the Conference, vol. 1. Salt Lake City: Deseret News Printing and Publishing Establishment, 1897.

Young, Ann Eliza. *Wife, No. 19.* Whitefish: Kessinger Publishing, 2003.

Young, Brigham. *Journal of Discourses.* London: Published by Brigham Young, 1860.

———. *Journal Of Discourses By Brigham Young V8, His Two Counsellors, The Twelve Apostles, And Others.* Whitefish: Kessinger Publishing, LLC, 2006.

Young, Brigham, and Church of Jesus Christ of Latter-Day Saints. *Journal of Discourses.* Liverpool: F.D. and S.W. Richards, 1856.

CHAPTER 14: GEORGE MACDONALD

von Balthasar, Hans Urs. *The Glory of the Lord: A Theological Aesthetics.* San Francisco: Ignatius Press, 1989.

Caldecott, Stratford. *Beauty for Truth's Sake: On the Re-enchantment of Education.* Grand Rapids: Brazos Press, 2009.

Chesterton, G. K. *All Things Considered.* London: Methuen, 1908.

———. *In Defense of Sanity: The Best Essays of G.K. Chesterton.* San Franscisco: Ignatius Press, 2011.

———. *Saint Francis of Assisi.* New York: Image Books, 1957.

Dearborn, Kerry. *Baptized Imagination: The Theology of George MacDonald.* Burlington: Ashgate Publishing, 2006.

Lewis, C.S. *George Macdonald: An Anthology: 365 Readings.* New York: Touchstone Books, 1996.

———. *The Lion, the Witch and the Wardrobe.* London: HarperCollins Children's Books, 2011.

———. *Surprised by Joy: The Shape of My Early Life.* New York: Harvest Books, 1955.

Lochhead, Marion. *The Renaissance of Wonder in Children's Literature.* Edinburgh: Canongate, 1977.

MacDonald, George. *David Elginbrod.* Christian Classics Ethereal Library, http://www.ccel.org/ccel/macdonald/elginbrod.toc.html (accessed January 9, 2012).

———. *The Diary of an Old Soul.* Minneapolis: Augsburg Publishing House, 1975.

————. *A Dish of Orts: Chiefly Papers on the Imagination, and on Shakespeare*. London: Sampson, Low, Marston, 1893.

————. *An Expression of Character: The Letters of George Macdonald*. Grand Rapids: Eerdmans Publishing Company, 1994.

————. *A Hidden Life and Other Poems*. Rockville: Prime Classics Library, 2004.

————. *Lilith: A Romance*. Grand Rapids: Wm. B. Eerdmans Publishing, 1981.

————. "The Miracles of Our Lord." Project Gutenburg. http://www.gutenberg.org/ebooks/9103 (accessed February 16, 2012).

————. *Poems*. London: Longman, Brown, Green, Longmans, & Roberts, 1857.

————. *The Poetical Works of George Macdonald*. London: Chatto & Windus, 1893.

————. *Robert Falconer*. Christian Classics Ethereal Library. http://www.ccel.org/ccel/macdonald/rfalconer.html (accessed January 9, 2012).

Macdonald, Greville. *George Macdonald and His Wife*. London: G. Allen & Unwin, 1924.

MacDonald, Ronald. *From a Northern Window: A Personal Reminiscence of George MacDonald by His Son*. Eureka: Sunrise Books, 1989.

Phillips, Michael R. *George MacDonald, Scotland's Beloved Storyteller*. Minneapolis: Bethany House, 1987.

Phillips, Robin. "George Macdonald and the Anthropology of Love." *North Wind: A Journal of George MacDonald Studies* 30 (2011).

Piper, John. *The Pleasures of God*. Colorado Springs: Multnomah Books, 2000.

Quiller-Couch, Sir Arthur, ed. *The Oxford Book of English Verse 1250–1918, New Edition*. Oxford: Oxford University Press, 1939.

CHAPTER 15: DIETRICH BONHOEFFER

Bonhoeffer, Dietrich. *The Cost of Discipleship*. New York: Scribner Book Company 1959.

————. *Letters and Papers from Prison, Updated*. New York: Touchstone, 1997.

————. *Life Together: The Classic Exploration of Christian Community.* New York: HarperCollins, 1978.

————. *A Testament to Freedom: The Essential Writings of Dietrich Bonhoeffer.* New York: HarperOne, 1990.

Colson, Charles, and Ellen Santilli Vaughn. *God and Government: An Insider's View on the Boundaries Between Faith and Politics.* Grand Rapids: Zondervan, 2007.

Hitler, Adolf. *The Speeches of Adolf Hitler, April 1922-August 1939.* New York: H. Fertig, 1969.

Pierard, Dr. Richard V. "Radical Resistance," *Christian History* 32 (1991).

Plummer, Alfred. *The General Epistles of St. James and St. Jude.* London: Hodder & Stoughton, 1891.

Rubenstein Richard L., and John K. Roth. *Approaches to Auschwitz: The Holocaust and Its Legacy.* Louisville: Westminster John Knox Press, 2003.

Tucker, Ruth A. *Parade of Faith: A Biographical History of the Christian Church.* Grand Rapids: Zondervan, 2011.

Watson, John Richard. *An Annotated Anthology of Hymns.* Oxford: Oxford University Press, 2002.

CHAPTER 16: ANTONIO GRAMSCI

Borst, William A. "A Nation of Frogs." Catholic Culture. http://tinyurl.com/7lfvhcl (accessed February 20, 2012).

Breitbart, Andrew. *Righteous Indignation: Excuse Me While I Save the World!* New York: Grand Central Publishing, 2011.

Conway, David, and Anthony Browne. *Retreat of Reason: Political Correctness & the Corruption of Public Debate in Modern Britain.* 2nd ed. London: Civitas, 2006.

Flynn, Daniel J. *Intellectual Morons: How Ideology Makes Smart People Fall for Stupid Ideas.* 1st ed. New York: Crown Forum, 2004.

Fromm, Erich. *Escape from Freedom.* Austin: Holt, Rinehart and Winston, 1961.

Goldberg, Jonah. *Liberal Fascism: The Secret History of the American Left, From Mussolini to the Politics of Meaning.* 1st ed. New York: Doubleday, 2008.

Horkheimer, Max. *Critical Theory: Selected Essays.* New York: Continuum International Publishing Group, 1972.

Horkheimer, Max, Theodor W. Adorno, and Gunzelin Schmid Noerr. *Dialectic of Enlightenment: Philosophical Fragments.* Translated by Edmund Jephcott. Stanford: Stanford University Press, 2002.

Huxley, Aldous. *Brave New World.* New York: HarperCollins, 1932.

Kolocotroni, Vassiliki. *Modernism: An Anthology of Sources and Documents.* Chicago: University of Chicago Press, 1998.

Löwy, Michael. *Georg Lukács—From Romanticism to Bolshevism.* London: NLB, 1979.

Lukács, György, Judith Marcus, and Zoltán Tar. *Georg Lukács: Selected Correspondence, 1902-1920: Dialogues with Weber, Simmel, Buber, Mannheim, and Others.* New York: Columbia University Press, 1986.

Marcuse, Herbert. *An Essay on Liberation.* Boston: Beacon Press, 1969.

———. *The Essential Marcuse: Selected Writings of Philosopher and Social Critic Herbert Marcuse.* Boston: Beacon Press, 2007.

Martin, Malachi. *The Keys of This Blood: Pope John Paul II Versus Russia and the West for Control of the New World Order.* New York: Simon and Schuster, 1991.

Phillips, Robin. "The Illusionist: Herbert Marcuse Is the Godfather of Political Correctness," *Salvo* 20 (Spring 2012).

Reagan, Ronald. *Ronald Reagan.* Washington: Government Printing Office, 1982.

Reich, Wilhelm. *The Mass Psychology of Fascism.* 3rd ed. New York: Farrar, Straus and Giroux, 1980.

Rowland Robert C., and John M. Jones. *Reagan at Westminster: Foreshadowing the End of the Cold War.* College Station: Texas A&M University Press, 2010.

Solzhenitsyn, Aleksandr. *The Solzhenitsyn Reader: New and Essential Writings, 1947-2005.* Edited by Edward E. Ericson and Daniel J. Mahoney. Wilmington: ISI Books, 2006.

Spielvogel, Jackson J. *Western Civilization: Volume II: Since 1500.* 8th ed. Belmont: Wadsworth Publishing, 2011.

Veith, Gene Edward. *Postmodern Times: A Christian Guide to Contemporary Thought and Culture.* Wheaton: Crossway Books, 1994.

Wiggershaus, Rolf. *The Frankfurt School: Its History, Theories, and Political Significance.* Cambridge: MIT Press, 1995.

CHAPTER 17: DOROTHY SAYERS

Alighieri, Dante. *The Divine Comedy Part 3: Paradise.* Translated by Dorothy L. Sayers. Baltimore: Penguin Classics, 1962.

Coomes, David. *Dorothy L. Sayers: A Careless Rage for Life.* Oxford: Lion Publishers, 1992.

Conlon, D. J. *G.K. Chesterton: A Half Century of Views.* Oxford: Oxford University Press, 1987.

Lewis, C.S. *English Literature in the Sixteenth Century, Excluding Drama.* Oxford: Clarendon Press, 1954.

Reynolds, Barbara. "Dorothy Sayers: 'The dogma is the drama,' An interview with Barbara Reynolds by Chris Armstrong." *Christian History* 88 (2005).

———. *Dorothy L. Sayers: Her Life and Soul.* New York: Macmillan, 1997.

Sayers, Dorothy Leigh. *Creed or Chaos?* Manchester: Sophia Institute Press, 1995.

———. *Further Papers on Dante.* (London: Taylor & Francis, 1957), 93.

———. *Introductory Papers on Dante.* New York: Barnes & Noble, 1969.

———. *Letters to a Diminished Church: Passionate Arguments for the Relevance of Christian Doctrine.* Nashville: Thomas Nelson, 2004.

———. *The Lost Tools of Learning: Paper Read at a Vacation Course in Education, Oxford, 1947.* London: Methuen, 1948.

———. *The Poetry of Search and the Poetry of Statement: And Other Posthumous Essays on Literature, Religion, and Language.* London: Gollancz, 1963.

Sayers, Dorothy Leigh, and P. D. James. *The Letters of Dorothy L. Sayers: 1951-1957 : In the Midst of Life.* London: Hodder & Stoughton, 2000.

Simmons, Laura K. *Creed Without Chaos: Exploring Theology in the Writings of Dorothy L. Sayers.* Grand Rapids: Baker Academic, 2005.

CHAPTER 18: JIM ELLIOT

Elliot, Elisabeth. *Shadow of the Almighty: The Life and Testament of Jim Elliot.* New York: HarperCollins, 1989.

———. *Through Gates of Splendor.* Wheaton: Tyndale House Publishers, 1986.

Hitt, Russell T. *Jungle Pilot.* Updated ed. Grand Rapids: Discovery House Publishers, 1997.

CHAPTER 19: ALEKSANDR SOLZHENITSYN

Aikman, David. *Great Souls: Six Who Changed the Century.* Lanham: Lexington Books, 2003.

Andrews, Robert, ed. *The Columbia Dictionary of Quotations.* Columbia University Press, 1993.

Pearce, Joseph. *Solzhenitsyn: A Soul in Exile.* Revised updated ed. San Francisco: Ignatius Press, 2011.

Radetsky, Peter. *The Soviet Image: A Hundred Years of Photographs From Inside the TASS Archives.* San Francisco: Chronicle Books, 2007.

Scammell, Michael. *Solzhenitsyn: A Biography.* London: Paladin, 1986.

———. *The Solzhenitsyn Files: Secret Soviet Documents Reveal One Man's Fight Against the Monolith.* Chicago: Edition Q, 1995.

Solzhenitsyn, Aleksandr. *The Oak and the Calf: Sketches of Literary Life in the Soviet Union.* New York: Harper & Row, 1980.

———. "I Am Not Afraid of Death: Spiegel Interview with Alexander Solzhenitsyn." Spiegel. http://www.spiegel.de/international/world/0,1518,496003,00.html (accessed January 9, 2012).

———. *The Solzhenitsyn Reader: New and Essential Writings, 1947-2005.* Edited by Edward E. Ericson and Daniel J. Mahoney. Wilmington: ISI Books, 2006.

Wilson, Alan. "Messianic Statism: A Political Terror." *Christianity & Society* VII.4 (October 1997).